SILENT CROSSROADS

Jem Duducu

Special thanks to Sandy for her incredible help and to Ted for believing passionately in this project.

This book is for Jonathan, Chris and Andy: only the good die young

2nd Edition 2018

Minor edits from the first edition 2017

All rights reserved. No part of this publication may be reproduced, transmitted or stored in a retrieval system in any form or by any means without the permission in writing from the author. This book is the sole intellectual rights of the author.

Prologue

He took in everything about the room. It seemed to be a hotel room, nothing special, quite drab in fact. The beige walls were bare apart from one framed picture, a poor quality print of some exotic scene involving merchants, camels and a desert oasis.

Light poured in through the half-open curtains and onto the bed to his right, a slash of early sunlight falling across the dark coverlet. He had spent the night not sleeping, just lying there staring at the invisible ceiling. His senses were heightened even though he was exhausted, and time seemed to pass in slow motion.

The linoleum floor looked tired, and the rug beside the bed was too threadbare to make out the pattern, something black against a faded red background. What had once been a fine example of weaving skills had long since been worn into a shabby memory of its glory days, much like the room and the man in it.

The room had certainly seen better days, but was it a hotel room or was he in barracks? It certainly wasn't a prison cell. Still, any roof over his head and a bed to sleep in were luxuries. He had long ago lost count of the nights he had spent under canvas or huddled in ditches.

He sat on a wooden chair that matched the same light wood of the desk beside him and thought about writing something down, some sort of explanation. But what could he say? He wasn't sure he could explain anything.

He thought he saw some lint on his filthy left sleeve and plucked at thin air. If he was going to die, it should be with dignity; he should try to look his best, but even without a mirror, he knew he looked far from his best. That blow to his head must have scrambled his brain if he was worried about his appearance. Why would it matter?

Memories streamed across his mind as he thought of other times and other places. He could be standing on a mountain ledge, drinking in the scenery: a lush forest valley below, a single bird of prey in silhouette against the sharp blue sky and distant snow-capped mountains bearing silent witness. That would be magnificent.

But then again, he could be lying in a hospital, surrounded by scores of men hacking out their diseased lungs, or he could be cowering in a muddy ditch, having wet himself and, in a flash of high explosives, ceasing to exist, no longer there. He'd witnessed that too many times.

He'd seen and done many things, but right now this room was his whole world. While it was no epic mountain view, it wasn't degrading squalor either. In the grand scheme of things, this dingy room wasn't a bad place to die. His thoughts were broken as he heard the key in the lock and saw the doorknob turn.

"Well," he sighed, "it's time."

Part 1: Kaiserschlacht

London 1914

Harry Woods read the headlines and ran as fast as his young legs could carry him down the winding West London roads back to his house. His mop of blonde hair bounced as he ran, the thick curls the only substantial thing about the scrawny youth. He waved the newspaper in the air as if it reported the greatest story ever told. "It's war!"

Harry was elated. Finally Britain was to turn her might on the evil Hun and, after a short, sharp battle or two, the British army would be victorious. There would be marching, there would be singing, there would be inspiring reports in the newspapers - there would be war heroes! It would be glorious.

Harry burst through the front door and ignored his mother as he ran straight past her. He wanted to find his father, the man who had fought in another great British imperial adventure. He arrived in the kitchen, the news exploding from his lips. "Father! Father! Have you heard the wonderful news? We're at war with Germany!" Harry stopped suddenly. The look on his father's face was not one he had seen before. It wasn't what he had been expecting and his face dropped.

Terence Woods was a man who appeared to be much older than his middle years. His mousey brown hair was thinning, and his features were sunken and sallow; he was sweaty even though the room was cool. His simple cotton shirt had a couple of buttons missing, and a stained woollen waistcoat hung from his slender frame. His whole demeanour was one of defeat. He sat hunched over at a kitchen table covered in the detritus of family life, an open bottle of gin in front of him. Harry had never seen his father drink anything stronger than tea, and it came as a shock to him.

His father looked at Harry with an expression of disgust, rose unsteadily from the table and lunged for his oldest child. His bony hands dug deep into Harry's shoulders as his father shook him furiously and shouted, "Don't ever say that war is 'wonderful'!" His sour breath reeked of the liquor. With each word Harry felt his father's grip tighten, and tears began to fill his eyes. What had he done wrong?

Terence's angry stare burned into Harry, but he relaxed his grip and pushed his son onto a chair, adding a bruise to his backside that would match those on his shoulders. His father took a lungful of air. All his terrible memories, all those moments he had tried to forget were being drawn out by his older son's youthful innocence. "Son, the British army flows through our veins like blood. The men in our family have been wearing the uniform since the time of Waterloo."

Terence was calming. He regretted his outburst, but he was in the grip of his emotions; he *must* make Harry understand before the seductive words of nationalism seeped further into his young mind. He wanted to save his son, but how to tell a thirteen-year-old about the crimes his father had committed? "So when it came time for me to enlist, I knew I was following a proud family tradition. But my war was different to those others. I served in the Second Boer War in South Africa. Notice that I used the word 'served' and not 'fought'. I never once fired my rifle in anger. I wasn't a soldier; I was nothing but a glorified prison guard."

Terence's voice started to rise and quiver. He caught himself as Harry's mother came in to deliver a cup of tea, a pretext to see what was happening. Terence grabbed the tea and slurped it, then grimaced. The leaves had been used too often and the tea was bitter. He wanted the gin to numb him, something no tea could do, but he needed a clear head to explain things to Harry, to make him realise what was at stake, and he resisted an urge to reach for the bottle.

Harry sat patiently. He had never heard his father talk about South Africa. All he knew was that he had come home a sick man. Harry was holding his breath, as if any noise he might make would break the spell. He wasn't enjoying this, but he understood that his father was about to say something important.

"Yes, a prison guard," Terence continued. "But the irony was that the people in my prison were innocent. It was us, the soldiers on the other side of the wire, who were the criminals."

The boy gulped. He'd never heard British soldiers being called 'criminals' before.

"I know, I know. This must all come as a shock to you, boy. I just have to tell you this because if I don't ..." He hesitated, thinking how to convey the storm of emotions that churned in his head and gripped his guts. "... because if I don't tell you this now, then you could make a big mistake later, and if there's one thing I want for you, it's that you get the truth from your old man.

"So to explain what I witnessed: We were fighting the Boers, a group of farmers who just happened to be farming the dirt on top of the largest gold and diamond deposits the world had ever known. So we took it from them ... because we could. The problem was that even though the Boers were small in number, they were well-equipped, and they knew the land better than us. They had everything to fight for and nothing to lose. You try tracking down a few dozen farmers on horseback in the wilds of the African countryside. We had to give them a reason to get within striking distance. So what did we do? We rounded up their families and put them in camps. 'Concentration camps', we called them.

"And you know what, Harry? It worked. Putting a man's family in prison is a good way to get him to give up. Problem was that with all those families huddled together in camps, disease broke out. And they had nothing – not enough food, no medicine, nothing. It was all women and children, so if anyone was going to get sick, it would be them." He paused. "That's how I got it; I caught it off them. I recovered ... mostly ... but thousands, and I do mean thousands, of those innocent people didn't." Harry was staring wide-eyed as his father told his story.

Overcome with emotion, Terence reached into his waistcoat pocket and shifted in his chair, concentrating as he slowly put some tobacco into his pipe. Harry could see the tremor in his father's hands as he raised the match to the bowl. He gripped the pipe and inhaled, then he continued: "All our ancestors were fighting to 'defend' Britain and yet they were always doing this 'defending' in another country. Do you think any of these people were about to attack Britain? No, they were doing whatever it is they do in their own country until we, the British, came along and started tearing chunks out of their land. So, yes, I've heard the news that we're at war again." He laughed a grim little laugh through a cloud of his own tobacco smoke.

"Again? Let's be honest. When isn't the empire at war? There's always some tribe we're snatching something from. But this new war will be different; it's going to be a big one; maybe it will be the one to put an end to all wars. The Germans have invaded Belgium, and France and Britain are going to fight them again. Everyone thinks it'll all be over by Christmas, but that's what they said when it was the British Empire against a bunch of farmers in South Africa.

"No, the Germans are far more dangerous than the Boers. This war will be a clash of the world's mightiest empires: France, Britain, Germany, Russia. Millions will fight in this war, Harry, and all the killing will be done to cheers and fanfares back home. If this war does last years, and if all the young men who will die are going be replaced by a new generation, then you, my son, you will be one of those replacements.

***

France 1918: three miles behind the German frontline

Katarina Rumpel had qualified as a nurse just before the start of the war and had had a year in London studying the latest techniques in sterilisation and germ theory. During her stay she had perfected her English, an invaluable tool as a front line nurse dealing with casualties from all sides, and her nursing skills had quickly earned her a promotion. As a medical professional who had been tending to the wounded for the four years since the start of the war, she thought she had seen everything. She had lost count of the numbers of wounded young men who had passed through her unit. It was more than a little ironic that she was a spinster at the age of twenty-six considering she spent every day surrounded by hundreds of eligible young men … eligible except for their wounds. The soldiers she saw were shattered souls, physically and often mentally. It would be unprofessional to show it, but she would never become accustomed to the constant background noise of coughs, groans and sobs that came with her day-to-day work.

Katarina's field hospital had been quiet over recent weeks, but now an ominous background noise, a rolling sound, almost like an arriving train, seemed to foreshadow the end of tranquillity. The noise was rhythmic and getting louder. She hurriedly finished taking her patient's pulse and rushed over to the window where she saw a column of German troops, all marching towards the front. At first there were dozens, then hundreds and, finally, more than a thousand men marching past, each man laden with equipment, each one carrying a rifle. Something big was brewing, and that meant she was about to begin another bloody cycle of triage, treatment and care, while trying to numb her feelings as casualties poured into the small, makeshift hospital.

She turned away and found Anna, the most capable of her nursing staff. "Men marching to the front can mean only one thing. We need a complete list of our medical supplies. Let's see what we have and what we will need to requisition. A storm is coming and we need to be prepared."

Anna, too, had been watching and understood the significance of the men going by. "I will have the report to you by the end of the day," she replied and walked off towards the stores.

Katarina stepped out of the dilapidated barn that was being used as a ward for the wounded and headed for her superior officer, Doctor Abels. He was a tall, broad-shouldered man in his fifties, with a thick grey moustache and hair turning to silver. He looked like he had slept in his clothes, most probably because he had. The doctor flicked ash from his trademark cigarette as Katarina approached and stood beside him. They were both assessing the column of German troops marching towards the trenches a few miles further west. "It's going to be a big one, isn't it?" Katarina sighed, knowing the answer.

Abels took a long drag on his cigarette. "This is the glorious *Kaiserschlacht,* the Kaiser's Battle. This spring offensive will be our last roll of the dice," he said in a matter-of-fact way.

"Why do you say that?"

"You know how many young men we've stitched back together and how many soldiers we've seen die in their beds. Now multiply that by every field station along the front, ours and theirs. We are running out of men. The troops you see in front of you now were all on the Eastern Front a few months ago. But they're it. They're all we have left … except for the elderly, the women and children. Germany has been bled dry. The men you see either win the war in one last assault on the Western Front or we run out of fighting men. It's as simple as that."

Katarina looked again at the men marching past, their boots kicking up dust on the dry earth road. "Good luck," she said under her breath, half in hope and half in prayer.

***

France 1918: three miles behind the British frontline

The troops had been marching for miles, their crisp, clean uniforms marking them out as new recruits. When they arrived at the supply camp, they were ordered to file into a an old brick storehouse, now being used as a briefing and training facility by the British Fifth Army, located just east of Bapaume. It was time to introduce these green Tommies to what lay ahead.

The fresh-faced young men chatted amongst themselves, sharing out cigarettes and stories as they waited for their induction to begin. A small raised platform and a military map of the front were already in place as an officer strode onto the stage.

His olive green uniform was immaculate; his cap with gold trim was that of a colonel. The murmurs of dozens of voices subsided in deference to the officer's rank. "I welcome you all," the colonel started in a measured voice. "I know you are new to this, and it is my intention that the men you are replacing are the last ones I will ever have to replace." The room went quiet with the colonel's reminder that these men were, literally, filling dead men's shoes.

"Unfortunately I have said that to every new group that has come through this briefing room. But you, the fresh recruits of 1918, have missed a lot of hard fighting and bloodshed because that's what it takes to win a war. For every mile we capture from the Hun, ten, twenty, maybe thirty thousand of our brave soldiers lie dead in the mud and ditches this war is so very good at making."

The silence was now an unnerving stillness. The troops were transfixed, partly in admiration, partly in horror at the grim realities being revealed by the man in front of them.

"The Germans started this war when they invaded neutral Belgium, but they have committed crimes much worse than we expect to see even in war. When Belgian troops had the temerity to try and defend their own country, the Germans used their bayonets to crucify them on farmyard doors, a true crime against all that's noble and civilised. Once the trenches locked down both sides, they were the first to resort to the sheer barbarity of gas warfare. And civilians ... civilian casualties mean nothing to them. They shot the nurse Edith Cavell for being a spy - a female nurse faced a firing squad! Their navy attacked our seaside resorts; their zeppelins have bombed London, and let's not forget that their submarines have been sinking dozens of ships, drowning thousands of men, women and children in the northern Atlantic."

The men's faces hardened; teeth were clenched. The litany of atrocities was doing its job. "So, yes, our men die, but they die to kick this accursed disease called the Hun out of France and Belgium. They die to save civilised society from Kraut barbarism; they die so that we can beat the Bosch! Our men may be dying, but theirs are dying in greater numbers. They are like carrion flies, buzzing around the borders of other countries, waiting to spread their disease into any country they can. We have stopped them. Now it's time to annihilate them!"

The men roared as the base feelings of war and blood-letting were unleashed. These men had been fed on stories of German outrages since they were boys, and now the first officer they had met in France was giving them permission to kill - kill the Hun, butcher the Bosch bastards!

***

Private Harry Woods was seventeen years old; he had reached his full height, but he had yet to fill out. His abundant blonde hair had a soldier's crop, and his young face still had a hint of the acne that was finally receding as his adolescence waned. His coarse uniform was too big for his slight frame; it appeared as if he had been lashed into it, his belt and puttees keeping him in.

The troops were bivouacked in a barn, able to spend the night on camp beds, the last bit of comfort before the trenches tomorrow. Harry sat chatting with his new pal Arthur Marsden, who was a few years older and a lot broader. The men were finishing off their evening meal and winding down after the march and the colonel's speech. A cloud of cigarette smoke hung over them.

"Tell you what, Art, that colonel gave us a good show, but he's not fooling me. Sure, the Krauts have been bastards, but are you telling me we aren't as big a bunch of bastards?" asked Harry.

"Look, Harry, you can have your own opinions in civilian life, but you're in the army now. We do what we're told, and those Bosch bastards don't care what your views are; they'll shoot you just as quickly as a real patriot ..."

"I know that," interrupted Harry, who was brimming with nervous energy, "but I don't plan on taking a Bosch bullet."

"I don't think anyone is *planning* on taking a Bosch bullet, but tell that to the thousands of poor bastards who already have. Listen, I may only be a squaddie, but the talk is that since Fritz has made peace with Russia, they've got hundreds of thousands of battle-hardened troops moving over from the Eastern Front to the Western Front. And you know what that means?"

"Peace at last?" said Harry, deliberately missing the point.

"Try a spring offensive with a million men," retorted Arthur, ignoring Harry's sarcasm.

"Jesus!" said Harry, pausing for thought. "You mean there could be a million veteran Kraut soldiers waiting to attack us right now?"

Arthur laughed, "Ah, Harry! There have always been a million Germans waiting to attack. Where do you think the Kraut army has been for the last three-and-a-half years? It's just that now they have friends. And those friends have been fighting the great Russian bear for three years - and have come out the other end as tough as tarmac."

"Alright, you two!" came a gruff voice. "Enough of the idle chit-chat. Lights out in five."

"Yes, sarge," both men replied automatically. Men packed away kit and settled on their cots. Some took a last drag on a cigarette; a few finished off letters to home. And so the lights went out at 22:00 hours on 20 March 1918. Six hours and forty minutes later, their world was thrown into complete chaos.

***

At first it sounded like faint whistling, then whistling followed by the rumble of thunder; but as the thunder grew closer, the noise changed into the unmistakable sound of high-explosive shells smashing into the ground, gouging out great craters of soil. The shells were falling like rain in a barrage that seemed to come from all directions.

The monster of war roared again and again outside the brick barn. The earth shook and the timbers trembled; dirt and plaster showered the sleeping men as they roused themselves to consciousness and leapt groggily out of their beds. Lost in panic and confusion, they grabbed boots and rifles and anything else that seemed to be of use.

The sergeant struggled for order. He'd been in similar situations before, but right now he was in a furious bombardment with a bunch of snot-nosed recruits. At least there was the saving grace of being a few miles behind the trenches. "Everyone calm down! Stop shouting and listen!" bellowed Sergeant Frall. While he was yelling as loudly as he could, his voice was barely audible over the whine of incoming artillery and the explosions that followed.

When order was restored, the men lay near their cots and waited for the barrage to finish, the vibrations of the shock waves from all the detonations reverberating through their chests. Harry gripped his steel helmet as if it would give him some kind of magical protection from the explosive fury. "You know those million Germans you were talking about?" shouted Harry to Arthur.

"Yes."

"I think they heard you," yelled Harry, a nervous grin on his face.

"Shut up, private!" barked Sergeant Frall.

The German artillery continued to rain down death not just on Bapaume, but for miles around. The ground was shaking so incessantly that it felt more like an earthquake than the commencement of battle.

Sergeant Frall tried to wrestle back the initiative with his men. "Alright, you lot, I've got good news and bad news." He paused as one of the windows blew inwards and showered a cot in glass. "The good news is this bombardment means their troops are getting ready to attack, but they aren't out of their trenches yet."

"How is that good news?" yelled Private Yorke.

"Shut your mouth, private. I suggest you don't interrupt the man trying to save your worthless lives. The bad news," continued Frall, shooting a meaningful look in the direction of Yorke, "is that as soon as it lifts, they will be moving out not only towards this area but, by the sound of things, for miles on either side of us. Therefore, as soon as Fritz stops, we will have to get down to the trenches to support the front line."

Harry and Arthur looked at each other from under their cots, Harry still gripping his helmet. They didn't have to say a word; their eyes fully conveyed the fear and apprehension everyone felt. This was it; this was their moment of truth. Would they walk away from this as veterans who had survived a tough fight, or would they become casualty statistics and telegrams to their mothers?

Dawn broke, revealing a sea of fog … and still the deadly hail slammed into the ground. The farmhouse could only just be seen through the grey murk. It had taken a direct hit and was now a blasted ruin; a split second was all it had taken to destroy a building that had been a family home since before the French Revolution. Corporal Perkins barely escaped when the unrelenting shock waves caused a corner of the barn roof to collapse.

The German artillery pounded on and on. The barrage lasted for so long and was so fierce that Harry felt as if he couldn't remember life before it. The never-ending noise was deafening; his body pulsated with the constant concussion of high explosives tearing up the surrounding countryside. His ears were still ringing from the blast that had demolished the farmhouse. He wanted to cry but was too scared to do so. He hoped the knot in his stomach was from the constant shock waves, but he knew it was fear. It was gnawing at him from the inside as an angry beast snarled at him from the outside. His plan to kill Germans seemed to have one tiny flaw: it looked like they were going to kill him first.

The oppressive wall of mist made everything more terrifying. Surroundings that should have been visible were hidden by the fog. It was as if some great war god had erased all the sights in the world and replaced them with the sounds of sickening thuds, the booms of near misses, the whizz of shells arching through the air, the dull crump of distant detonations. For any man brave enough to look out of the window, all that could be seen was part of the farmyard and the ruined hulk of the still-smouldering farmhouse.

Then, finally, one of the most intense artillery bombardments of the whole war, indeed, one of the most explosive in the whole of human history ended abruptly. After hours of bludgeoning, their senses took several seconds to register the silence and a terrible, foreboding stillness, which could not last. As soon as it had settled on the cowering troops, it was broken by the tell-tale percussion of rifle and machine gun fire. The German assault had started.

***

"Okay, men, helmets on and rifles at the ready," ordered the sergeant.

What had so recently been a cringing and confused mass of adolescents transformed into a fighting unit. Their training had soaked into their very bone marrow to become second nature. The platoon moved out into the farmyard, where other platoons, only just visible through the thick fog, were emerging.

"How are we going to see where to go?" whined Yorke.

"That, private, is not your concern," warned Frall.

Lieutenant Watkins ran up to the unit, a revolver clenched in his hand. "Casualties from last night?"

"None, sir."

"Very good, sergeant. Men, it looks like the Germans have decided that the war is going to start a little sooner for you than we had planned, but you are well-trained, well-equipped and fighting fit." As the lieutenant spoke in his confident manner, the sounds of battle were approaching.

"Sir, the Huns sound like they're getting closer!" blurted Corporal Murphy in his broad Yorkshire accent.

"Interrupt the lieutenant again, corporal, and I'll put you on report," snapped Frall.

"It's okay, sergeant," said Watkins, pausing to listen to the noise of the gunfire. "The corporal has a point … but why does the shooting sound like it's coming from the supply trenches?" The last part he said almost to himself.

The lieutenant and the sergeant split the platoon into squads and ordered everyone to advance to the eastern edge of the farm compound. The battle was now near enough to hear shouting as well as exchanges of fire. Snippets of calls drifted through the heavy mist:

"Jesus, they're here!"

"I'm hit, I'm hit!"

"It's a breakthrough!"

The more intelligible shouts were mixed with screams and the sharp crack of gunfire. The men could hear German too. Watkins and Frall quickly discussed tactics just out of earshot of the men. Their brief conversation ended with Frall saying, "Very good, sir," and he turned to the troops.

"Corporal Murphy, get the Lewis gun up to the first floor window of what's left of the farmhouse so you can cover the field ahead of us. You lot," he said, pointing to a small clump of Tommies, "I want you to go to the north side of this wall. Get anything: boxes, bales of hay, anything to make a firing step so you can shoot over the top. The rest of you, same drill but on the south part of the wall - and use the farmhouse ground floor too."

As the men ran to their designated positions, he added one more order: "Woods and Marsden, get as much ammunition as you can find. Pile it up in the barn and keep resupplying everyone else. Make sure the Lewis gun is your priority; it'll be chewing up the ammo faster than anything else."

"Yes, sir," the two privates said in unison. Woods and Marsden found crates of ammunition and hand grenades on the back of a cart. They carried them as fast as they could, one box between them, each holding onto a handle while trying to keep their rifles slung over their shoulders. The shooting had subsided but not the calls and screams. It was clear that there were no more British troops between them and the Germans.

The two Tommies were making their third trip to the barn when the Lewis gun roared into life. It sprayed high-velocity fire into the oncoming troops, invisible to everyone else, but in particular to the two men hefting the crates just behind the rest of their platoon. The Germans obviously had a new tactic as no one had heard of such a rapid advance. Harry and Arthur were just entering the barn, when Harry heard a strange, swooshing noise. Out the corner of his eye he saw something arch through the air and land just behind the men on the makeshift firing step to the north side of the wall. Yorke glanced down to see what had just landed next to him. His eyes opened in horror. "Grenades!"

This was to be his last word as, the instant he shouted the warning, it detonated by the heel of his left boot. His body took the full force of the white-hot shrapnel that ripped through his half-turned torso and into his face. The power of the blast pushed him up off his feet and into the wall. His body crumpled to the floor, leaving a wet smear of blood on the weathered bricks. More grenades detonated almost simultaneously. In the confusion that followed the explosions, men were seen slipping over one of the walls. They wore grey uniforms and steel bucket helmets.

Arthur was already in the barn, but Harry was frozen to the spot. He saw one of the grey-uniformed men raise a weapon. It was unlike anything he had seen before, much shorter than a standard rifle, with what looked like a black metal box sticking out at a funny angle. The man was aiming it towards Sergeant Frall, who was, similarly, bringing round his rifle to take a shot. The German got there first, and his rifle fired a burst of fully automatic gunfire. The sergeant's face creased in agony as three rounds of .30 ammunition tore through his chest, one ripping through his left lung, another shattering a rib and the third piercing his heart.

Harry snapped out of his stupor and dived into the barn as a burst of gunfire sizzled past him. He crashed into a cot, making Arthur spin around in fright and raise his rifle in anticipation of what else would come through the door. Instead, another grenade came hurtling through the window, this one detonating in mid-air. The crates absorbed most of the blast and deflected much of the shrapnel, but the shock wave knocked Arthur senseless to the ground, and hot metal shrapnel lacerated the left side of his waist.

A soldier armed with a submachine gun appeared in the doorway and, seeing Arthur, raised his gun towards the moaning Tommy, but he failed to spot Harry, lying in a tangle on the floor. Instinct took over as Harry lifted his rifle and fired. The bullet, coming from almost point-blank range, tore through the man's head from the base of the jaw, into his brain and out through the top of his head and helmet. He fell to the floor as if in slow motion, the stunned look on his face mirroring Harry's own. The German's rifle clattered to the floor as his body collapsed in a heap.

Harry wrestled himself out of his prone position and stood up. As he reached for the bolt on his rifle, he noticed that his hands were trembling uncontrollably. He could still hear Arthur groaning on the floor behind him. At that moment a second man appeared into the doorway, about to fire his weapon, when Harry swung his rifle and knocked the barrel of the German's gun to one side, exactly as it let off a number of rounds. Then there was an audible click.

Harry pulled back his own rifle and, with still shaking hands, frantically tried to work the bolt of his Lee Enfield. What he had done hundreds of times before now seemed dauntingly complex. His fumbling gave the German enough time to spin around and ram his weapon into Harry's face. His head exploded in pain, and there was an audible crack as hard wood connected with Harry's soft tissue. The last thing Harry remembered was the man swinging the rifle again, brutally smashing the butt of his gun into his face a second time. After that there was only darkness and pain.

***

Harry was lost in a swirl of memories. The one that came back, again and again, was an anxious time when he was eleven; his brother Alfred was nine, and his little sister Nancy was eight. Their father lay gravely ill in bed, and their mother was beside herself with worry. Father's fever had returned, and there wasn't money for costly doctors or medicine.

Harry, like his siblings, was wrapped up in worry that Father would die, so by way of distraction, he coaxed them into following him across London to a place unlike any other he knew. They had all scampered on and off trams and auto buses many times; they all knew how to dodge paying fares, and an hour later, they had travelled from their home in Acton to the city's docklands. Hundreds of ships were moored along the Thames, and thousands of labourers worked to load and unload their cargoes. The children stared agog at the huge cranes moving great roped bales from all over the empire and beyond.

When he turned to look at his siblings, Harry realised Nancy had wandered off. His heart sank. The docks were no place for a little girl on her own; the possible consequences were unthinkable. He was the oldest; he was responsible, and he *had* to find her. He and Alfred quickly decided to split up, scour the immediate area and meet back in the same spot.

Harry dashed around, searching frantically and accosting some of the dock workers to ask them if they'd seen a little girl. Their bemused answers were always 'no'. But after twenty minutes, just as anxiety was becoming panic, Harry saw a flash of tiny blue skirt from behind a crate. He sped round the corner to see Nancy, couched behind a tea chest, clutching something in her hands. "Nancy! Where have you been? I've been looking everywhere!" cried Harry.

Nancy looked bewildered but gleefully produced a bottle. "It's medicine. See, it says so on the bottle. I know it's stealing, but it's to help Father," she explained, showing surprising moral dexterity for an eight-year-old.

"Where did it come from? How did you get it?"

"I saw some men with a broken a crate. They were busy gathering up the bottles, so when I saw a chance to grab one, I did!"

Harry looked at the bottle. It was medicine, alright; it said 'laxative' on the label. Harry hugged his sister, and together they walked back to the meeting point where a worried Alfred stood waiting.

The memory faded as overwhelming pain stabbed Harry's face.

***

Katarina's worst fears had been realised. It was not a steady flow of casualties but a flood. The barn had been filled on the first day of the assault, and by the end of the week there was a sea of men, filling every bed, lying on stretchers – even propped up against walls – wherever there was space. Everywhere men writhed in pain from every kind of injury imaginable - and others that were worse.

The wounded were both German and British, but nationality was unimportant to the hospital staff. To Katarina the men were just men, patients with no names; the numbers were too great. At this point one face blended into another; she couldn't keep them straight, nor did she want to. It was the only way she could cope, the only way she could care for her patients, the only way she could do what she needed to do to keep them from slipping into the abyss. Just do what you can and move on to the next one … and the next, she reminded herself.

On her way to the stores for yet more bandages, she walked past the British soldier wounded on the first day of the big offensive. She had passed his half-bandaged face many times. His wounds were nothing unusual, something she had seen many times … but just at this moment he happened to be lying in a shaft of spring sunlight as it poured through a blasted hole in the barn roof. The part of his face that was visible was boyish and handsome, his good eye closed as if in blissful slumber. His soldier's haircut was topped by a crown of golden curls, and the sunlight appeared to make it glow. He seemed impossibly serene, like a sleeping angel. As an experienced nurse she knew he was unconscious as the result of his head trauma, but there was something about him, something that broke through her protective defences and long-suppressed emotions. She couldn't dismiss the feeling that here was a fallen angel in an ocean of unbearable pain and misery. He was beautiful. Right, she promised herself, I'm going to be here when he wakes up – if he wakes up.

During the hours that followed, Katarina used every opportunity to check on the Tommy. When she saw him stirring as she checked the stitches of a nearby patient, she called Anna to take over. In the next instant she was at his bedside.

Harry winced in agony as talons tore away at the left side of his head. He was trying to work out where he was, what was going on, why he couldn't see through one eye. He could hear noise all around him, but he couldn't make sense of it. Had he lost his faculties? In the midst of the roaring pain that pounded away in his skull, Harry's ears began to tune into the sounds. He hadn't lost his faculties. It was German; he was surrounded by Germans! Just as he grasped the horror of this, a gentle hand touched his shoulder. He turned to look into the face not of some vicious German soldier, bayonet drawn, ready to finish him off, but the face of a smiling woman. To his still-focussing eye, she seemed like a lovely mirage.

"Hello, I am Sister Rumpel. What is your name?"

"Ah," Harry hadn't lost his memory, but he was still badly disorientated. "Woods, Private Harold Woods."

"Well, Private Voods, you have a serious injury to your head. You should recover, but in the meantime, lie back and rest. You need to rest and heal."

***

Now, along with his pain, Harry had an irresistible itch. While the logical part of his brain knew that any scratching near his wound would provide only short-term relief and then add to the pain, he found it hard to resist the growing urge. Harry raised his hand to the bandage and began a delicate probing. He felt a searing pain but also the beginning of relief. He was about to give it a second try when a hand came from nowhere and slapped his prying fingers away from his face.

"That's enough, private," came the firm but soothing voice of Katarina.

"But it itches so much," whined Harry, who had been surprised and delighted to find his nurse was a fluent English speaker.

"Good, that's a sign the wound is starting to knit together. You are not to touch it; the short-term relief from your discomfort will only increase the long-term damage to your face."

"But ..."

"No 'buts'; it's doctor's orders.

"It's so unfair! It's not enough I have to deal with the pain, but now I have an itch too."

"Harry, look around you. While your injury is serious, it is neither life-threatening nor life-changing."

He winced with the movement of his head as Katarina propped him up. She pointed diagonally from the foot of his cot. "Do you see that patient, just there?" The man had a few scratches on his face, and the rest of his body was tucked neatly under a grey army blanket. At a glance he looked okay, but his eyes were sunken and seemed to stare straight through his surroundings. "His name is Sergeant Eisenhändler, and two days ago he was as fit and as active as you were. But a British artillery shell landed by his left foot; he is now missing his left leg from the thigh down and his right leg from the knee down. He'll live; he may make it to the age of seventy, but he will always be either in a wheelchair or on crutches. Will he ever work again? Will he become a beggar? Will any woman ever love him as he is? All those things are running through his mind right now, and you, Private Woods, you have an itch!"

Harry was silent. He was concentrating on the injuries around him: some were missing arms; others, legs; some were covered in bandages. British or German, mute or moaning, each was lost in his own world of pain and torment. Self-absorbed as he had been, Harry was only just beginning to realise that he was but one amidst a host of shattered young men. He wasn't the least injured, but he wasn't even close to being the worst.

Katarina let him soak up the reality of the field hospital. She realised that for her, Harry was becoming rather like a china vase: something beautiful, something to covet and something to shield from harm. She was spending a disproportionate amount of time with this enemy soldier, and if she was honest with herself, she was enjoying … no, *loving* every second of it! Her emotions were clouding her professional judgement when it came to a patient she was undeniably drawn to and whom she desperately wanted to help. She was intoxicated with desire for this handsome young man, this angel. She knew it in her heart but was afraid to admit it, even to herself … especially to herself. For some unknowable reason, Harry had made a connection with Katarina that was deep and intense.

***

Katarina had had a busy day and she was exhausted, barely able to talk. After working a sixteen-hour shift, she made her way to the quarters she shared with Anna and collapsed on her bed, still dressed in her uniform.

The small room in an abandoned out-building had been turned into their little retreat from the real world. Hanging on the wall was an oval mirror with a crack straight down the middle. In front of the mirror, on a commandeered dresser, sat some candles, their light reflected in the glass. Three-day-old flowers had been placed in an empty shell casing on a small wooden stool in the corner of the room. The only other furniture was two single beds; they were small, but most importantly, they were real beds, not army cots … much coveted luxury, for all it mattered. Since the *Kaiserschlacht*, they were so drained by the time they returned to their room, they could have slept on sacks of potatoes.

Anna was pouring schnapps into a metal mug when she saw her shattered roommate and superior officer come staggering into the room. "A little night cap before you retire for the evening?" Anna asked, keeping her voice light, trying to get a smile.

Katarina made a herculean effort and manoeuvred herself so that she was now sitting on the side of the bed. "Okay, it would be rude not to."

Anna poured a second mug and handed it over to the almost comatose Katarina. She recognised the look and knew she was not far behind. She was glad Katarina had accepted the drink because, tired as they both were, there was something she wanted to discuss. "I've noticed you've been spending quite a lot of time with that English soldier, the one with the wound to his face."

"Private Woods, yes. What of it?" Katarina asked, now alert and already on the defensive.

"Oh, please, Katarina, you may be my boss, and there may be a war on, but relationships between men and women have been around for a very long time."

"I..." Katarina began but realised she had nothing to say.

"Look, I think it's great. Unlike me, you don't have a man back home, and who cares if he's English? This war will be over soon enough, and with the amount of German casualties we're getting, I figure the spring offensive has stalled. If that's the case, our last big chance to end things on our terms has failed, so it won't be long before you and the Englishman can be on the same side."

"Is it really that obvious?"

"There are times when I think you're going to get into the bed with him!" said Anna, raising her drink in a mock toast.

"What a scandalous idea!" Katarina said, genuinely shocked.

"I would prefer to see a man and woman in bed together than all the damaged young men we have in those cots." The conjured images led to a sobering silence between the two women. They sat lost in their thoughts as they sipped their schnapps.

It was Katarina who broke the silence, "Well, Nurse Frosch, thank you for the drink. I will now be going to bed and sleeping on your observations."

"Just be careful, Katarina. For all kinds of reasons, just be careful."

And with that, the exhausted nurses blew out the candles, pulled off their boots and were sound asleep within seconds.

***

Whenever she could and whenever he wasn't sleeping - and even sometimes when he was - Katarina would stop by to see Harry. She was nearly ten years his senior, and he was an enemy combatant, but that just didn't matter, not to her. "Why did you join the army?" she asked, wondering why someone so young would want to go to war.

"Didn't have a choice; I was conscripted."

"You didn't want to fight for 'king and country', a phrase I have heard often enough from your Tommy friends?"

"A lot of men did, but me, I'm not so sure about all of that. I am in no doubt that France doesn't belong to Germany, but this is a problem for the Kaiser, the French and Lloyd George. What's it got to do with me?" Harry tried to smile, but he winced instead, his face a livid bruise underneath the bandages.

Katarina smiled at the idea of the politicians having to do their own dirty work and wondered aloud, "Imagine if they all declared war and nobody turned up."

Harry snorted with laughter but was cut short by the agony from his wound. "What about you? Why do you want to be surrounded by all this pain and suffering?" he asked, directing the conversation back onto Katarina.

"Well, I was a qualified nurse before the war broke out, and isn't it a nurse's duty to help the sick and suffering? I certainly think so, and while a part of me would like to be on the other side of the planet from this godforsaken place, this is where I have to be, otherwise ..." Katarina let the end of the sentence hang in the air as she thought about the implications of neglecting her duty. The question really was 'where did duty lie?' Did she owe it to her country, her profession, the men?

Maybe she was kidding herself. A promotion to Sister on the Western Front would get her pretty much any job in any hospital anywhere she wanted to work after the war. Could she be that callous? She didn't know any more. And yet, despite her doubts, here was a young man who seemed to epitomise her longing to do the right thing. He inspired her anew in her desire to heal as much of the damage caused by the war as she could. If she could save only this lone British soldier, maybe he would be enough; maybe that would be her duty done. She leaned over her angelic Harry and smoothed his thick locks with her hand, a gesture that felt immeasurably intimate to both of them, and yet it was a trifle. Her warmth on his forehead reassured them both. Each wanted to be with the other; they needed each other.

***

Assisted by a couple of male orderlies, Katarina and Anna had just hauled the last stretcher onto the back of a truck taking the wounded soldiers home to Germany. The orderlies lit cigarettes and sloped off to have a quick break, leaving Anna and Katarina to head back to the overflowing field hospital. Katarina wiped her brow following their exertions to lift nearly a dozen men into the truck. "Glad that's over."

"Yes, that's another bunch of young men we've patched up." Anna continued, "It will be hard for you to see your Englishman leave with an armed escort."

Katarina had yet to confront the fact that Harry would not be staying, nor would he be going home. He would be sent to a POW camp, and she'd never heard anything good about their conditions.

"Yes ..." Katarina hesitated, a little flustered, unsure how to respond.

"But suppose that's not the end."

"What do you mean?"

"Look, Katarina, you've been here for years. You've been promoted as high as you can go. Quite frankly, the army owes you."

"You may have noticed that the army isn't big on favours," snapped Katarina, but her mind was already working.

"That's true, but if you request a transfer to the prison camp where your Tommy is going, you could follow him there. My God, his wound is bad enough to need some special attention!"

Katarina hesitated as she mentally worked through the details. She had not dared to think of such a solution to the looming problem of separation, but now that Anna had voiced the possibility … The plan didn't seem to have any discernible flaws, and the transfer would be legitimate. She just needed to convince Doctor Abels, but had she built up enough credit with him to get what she wanted? "But who would take my place here?" And then it dawned on her. "Wait a minute; is this just an elaborate plot for you to get my job?"

"No, this not *just* an elaborate plan to get your job … although there would be that positive side effect for me. Katarina, I've known you for two years, and I've never seen you show anything other than a professional interest in your patients. I think, after all the thousands of potential suitors you've nursed, you've found someone special, and it will be the biggest regret of your life if you don't follow him."

 Katarina was silent.

"What do you see in him?"

"I don't know. He's young, hopeful, innocent …"

"… and good looking, with that lovely blonde hair!" Anna added, a big grin on her face.

"It's not like that."

"I'm kidding. My Oscar is a handsome man, not that I tell him. It's always best to keep a man guessing just a little." Anna reached over to put her hand on Katarina's arm; the smile had dropped from her face. "I'm serious. It won't be long until they rotate him out of here, so I urge you to act … not because I want your job, but because you deserve the chance to find your happiness."

Katarina nodded. Anna's encouragement had given her all the motivation she needed to make the leap of faith.

***

Katarina had the outline of her case in her mind as she set off to see Dr Abels, who was, as always, puffing on a cigarette while he completed his paperwork on a desk he had dragged outside under a tree. No matter that the forms were drenched when it rained or that he kept the papers in place with rocks, across the desk he had a perfect view of unspoilt countryside. This was his way of wiping away all the images of man-made horror in the hospital.

Dr Abels waved as Katarina approached him, but the smile faded from his face when he saw her determined look. He knew she wanted something, and he knew he wasn't going to like it. Dispensing with the usual courtesies, he blurted out, "I know that look, so let's get it over with. What can I do for you?"

"Herr Doctor, as you know, I am well overdue for some leave …"

"Yes, yes, I'm sorry, but the spring offensive has kept us all rather busy."

"If you would let me finish, Herr Doctor. I have taken hardly any leave in the last four years because, if we haven't been throwing our men over the top, the French and the British have been finding them where they are. I work very hard. I have never asked for leave, and you've had to sign me off only when I was clearly at breaking point."

"And I have never said otherwise, Katarina," Abels acknowledged, slightly puzzled.

"We have a wounded British soldier who's about to be sent to a prison camp near where I live. He has a serious head injury, and we both know that the medical care in our prison camps is rudimentary. Since I have nursed him to this point, I feel a further responsibility to see that this soldier continues his recuperation, and I would like to be closer to my family. I want to request a transfer – as a member of the medical staff - to the camp where the patient will be sent."

"And who is going to replace the best team leader I've ever had?"

Katarina had anticipated the question. The fact that it had come sooner than expected must mean things were going her way. "Anna Frosch. She's been on my staff for two years as you well know. You also know that she's an exceptional nurse; it's only the fact I'm still here that's prevented her from being promoted."

"… a prison camp full of English soldiers … what about your safety?"

"I'll be as safe as any of the guards; the English prisoners are, of course, unarmed. After all, there are weapons everywhere here at the field hospital. What's to stop any of our patients, whatever their nationalities, from holding guns to our heads?" Katarina asked with a look of steely determination.

Doctor Abels sighed with the realisation that defeat was inevitable. "You've thought of everything, haven't you?"

"Yes, Herr Doctor, I have."

"When is the patient being transferred?"

"The day after tomorrow."

"And you can have everything in place by … " Abels stopped himself; he already knew the answer.

"You know I can," Katarina said with a smile. "I just need you to sign the papers," she said, producing the necessary forms from her pocket. Abels took them, placed them on the desk and signed them. "It's interesting," mused Abels as he handed over the papers, "you spoke more of the patient than you did of your family."

Katarina didn't reply. Smiling to herself, she nodded her thanks, turned on her heels and strode off, triumphant that her plan - or was it Anna's - had worked!

***

Harry's body swayed back and forth in time with the train as it chugged across the German countryside. Opposite him sat Katarina; they were in deep conversation. "I used to sit underneath Eros in Piccadilly Circus, watching the never-ending traffic rush past me - buses, automobiles, horse carts. It was best in the evening, when everything was lit by the giant Bovril sign," laughed Katarina.

"You know what? I did that too!"

"You're just saying that."

"No, I'm not. I love London; it's like nowhere else, all those people rushing to somewhere I always thought must be very important. Where better to watch them than right in the middle of things?"

"We could have been sitting next to each other and never knew it."

"I was quite a lot younger then; you probably wouldn't have noticed me," Harry said, blushing slightly.

"Sometimes I would go to a little restaurant and order a rich, red wine – French, of course."

"I'm a beer man myself. Never tried wine."

"Is that so? Well, maybe after the war, I could introduce you to a nice Merlot."

"A what?"

"A Merlot. It's a type of grape used to make wine. I drink mostly white wines in Germany, but the French have the best reds."

"I would like to try your Merlot," Harry replied, suddenly feeling awkward.

Talking about 'after the war' seemed like a dream, something almost too good to be true. And here was this beautiful, sophisticated woman taking an interest in him, a wiry kid with a shattered face. He may have been on a German prison train, but he felt like he was in heaven. Harry decided to test the water. "If we're sharing a bottle of wine, could I make it part of a dinner and then, maybe, a dance?"

But before Harry got his answer, a German soldier appeared and towered menacingly over them. The carriage was full of mostly sleeping wounded soldiers, and Katarina and Harry were becoming animated. The guard fixed Harry with a stony look. "*Stille*!" barked the guard to Harry.

The frivolous mood of only minutes before evaporated. Harry turned his head to see that Katarina's smile had melted away as she apologised to the soldier, who stalked back to his seat and sat down with a grunt.

After a few minutes Harry dared to look back at Katarina and found her smiling at him. "That would be wonderful, Harry," Katarina whispered. Anna had been right; she had earned this.

Was Harry imagining it, or had she blushed a little when she answered?

***

Doctor Gerhard Jülicher sat behind his desk, his wire-framed glasses perched on the top of his brow, just below his retreating chestnut hair. He felt that, in his mid-thirties, he was too young to be going bald and blamed it on the difficulties of his work. He rubbed his eyes wearily and let out a long sigh, then cradled his head in his hands. Finally, he added a long, slow yawn. His uniform was worn and his desk was unlit. Rationing, shortages and intermittent supplies had made everything slow and difficult. He knew things were bad all over Germany, but as a doctor in a POW camp, he was low on any list of priorities.

His thoughts were interrupted by a resolute and persistent knock on the door. *"Komm herein,"* he said, somewhat indifferently.

The door pushed open to reveal Sister Katarina Rumpel. "Good morning, Herr Doctor."

"Good morning, Sister Rumpel."

"I am reporting for duty," Katarina said neutrally. Jülicher was an unknown quantity. Had she made a mistake following her wounded foreigner to a prison camp? Had she jumped from one nightmare, only to land in another?

"Sister Rumpel … may I call you Katarina?" Jülicher asked as he offered her a chair.

"Please, do," she replied with a polite smile.

"Your former superior, Doctor Abels, speaks of you in the highest regard," said Jülicher, attempting to put the young woman at ease. "He says that I can be confident in giving you complete autonomy in the conduct of your duties and that if anything untoward were to happen to you, he would personally hold me responsible and hunt me down. It seems you inspire both loyalty and admiration in those around you, and I see no reason to doubt Doctor Abels' comments."

"Thank you, Doctor Jülicher."

"Please, call me Gerhard. You cannot imagine how delighted I am – finally - to have an able medical assistant. I have been working entirely alone, but even now that you're here, we will be very busy looking after hundreds of men - and many of their wounds aren't just physical, either."

"During my years in the field hospital, I had wide experience of the physical and emotional toll that war takes." She paused and then continued, "On a practical note, what do we have in the way of supplies?"

"To be honest, not a lot. British soldiers aren't important to the Kaiser. I have been using boiled and shredded sheets for bandages. In terms of medicine, I have little stronger than aspirin and medicinal alcohol, and even those are in short supply. Any restocking of our meagre stores is infrequent, and the gap between deliveries grows ever longer, so I make do with what I have. But let me say again how good it is to have you on board. Before your arrival, I've had only the help of a few well-meaning guards."

"What do we have currently in the beds?"

"It's relatively quiet just now. There's an English private in isolation with TB, and then there's the new arrival who came with you."

"I can take care of changing his dressings, but Private Woods mostly just needs time to heal. At the moment he's recovering from the journey."

"Good, good. Well, I will let you settle into your quarters. Once you are ready, I'll show you around our little empire," Jülicher said this while raising his arms dramatically, with a knowing smile.

"Thank you and good day to you," Katarina said as she stood and turned to the door, leaving Gerhard to his work.

Jülicher couldn't quite believe his luck. At last, someone else with medical training to help with the ever expanding prison population, Jülicher thought to himself. He also knew, however, that she hadn't been impressed with his lack of medical supplies. Who would be? No sooner had he returned to the papers on his desk than there was another knock at the door. "*Komm,*" said Jülicher.

A young private, barely out of his teens, saluted nervously as he entered.

"What is it, Private Obermann?" sighed the doctor.

"The new prisoner with the head injury is awake now, sir."

"Ah, yes, thank you. I'll be along shortly."

Jülicher rose from his desk and went over to his black bag. He looked into it even though he knew what would be there: stethoscope, the bandages made from torn sheets, a scalpel, a pair of tweezers, a half-empty bottle of aspirin, a metal spoon and a bottle of 'medicine'. The 'medicine' was actually one-part vinegar to five-parts of water, with a drop of medical alcohol. It was a placebo, but it tasted medicinal enough to fool the soldiers into thinking that it was something more potent. It had worked wonders on minor ailments. He snapped the bag shut and left his office, closing the door behind him.

Jülicher had noticed that time in captivity changed men. At first they were frightened, then they became cowed. Some never got over the blow of having been captured - as if it was a fate worse than death. Most of those who had been here for two or more years had mentally adjusted and seemed to think of the prison as a kind of long-stay hostel or encampment. Throughout the war nobody had escaped.

Part of Jülicher's job was to check every man coming into the camp, primarily to stop any carriers of infection from spreading it. Cases of cholera were rare as was TB, but he had spotted a few and made sure those men remained in strict quarantine. He'd always patched up the lightly wounded, but with this new offensive, the prisoners had been moved with such speed to the rear that he was carrying out some of the most complex procedures he'd done since before the war, with only the most basic of amenities.

The doctor crossed the corridor and entered the small hospital ward with just twelve beds. It was almost empty, but each bed was given a little privacy with blankets hanging down from the ceiling on either side. He nodded to the guard, a private who came to with a start and quickly jumped to attention. Jülicher walked over to number four and looked down at the man occupying a chair at his bedside, his face largely obscured by bandages. A groan came from underneath the dressings.

As he scanned the patient's notes, Doctor Jülicher spoke slowly and clearly in good English, knowing that the man would be in a lot of pain and, probably, a little disorientated. "Private Harold Voods, my name is Doctor Gerhard Jülicher, and I am in charge of the prison hospital."

Harry stared at this expressionless German doctor; he didn't know what to expect. Was he another Katarina, or was he more like the German soldiers who had either glared at him with hatred or tried to kill him? Harry sat silently, waiting to see if the doctor would reveal his hand.

Jülicher recognised the suspicion in Private Woods' eyes. The propaganda in Britain was clearly as brutal and as effective as that in Germany. Woods was not the first to think that he, a doctor who had qualified at the top of his class from the University of Munich, could be some kind of blood-thirsty barbarian. "In my role as a medical professional, my only purpose is to help you recover from what is a serious head injury."

More silence from Harry.

Jülicher sighed. He'd like to get this prisoner to trust him, but it was an uphill battle, given that Woods was a POW, and Jülicher was wearing the uniform of the enemy. Then the doctor was struck by a bit of inspiration. "Let's get three things clear, shall we? I know what your British press says about us, so I thought I'd clarify some misconceptions. One: my name is Gerhard, not Fritz. Indeed, Germans have many names other than Fritz. Two: Huns come from Hungary. I am from Bavaria, which makes me German. Three: I do, however, like sauerkraut, particularly with *Weißwurst.*"

There was a splutter of laughter, followed by a wince of pain from Harry.

"Good, I see you haven't lost your sense of humour. Now, allow me to explain what's happened to your face."

"It's okay; I remember. I got smashed in the face with the butt of a rifle."

"That would do it, but you are a very fortunate young man. Your cheek bone has a compound fracture, which will knit back together; but the trauma to your face is such that you are likely to have a permanent scar. Your nose is broken, but that's healing – and can always be fixed later. You may not feel like it, but you are lucky - a centimetre higher and you would be blind in your left eye. As it is, the orbit of your socket is severely traumatised, and you must keep that bandage over the eye if you want it to heal properly.

"I can only imagine how much pain you must be in, and I would love to give you more powerful painkillers; but with regret, your Royal Navy is doing a rather good job of blockading our ports, and I just don't have everything I need. We can keep your wounds clean, and we will keep an eye on the stitches put in at the field hospital; but in the meantime, I can give you two aspirin and some of my medicine." As Jülicher rummaged around in his black bag, a whisper leaked from Private Woods' mouth.

"Thank you."

Gerhard leaned over and put his hand on Harry' right hand to reassure him. "You're welcome. Now all I have to do is figure out how to get both the aspirin and the medicine into your mouth, which is half-hidden under all those dressings."

***

Spring 1918

Dear Harry

We were all so happy to hear that you are safe. Well as safe as you can be in a prisoner of war camp. The fact you can write means we know your wounds can't be too bad. But seriously Harry between us two how are you? I'll tell Mum and Dad whatever you want me to but I hope you will tell me the truth and I hope its not too bad. Dad keeps telling his mates down the pub how the army has let you down by allowing you to be captured. It frightens Mum but she actually seems happier now that your out of danger.

Nancy is growing up fast. Its hard to believe that our little sister has just had her 14th birthday. Mum outdid herself. Such a beautiful cake - it was delicious too. I managed to get two helpings. I ate the other one for you.

Mrs Turner next door saw Nancy walking down the street with Jonny Lewis the other day. Dad really tanned her hide after that. I don't think she'll be going anywhere near Jonny in the future.

The newspapers are all talking about the German spring offensive. They have driven a wedge between our forces and the French but it seems to have run out of steam. Looks like our lines buckled but held out and now its time for payback. I guess you'll be missing all of this as you sit there getting bored of sausages.

Write when you can and stay safe.

Your loving brother

Alfred

***

The prison camp was little more than some wooden huts, a large open yard and four towers, one on each of the squared-off corners. The perimeter 'walls' were a double layer of barbed wire fifteen feet high. Anti-personnel mines had been laid in the gap between the wire fences; at least that's what the signs said. Nobody knew for sure and nobody wanted to be the first to find out.

The camp was located on an exposed plain. The lack of surrounding trees or sheltering hills meant not only that there was nowhere to hide if an escape was attempted, but also that a stiff, cold wind blew down from the northeast and swept across the camp, unhindered. Even now, as summer was approaching, the wind could be bitter.

By day, the prisoners milled aimlessly around the camp. There were attempts by the officers to keep some semblance of military discipline, but most of the men looked forlorn, their spirits crushed. A few held the distinction of having been in the camp since the summer of 1914 and had become institutionalised, dependent on the strict, unchanging daily routine.

The British army had brought men together from all over the world, but most nationalities stuck together. The largest group was the British, then the Canadians. There were also Australians, New Zealanders and South Africans as well as a few sepoys from India. Just recently, a few Americans had come trickling in. The camp was getting crowded. It was at capacity and yet still more prisoners arrived. It was as if the German authorities had remembered enough about the camp to send prisoners but not enough to do anything about the poor conditions.

For some, internment was a chance to flex their muscles. Gangs formed; their leaders were the prisoners who had reached the top of the heap not through military rank, but by that much older path to power, brute strength and callous violence. One of the worst was Sergeant Hannigan, a man of powerful build from his years as a dock worker in Liverpool. Hannigan was a man of dubious morals and had joined the army to see if he could use his animal strength and love of fighting to improve his lot in life. He was utterly contemptuous of everyone, and all but a few officers were terrified of him. Back in Liverpool, he'd had a fearsome reputation not only for the copious amounts of alcohol he could consume, but for the consequences if anyone crossed his path after he'd spent an evening in the pub. Hannigan had been in the camp for over a year, which meant he'd not had a decent drink for at least the same amount of time. Abstinence did not suit him, and without the discipline of military life, he was inclined to give full rein to his foul temper. Unfortunately for Harry, he had been assigned to Hannigan's hut.

Harry did his best to avoid potential trouble. His still-bandaged face meant he was seen as an invalid, and everyone left him alone. The man in the bunk above him was David Goldstein, a friendly Jew from the East End of London. David was short and stocky, with thick black hair and a luxurious moustache which, when he had the opportunity, he would wax to resemble Lord Kitchener's. David had befriended an Indian corporal, Atul Seth, who was also short, but slim and bony, with rounded features, a neatly trimmed beard and a grin as wide as the prison yard. Seth was used to the climate of northern India, where the monsoon rains marked the cycles of village life. He remembered that when he was ten, the men had hunted down a tiger that had killed one of the women - and now, here he was, standing on a windswept plain in Germany. It was all so alien he might as well be on the moon.

David and Atul were two outsiders, drawn together by their otherness. Now they had the wounded Englishman, another misfit, in their little band. The three of them stood looking out over the barbed wire at the fields beyond, where the prisoners had spent weeks ploughing and sowing in the surrounding countryside. They were free and much-needed labour in a nation where most of the young men were fighting, wounded or dead.

The resulting crops were reaching for the sun, no longer fragile shoots. Their gradual transformation fascinated the prisoners, partly because so many came from urban areas, partly because the simple beauty of the fields was in such contrast to their more immediate surroundings and partly because there was little else to do.

"What is it?" Harry asked as he surveyed the field closest to them.

"Could be barley, maybe wheat or rye ... I don't know. My family are hat makers; I didn't see much of the countryside before the war," remarked David.

"It's wheat," said Atul, puffing on a cigarette.

"Well, why can't it be barley?" enquired David, somewhat tetchily.

"Because it's wheat," said Atul, again, in a matter-of-fact tone.

"And how would you know?" enquired Harry.

"Because the Jewish hat maker here forgets that I grew up on farm, and you know what? We don't just grow tea and rice in India."

David petulantly kicked the ground but smirked nonetheless. Atul was about to continue when the conversation was interrupted by a loud "Oi!" The three men turned around to see the massive bulk of Sergeant Hannigan bearing down on them.

"You, fucking new boy!" Hannigan snarled at Harry. "I want your spoon."

Harry was completely flustered. He didn't understand; was this prison slang for something? "I …ah…beg your pardon?" stammered Harry.

"For fuck sake, I want your spoon," Hannigan growled through gritted teeth.

Harry was totally bewildered. Every prisoner was issued with a spoon, which he kept with him in case he could scavenge an extra bit of food, but why would this bruiser need Harry's spoon? Was this a test or did it mean something else? "My spoon … you want my spoon?" Harry asked, trying to make certain he understood correctly.

"Yeah, your fucking spoon. Jesus Christ, did that head wound cripple your brain? Are you fucking stupid? You have a spoon. I am taking that fucking spoon because I need your fucking spoon." Hannigan said all this with measured precision as if talking to a child.

"Why do you need the spoon?" interjected David, hoping to take some heat from the situation.

"Never mind why, Jew boy. I need the cripple's spoon."

With a baffled shrug of defeat, Harry delved into his trouser pocket and handed over his spoon.

"Ta," Hannigan said with a wicked smile and ruffled Harry's blonde locks in a gesture meant less as a 'thank you', more as an act of subjugation.

"Guess you're eating with your hands now," Atul observed.

***

Katarina leaned close as she changed Harry's dressing. The greatly reduced bandage reflected the successful healing of the livid bruises that had once covered almost the entire left side of his face. As she worked within centimetres of Harry's head, he could smell her soap and feel her warm breath on his skin. It was electrifying. For Katarina also, this normal nursing duty had become an act of intimacy. She had tended to hundreds, if not thousands, of men's dressings, always in a professional manner, never thinking of anything but the job in front of her. Now she was finding reasons to linger, relishing the close proximity of Harry's young body. She cradled his head with a lover's tenderness and ran her fingers through his hair, smoothing it down over his bandaged forehead. This was not part of any medical procedure, but Harry wasn't objecting. Did she spend just a little longer than necessary moving her hand through his golden hair?

Once she had finished, their eyes met; the intensity of the gaze was mutual. Did they, imperceptibly, tilt their heads a little closer together, an outward sign of a subconscious yearning to embrace and kiss? "When this war is over, we will have that dinner and a glass of wine, won't we?" Harry managed to choke out.

"Try and stop me." Then, "You're healing nicely, Harry. What was once a gaping wound will eventually become a faint scar on your cheek."

"Will I … " Harry wanted to ask the question, but he was afraid of the answer. "Will I be ugly?"

"Harry, you're a handsome man. The scar and your broken nose will … how would you English put it … they will add character."

"Good morning!" Jülicher's voice broke the spell. How much he had seen, neither could say.

"Private Woods, you are done. Private Obermann will escort you back to your quarters," Katarina said, mustering all the professionalism she could for Jülicher's benefit.

***

The prison camp was in uproar. At first there had been apprehension, bordering on panic, when an entire platoon of heavily armed soldiers, flanking the camp commander and Dr Jülicher, marched in. The commander shouted out a speech in German and Jülicher translated. Katarina stood off to the side, mouthing to herself her own translation of what was being said.

It transpired that the extra security was not there to cause trouble or carry out some terrible act of violence. A German news agency had come to take moving pictures of the prisoners for a news reel, and a journalist was there to write about the conditions in the camp. The soldiers jostled for positions at the front; there was always a chance their faces would be seen back home. The pushing and shoving became so heated that the camp commander ordered troops to break up the scuffles.

Doctor Jülicher pointed to Harry. "You, Private Woods and all the other walking wounded, please come to the front. We want to show that we are looking after the injured men."

Harry walked past a number of men, including Hannigan. "Got a fucking Kraut friend, have you?" Hannigan muttered under his breath.

"So what, Hannigan? The boy's got to be nice to the doctor who's fixing his face, hasn't he?" David blurted out as Harry moved past.

Hannigan clenched his fists and glared at David but did nothing; there wasn't much he could do with a platoon of soldiers and a camera crew nearby. The line of German soldiers moved apart, and a camera man, photographer and journalist stepped forward.

The photographer was a drab-looking, middle-aged man in a shabby coat, who began checking his equipment. The motion picture camera operator was large and fleshy, with luxurious mutton chops; his intricately carved meerschaum pipe puffed out clouds of tobacco smoke as he set up his tripod. He grinned at the soldiers and waved his hat at them; he got some cheerful smiles and a few raised caps in reply. But it was the woman journalist who got the biggest response.

As a woman, Katarina's arrival in the camp had caused a flurry of excitement, followed by a sudden outbreak of minor ailments, but these transparent attempts to see the new nurse had been thwarted by the stern Sergeant Weick. And, of course, Katarina dressed in the drab uniform of a military nurse. The journalist was different, and her sudden appearance in civilian clothing caused quite a stir.

Klaudia Meyer was tall and probably slim, but it was hard to tell because of her thick jacket. She had tucked her hair up under her hat, and her appearance was distinctly tomboyish, which, given her surroundings, might have been an attempt to downplay her femininity. If so, the attempt failed as the prisoners thought she was a goddess and a shocking reminder of what they were missing. As she moved towards the front of the assembled prisoners, there was a unanimous roar of approval, but she studiously ignored their catcalls and whistles. She was prepared for such behaviour, and while hundreds of men cheering and shouting must have been unnerving, she was a complete professional and gave no outward indication of anything she might be feeling.

The crew was practiced in its work and quickly got what they needed, after which the commander spoke again. Apparently the authorities had recognised that the camp was at capacity, and work details would be created to build a new camp half a mile away. It was something different, and in a prisoner's life, different usually meant diversion, and that was – usually - good. High on excitement, there was a last cheer from the POWs.

The crew had been at the camp for only an hour, but the time had seemed even shorter to the elated prisoners. The chubby cameraman had been particularly good at getting the men to cheer and wave to show they were happy in the camp. Despite the briefness of the visit, the whole experience was the only thing anyone could talk about for the next week. As diversions went, it was hard to beat. The newly formed work crews laughed and joked about the female journalist as they marched along to the new site. Memories became exaggerated until she had become a busty blonde in a revealing dress, blowing kisses to all the men!

***

Katarina arrived at Jülicher's small office for their Monday morning meeting. She liked the regular routine of prison hospital life. Unlike the field hospital, medical care here changed little from day-to-day, and she had been lucky. Jülicher was a talented doctor and a kind man. If it was not for Harry, he might have even caught her eye in a different way.

"Ah, good morning, Katarina. Please take a chair," Gerhard said with a wide smile.

"Good morning, Gerhard."

"Well, here we are again. What have you got to report?"

"The work on the construction site has led to an increase in … I guess we should call them 'labour-related injuries'," Katarina began. "Apart from Morgan, still in isolation with TB, and Private Woods, whom we both know about, we have had, once again this week, close to a dozen minor injuries. One man fell from scaffolding and dislocated his shoulder; there have been a couple of nasty splinter cases, and poor Corporal Jones broke his thumb when he was distracted while using a hammer."

"I beg your pardon?"

"It appears Jones was rather enthusiastically banging in nails, when another soldier called out to him. He missed the nail and hit his thumb, right on the knuckle."

Gerhard snorted but regained his composure. "Ah, the horrors of war," he couldn't resist adding, in mock solemnity. He stopped and looked down at his desk as he thought of the right words for what he wanted to say next. "Katarina, we've only known each other for a short time, but something I have observed forces me to give you a warning."

Katarina froze. What did he mean? Her mind was racing.

"I have seen you with Private Woods, and I have seen you with other patients. I don't need a medical degree to know that you have feelings for him." The words hung in the air. The atmosphere in the office had gone from light and good-humoured to one thick with meaning. "I, too, have spent time with Private Woods, and he's unusual. Yes, he's fresh and innocent, but these traits alone do not account for the fact that he's a rare species, especially when it comes to soldiers. His views on life and the war are remarkably nuanced for one so young. I enjoy spending time with him and, like you, I've been teaching him a little German, but let's be honest about the situation; you enjoy his company in a different way than I do."

"But I …" Katarina murmured, feeling exposed.

"Please understand, I am not criticising you or Woods. For years, all I have seen is suffering soldiers, broken men, roaming aimlessly behind barbed wire. You have reminded me of that most important and powerful of human emotions, love. It's like finding a flower in a muddy field, but it makes you vulnerable, both of you. If the guards find out, they will make Woods' life worse; if his fellow prisoners find out, they will make his life unbearable. If this ever got out, you could be arrested and imprisoned."

While Gerhard stopped to gather his thoughts, the silence in the room solidified. Katarina sat as still and as stiff as a statue; her face was an impassive mask concealing a rising panic that threatened to engulf her. The only clue to this inner turmoil was a gentle blushing on her cheeks.

"I can't turn a blind eye to this situation because of the possible danger to you both. Under normal circumstances the two of you might make a good match … but these aren't normal circumstances. I'm asking you, Katarina, to keep these emotions in check and ensure that nobody else becomes suspicious. Remember the consummate professional that Doctor Abels referred to me."

Katarina nodded as Gerhard spoke. Tears began to well up in her eyes. She fought them back; this was no time to add another layer of humiliation to an already fraught conversation. She breathed in deeply, filling her lungs with fresh air in an attempt to control her emotions. "You are absolutely right, Herr Doctor. I apologise profusely for my unprofessional conduct."

She stood up to leave when Gerard reached over to touch her arm. Their eyes met, his pleadingly honest, hers quivering with the effort it took to hold back her tears. "I will speak of this to no one. I only raised it because I don't want two people I care about to get hurt."

Katarina nodded acknowledgement and sniffed back the tears that were still threatening to spill out. "Thank you, Gerhard," she whispered, slipping away from his touch and out through the door.

Jülicher collapsed back into his chair and let out the longest sigh of his life.

***

Richard Barley was physically ordinary. He was of average height and build, with brown hair, a thin moustache and blue eyes behind thick glasses. He wore a nondescript three-piece suit with a white shirt and a drab tie. But Richard Barley was exceptional in at least one respect: he was a genius, a graduate of Oxford, with a double-first in German and Arabic. He had, of course, been approached by the Secret Intelligence Service (SIS) and had accepted their offer not only because he considered this to be his patriotic duty, but also because he liked challenges, and he was reasonably certain that the intelligence services would provide some of the most cerebral challenges available anywhere.

However, even the most brilliant of men must start somewhere, and a career in the secret service started at the bottom. At the moment Barley was on the lowest rung. He had been given the task of checking the German newspapers to monitor their versions of events to see if anything could be gleaned concerning the mood in Germany. He munched absentmindedly on a corned beef sandwich as he read an article about prisoners of war by Klaudia Meyer in the *Munich Zeitung*. It seemed they were being treated as well as could be expected, but reading between the lines, there was a danger that as Germany ran out of resources, the prisoners would come last on any list of German priorities. Malnutrition and diseases associated with overcrowding, such as cholera and TB, could become a serious threat.

Barley made a note of this in a report he feared would come last on any list of Allied priorities. Then he read the note that had been attached to the article. Apparently there was a news reel from the same prison camp. Copies had been released to German cinema audiences, and the SIS, with its many mysterious sources, had managed to get a copy back to England only six days after its initial release.

Barley sat down in a darkened room with a few other men, all ready to take notes as they viewed the smuggled footage. The white screen flickered to life, and there they were, hundreds of imprisoned men, waiting for the war to end so they could get back home. It was shocking to see so many. Although incarcerated behind barbed wire like common criminals, the men were guilty only of being on the losing side of a battle. They had fought for their country and were now being held captive in another country. There, in the front, were the wounded, men with missing limbs and another, with bandages on his face, presumably because he'd had half of it blown off.

While the men looked cheerful enough, the whole thing was obviously staged and was simply too shocking for release to the general public in Britain. This news reel would be seen only by a select few, but Barley didn't feel particularly privileged. He didn't do emotions. It was easier just to make notes, to observe and assess.

***

The men chosen for the work detail at the new POW camp were selected on the basis of three main criteria: they had to be fit, strong and compliant. This meant that the wounded, like Harry, and the serious trouble makers, like Sergeant Hannigan, were left behind. While Atul and David were both labouring at the building site, Harry was in the hospital having his dressings changed again; but as far as Harry and Katarina were concerned, it was another welcome chance to be together.

Meanwhile, the camp's routine for lunch continued as it always did. Two men emerged from the kitchen carrying a huge cauldron of steaming broth; once it was set up, one of the men banged the side of the cauldron as if it were a gong, and the prisoners queued with their bowls and spoons.

Supervising all of this were Corporal Holt and Private Sigmund, who were also there to guard the coarse dark bread. They were friendly and everyone liked them; their faces had become associated with being fed. Both Holt and Sigmund were naturally affable and liked to use their broken English to engage the men in conversation, while also encouraging the prisoners to try a few words of German - but not the rude ones. For more than one reason, lunchtime with Holt and Sigmund was the highlight of the day for many prisoners.

The men lined up anxiously, awaiting their turns. As Hannigan got to the front of the queue, Holt said simply, *"Guten auben."* Hannigan grunted in reply and waited for his bowl to be filled with the thin soup that passed for a meal. Then, in one swift motion, Hannigan threw the hot contents into Holt's face. The corporal screamed and everyone looked in his direction. Hannigan pulled something out of his pocket and slammed it into the stunned Sigmund's throat. He tried to scream but only gurgled as the carotid artery filled his throat with blood.

Hannigan yanked the makeshift weapon out of the private's throat and turned on Holt, who was wiping the steaming liquid from his face. He was temporarily blinded and in pain from his burns. Hannigan grabbed the man and jerked his head up, once again tearing open the throat of a German soldier, sending a spray of blood into the air. Hannigan snatched the rifle from Holt's still twitching hands and turned to his gang, "Someone grab the other rifle. The rest of you, head for the hospital as planned."

Chaos reigned. The prisoners scattered in all directions. The guards in their towers couldn't see what was going on, but they knew there was trouble and called out, "Alarm!" Their cries didn't reach Katarina and Harry, wrapped up as they were in their private moment.

As the German guards shouted their warnings from the towers, Hannigan dropped his makeshift weapon. If Harry had been there, he would have seen his spoon, now a crude, sharp shank, the weapon Hannigan had used to stab the two guards. The blood-covered piece of metal fell to the ground, where it was trampled underfoot.

By now the German sentries had worked out what was going on. They were not the best shots in the army, and it was taking time for them to get their bearings. Eventually they began firing at the group of British soldiers crossing the compound, and one of Hannigan's men fell with a scream when a bullet ripped into the small of his back and severed his spinal cord. If he didn't bleed out, he would never walk again. Hannigan and the other five men made a dash towards their hospital target.

It was the crack of rifle fire that shattered Katarina and Harry's cosy chat. Jülicher also heard the shots and jumped up from behind his desk, sending paperwork fluttering to the ground. He ran to the window and peered out to see a group of Tommies rushing towards the hospital. At the same time he saw Private Obermann burst out of the front door and race towards the barbed wire gate that separated the medical building from the rest of the prison compound. Obermann had realised he hadn't properly closed it when he'd let Harry in. Who would try to break into a prison hospital?

Hannigan had previously noticed that Obermann was a man of sloppy habits. He'd seen Harry go in and was counting on the private's carelessness. As Hannigan watched Obermann running for the gate, he stopped, brought the rifle to his shoulder and squinted down the site. A shot rang out and Obermann stumbled. The private fell to his knees, a red patch forming around his left breast. Hannigan had shot him through his heart. "Keep going, boys; we're nearly in! Jock, get the dead Kraut's rifle and bullets," bellowed Hannigan.

Jülicher witnessed all this and caught his breath when he saw Obermann fall to the ground, probably dead. He turned to his desk, frantically looking for his service pistol. He was a doctor, not a soldier, but he had to protect the hospital. He flung open the desk drawers and got a splinter in his finger for his trouble. He winced in pain but continued his desperate search. Pull yourself together, Gerhard, and don't be stupid, he thought to himself. A half-dozen murderous Tommies are heading straight towards you, so don't worry about a splinter!

Hannigan and his crew rushed through the gate that Obermann had been trying to lock. Bullets whizzed past their heads, throwing dirt in the air where they hit the ground. Seconds later, the gang was inside the building. "Find the back door," ordered Hannigan as his men moved into the building like a pack of wild animals.

One of Hannigan's men shouted, "Found it!" As he opened the door, he was immediately cut down by a hail of bullets. The guards had rallied and, while the rest of the prisoners had been ordered to return to their huts, a second platoon of soldiers had recognised the hospital as the gang's target. It didn't take them long to surround it.

Hannigan now had just four men and three rifles. As they swept through the building, they came to Jülicher's office. Hannigan opened the door and Jülicher fired. Considering that the doctor had managed to catch Hannigan by surprise and that Hannigan himself was over six feet tall, the fact that the doctor's shot hit the door frame proved Gerhard did not have a flair for weapons. As the wooden frame splintered and spat fragments, Hannigan lunged forward and snatched the pistol from the doctor's hands. "Give me that, you twat!" barked Hannigan as he tucked the gun in his trousers and punched Jülicher in the face. The doctor doubled over, clutching his head.

***

Harry and Katarina heard the gunfire without knowing what was happening. Whatever it was, it wasn't good, and Harry begged Katarina to hide. But where? As the murderous soldiers roamed the building, the pair glanced around quickly, deciding on the far corner of the room where they could use some dirty sheets for cover. Katarina tucked herself into the foetal position, and Harry did the rest. It wouldn't withstand close inspection, but hopefully, at a glance, it would look like just a pile of laundry.

Harry tore off his bandage, hoping the livid scar on his face would be enough to divert the attention of anyone who came in. No sooner had he done so than a stocky Scottish corporal came bounding through the door. The corporal's name was Smith, but everyone called him Jock.

"What's going on?" Harry asked with a look of confusion that was not entirely feigned.

"Break out," Jock replied curtly, his face a mask of concentration as he scanned the room. "Where's that little nursey?"

"Gone to get new bandages," Harry said, pointing to his face.

Jock leered at Harry's left cheek. "Jesus! They sure hit you with the ugly stick, didn't they?"

Harry shrugged, trying to remain calm.

"Men, to me!" roared Hannigan as he strode into the room, dragging Jülicher behind him. Hannigan set eyes on Harry. "Fuck me! I didn't know you were hiding that mess under your bandages," Hannigan said, staring at Harry's wound. "Where's that nurse?" Hannigan snapped at Harry.

"He says we just missed her; she's gone to get some bandages," said Jock, trying to be helpful.

"Bollocks! We need to find her," spat Hannigan. "The private here is a Kraut lover, isn't that right?" The last part was aimed at Jülicher. Hannigan had yanked up the doctor's head and shouted it into his face. All Gerhard could do was grimace.

Another one of Hannigan's crew came into the room. "The whole place is clear except for one guy at the far end in a room on his own," he reported.

"Bring him in here. This is where we'll rally," ordered Hannigan.

"No! Don't do that!" Jülicher cried.

"Why the fuck not?" Hannigan asked threateningly.

"Morgan is in isolation. He has TB. You want us to all catch it?"

"Listen, Fritz, my plan hasn't worked out too well. We're surrounded and we've already killed three guards. If I live long enough to die from TB, I'll be happy." Hannigan turned to the man in the doorway. "Could he be trouble?"

"Nah, he's lying there with a fever."

"Leave the fucker there. Jock, you checked under the beds?"

"Yeah."

"And what about those sheets?" asked Hannigan, who had pulled out Gerhard's pistol and used it to point at the pile that contained Katarina. Jock was walking over to it when they suddenly heard shouting in German. "What's he saying?" demanded Hannigan to Jülicher.

"It's the camp commandant. He says you are surrounded, and if you throw down your weapons and come out with your hands up, they won't shoot."

"What do you think, boys, do we trust the Bosch bastards?" By now all of Hannigan's men were in the same room, and they all shook their heads. "We've got three rifles, one pistol and their doctor as hostage," Hannigan summarised.

Jock was now standing over the pile of sheets. He pulled at them and exposed a human shoulder. He jerked more away and revealed Katarina, her face a picture of terror. "Make that *two* hostages," Jock said, triumphantly.

Katarina shrieked as she was dragged from the tangle of sheets. Hannigan turned to Harry. "You lying little fuck!" he said angrily. He moved towards Harry and swung his meaty fist into Harry's face. His bone-hard knuckles crunched against Harry's left cheek. In his head Harry heard the crack of newly knitted bone, followed by a white-hot pain that consumed him. Harry cried out and fell to the floor, blood oozing from the freshly ruptured sutures on his face.

Katarina screamed, "*Nein!*" and lunged towards Harry.

Jock reacted instinctively, brought his rifle around and fired. Jock's aim was true. Katarina never made it to Harry. The shot entered the back of her head and exited her temple. She slumped to the floor, lifeless, blood flowing freely from the wound in her head. Gerhard stared on in shocked disbelief. The two people he cared most about in this godforsaken place were now lying on the floor in pools of their own blood.

The soldiers outside, hearing the screams, began firing, and a platoon of German soldiers stormed the building. The shoot-out was swift and intense. Hannigan's last words were lost as he fired into the oncoming soldiers, intent on taking as many guards as he could with him. Jülicher lay on the floor staring at Harry. The private was absorbed in his own agony, oblivious to the fact that he was writhing around in the blood of his beloved.

Katarina Rumpel lay there with dead eyes and a gaping hole above her right eyebrow.

***

Jülicher had managed to scrounge a small amount of chloroform and had used it on Harry to make certain he was completely unconscious. This drug-induced sleep had given Gerhard the chance to re-stitch his wounds and do what he could to mitigate the damage inflicted by Sergeant Hannigan. The doctor knew, however, that no matter how skilfully he dealt with the physical aspect of Harry's injuries, the devastating emotional blow was beyond his capabilities. Harry had been in so much pain, Jülicher didn't know if he had seen or understood what had happened to Katarina, and so he sat by his Harry's side, waiting for him to wake up.

As Harry began to stir, Gerhard leaned towards him. He had fashioned a new bandage that allowed Harry to see out of both eyes, now blinking open. Harry groaned and reached for his cheek. Gerhard gently but firmly stopped him. "Now, now Private Woods, you leave the bandages alone, please." Jülicher said, soothingly.

Harry was obviously searching his memory as he struggled to speak. "Hannigan ... smashed me in the face ... then gun shots," he croaked.

"I knocked you out with some chloroform and you slept for eighteen hours; you've missed almost a day." Gerhard spoke slowly and deliberately, giving Harry time to orient his thoughts and regain his faculties. The doctor dreaded what was coming.

"Where's Katarina?"

"First I need to tell you about your wound."

"Why isn't Katarina doing this? Is she okay?" Harry hesitated, piecing together what he could remember. "Jock found her, didn't he? She's alright, isn't she?"

Jülicher sighed. It was almost as if saying it out loud made it real, as if not saying it meant that what had happened could be changed, but nothing was going to alter the devastating news. "Katarina didn't make it. She's dead."

"What? Wait! No! That can't be!" shouted Harry. As he jerked up from where he lay, the sudden movement stabbed him, and he let out a scream caused not entirely by physical pain.

"Who ... who killed her?" he demanded.

"It doesn't matter. It was quick, and I'm making arrangements to have her body returned to her parents," Gerhard said, desperately trying to get past the initial shock of the news.

Harry wasn't listening. "Who killed her?" This time the demand came with an implied threat.

"It was Corporal Smith," Gerhard almost whispered.

"I'll kill the bastard!" roared Harry.

"Harold, he's dead too. They're dead; they're all dead. Hannigan ensured the guards were in no mood to take prisoners. You and I are the only survivors."

Tears streamed down Harry's face as he lay back on the bed, muttering, "No, no, no, no, no ...." His head was swimming with both physical and emotional agony. The one decent thing that had happened to him was gone. Katarina was gone.

"It's alright, Harold, it's alright. You'll be staying here for a few days, and I'll be right here with you. Now, please, lie back and rest. Time heals all wounds; I promise you it does."

***

Jülicher kept Harry under close observation for several days before believing he was fit enough to return to the general prison population. The camp was abuzz with the story of Hannigan's attempted breakout and his last stand in the hospital, and Harry had become a celebrity, the only British survivor of the shootout. As soon as the guards' backs were turned, the questions came pouring out: How did Hannigan and his crew get into the hospital compound? Why was the doctor alive and the nurse was dead? How many did Hannigan take down with him?

Their curiosity was never-ending, and for Harry the questions were overwhelming. He was in mourning, absorbed in his grief and able to think only of Katarina and what he had lost. When he eventually met up with his friends, they took their evening broth outside to get away from the constant scrutiny of their fellow prisoners. Atul and David were bewildered by Harry's reluctance to discuss what had happened, but they understood he was tired of talking about it – and they knew he was in pain. They ate in silence as the sun set, the early summer crops now a golden glow in front of them.

"I heard Hannigan killed two men with a spoon," David said, breaking into the quiet.

"Probably your spoon, Harry," Atul observed, unnecessarily.

Harry had already realised that the deaths of Holt and Sigmund at the start of the violence had been caused by the spoon he had so easily handed over. A spoon – *a spoon!* – had led to so much death and the loss of Katarina. The comment only made him feel worse.

"Why didn't you help Hannigan?" blurted Atul.

"What? What are you talking about!" snapped Harry. "The man killed two soldiers with my spoon and then proceeded to tear apart a medical facility. He punched me in the face and then killed ..." Harry felt tears welling up but fought to gain control of his emotions. He knew showing too much sympathy for a German nurse wouldn't be understood. "... then killed a defenceless nurse."

"People are saying he's a hero, reminding us of our duty," said Atul meekly.

"What? Hannigan killed those men just for the sake of it. His escape plan was doomed from the start. Eleven men and one woman died for no reason."

"There's a war on, in case you hadn't noticed, and Hannigan, a British soldier, killed German soldiers. They were armed with rifles, and he had a bowl of gruel and a spoon. Then he took a group of men and tried to lead a prison camp breakout. If this gets back to Blighty, they'll call him a hero and give him a posthumous medal," David said, explaining what seemed to be obvious to everyone but Harry.

"But it didn't happen on a field of battle or for noble reasons; it happened during lunch and the breakout was led by a thug," Harry retorted angrily.

Atul was still chewing a fatty lump of gristle as he waded into the debate. "David's right. This is a war, and regardless of the location, the Germans are the enemy. Hannigan did his duty, his patriotic duty, to kill the enemy."

"That's just crazy talk," said Harry defiantly. "We were told the Germans are barbarians, looking to kill and rape their way across Europe. You know what? Since being captured, I've been treated with greater kindness by the Germans, by Jülicher, Rumpel, Holt and Sigmund, than I have by a lot of our own guys. You know, we *all* know, that Hannigan was nothing but a brute and a bully!"

"I didn't come half-way around the world and freeze my ass off in a muddy trench to hear an Englishman defend the Kaiser!" exploded Atul.

"I'm not defending the Kaiser. To hell with the Kaiser! But the German people are not our enemy. You weren't there; you didn't see what I saw. Hannigan murdered those men because he could and because he liked it, and Sister Rumpel was shot by Jock. What did she do to deserve being shot in the back of the head by a prisoner of war? Remember Edith Cavell? How is Germans shooting a British nurse wrong but a Scottish prisoner shooting a German nurse right? I don't care whose side they were on. As far as I'm concerned, Hannigan and his gang were all murderers!"

"In war you stick with your own side," David said simply.

"I agree with that," Atul said, with a nod to David.

"It can't be right that simply because of nationality, we have to defend people like Hannigan, and that the Germans are bad just because they were born in a different country. That's insane," said Harry as he got up to leave.

"Wait, Harry," said David in a loud whisper.

Harry ignored his friends. Was everyone blinded by patriotism? Could no one think for themselves? Why wasn't there anyone else who felt like he did? He walked away, his hands dug deep in his pockets.

***

Gerhard leaned over Harry's face. His nose and eye had healed; all that remained was a purple scar, about two inches long, across the top of his left cheek. Over time it would lose its vivid colour, and Harry would look almost as he had done before. They were both in Gerhard's office, sun streaming through the window.

"Excellent, excellent!" exclaimed Gerhard as he admired his own handiwork. "You youngsters heal so quickly; it really is like looking at a miracle."

"I think it's all down to the doctor," replied Harry gratefully.

"Oh, nonsense, nonsense, but I will still quote you on that," Gerhard said with a wink.

"The longer I'm here, the more German I pick up. Should be useful after the war."

"Ah, *after* the war, what a wonderful idea," Gerhard sighed wistfully. "I am sure you've heard that the great offensive, the *Kaiserschlacht*, failed. It was our last chance of success. The cream of our army used as *Sturmtruppen*, and now more than a half-million of them are casualties. If it had worked, it would have allowed us to dictate terms. Too much blood was spilt, with no decisive victory. Now it will be our turn to be attacked, and this time you will have fresh American troops joining in their hundreds of thousands."

"So the war will be over soon, and then we can all go back to our real lives," said Harry, trying to say something encouraging to a man he now considered a friend.

"But not before a further colossal loss of life. Not before we add another million crosses to the cemeteries of Germany, France, England and America." Jülicher hesitated and then said, "Listen, Harold …"

"Harry," interjected Harry. "Please, only my mother calls me Harold, and even then, only when she's angry with me."

Gerhard smiled. He had become fond of this teenaged Tommy, and they were now bound by the dreadful events of Hannigan's prison break. "Listen, Harry, this war has been one of the most destructive in history. Millions of men from across the world have been torn to pieces in this conflict. What was meant to be over by Christmas 1914 has bogged down into four years of trench warfare, and it's not over yet. I am resigned to the fact that we are going to lose this war; I just want the end to come quickly so we can begin to resume our normal lives."

"I remember things from before the war, things like the king's coronation, but they all seem so distant, like the dreams of a child," began Harry.

"You *are* a child!"

"Just a minute, doctor, let me finish. I was thirteen-years-old when war broke out. All I can really remember is this war … a tank in Trafalgar square, all the men going abroad, women wearing workmen's clothes … the newspaper headlines declaring victory at Jutland and the casualty lists from the Somme. One of my uncles was killed in Gallipoli and the other is in the Royal Navy. To me all of this is normal. When war ends, I won't really know what *is* normal."

"Anything is better than this."

"That may be true, but I am a prisoner in a foreign country, and I have a scar on my face. For what? Everyone back home said the Germans are evil and only want to kill us, but the most brutal violence I've seen has been carried out by my own countrymen. Now the closest thing I have to a friend is a bloody German doctor!"

Gerhard chuckled, "Friend, eh? I'm flattered."

"Oh, 'cos that's not giving me any shit in the camp! What started as 'Harry, tell us what happened!' has turned into, 'Why didn't you go down with them?' It's turning ugly."

"You tell me who's intimidating you, and I'll have them put in solitary confinement."

"Oh no, no! That would make things even worse. Then it would look like I was working for you, and I'd be a Kraut spy. Besides, you'd have to put most of the camp in solitary." Harry hesitated before continuing, "Look, I really appreciate your concern; it's very kind, but as you said, this is war and it isn't over yet."

"Okay, I understand. Well, Private Woods, you are dismissed and take care."

Harry got up and moved to the door where a soldier stood waiting to escort him back to the prison compound.

***

A sneering face hovered nose-to-nose with Harry. Foul spittle sprayed onto his cheek as Sergeant Cosworth spat out the angry words, "You Kraut-loving traitor!" The sergeant was one of Hannigan's many sympathisers, and his face contorted in fury as he threw a punch at Harry's gut. He was being held by two men and was surrounded by a dozen more, all jeering and shouting inside one of the huts. It was the middle of the morning; Atul and David were off working at the other camp.

Cosworth had perfectly timed his attack. "You're a traitor put in here to report on all of us!" snarled the sergeant as he directed another blow at Harry's abdomen.

"Well, in that case, I'm not doing a very good job of blending in, am I?" Harry gasped and spluttered.

"*Halt!*" barked a voice from behind the pack of angry soldiers. The noise from the hut had attracted the attention of the guards. A squad of German soldiers had just entered the room, rifles drawn, suspicion glinting in their eyes. One of the soldiers pointed to Harry. "*Kommen!*" he ordered tersely.

Cosworth reluctantly let go, and as Harry extricated himself from the mass of Tommies, several of them spat in his direction. The atmosphere was tense. The Germans wanted an excuse to fire at the bastard prisoners who had killed their comrades and a nurse. The prisoners wanted revenge for the deaths of their mates, but especially for the death of Hannigan, who overnight had gone from being a vicious thug to a hero, a brave soldier who had given his life for king and country.

Harry moved between the two groups, a man who belonged to both sides and yet to neither. He walked over to the German guards and left, surrounded by them.

***

Colonel Wilhelm von Thoma was a tall, thin man, who sat awkwardly in the padded leather chair he had been offered. He was still recovering from surgery to remove grenade fragments he'd received during his last battle, and while he welcomed the comfort and luxury of his grand surroundings, he really just wanted to be in a *Bierkeller*, trying to drink away the war and his wounds. He had only a vague idea of why he had been asked to this meeting, but he sat as starchily as his surgery would allow, all too aware that he was being assessed by the general sitting behind the large antique desk. They made idle chit-chat as they awaited the arrival of the third and final member of the unlikely gathering.

General Otto von Below was anxious to get the meeting under way. He had been involved in the war from its earliest days and, lately, with the failure of the *Kaiserschlach*, the final German attempt at a decisive victory. Now an Allied summer offensive was inevitable, and he was worried about how it could be stopped. He knew the simple answer was that it couldn't, but Germany and Prussia hadn't lost a war in generations, and the thought that he might yet be a general in the defeated German army made him sick every time it seeped into his consciousness. Still, with talented commanders like Thoma, maybe there was hope. There must be hope.

Both men were grateful for the interruption when a knock at the door signalled the arrival of Gerhard Jülicher. "Herr Doctor, you are late," Below chided.

"Apologies, Herr General. Transportation is a bit erratic; it's almost like there's a war on," Jülicher said as he saluted.

"Thank you for the apology and the sarcasm," Below responded with a cold smile. "Now allow me to introduce you to Colonel Wilhelm von Thoma."

"My pleasure, colonel, and thank you for agreeing to this meeting," Jülicher said, saluting again.

"Herr Doctor, even from the little I have heard, I have to say I am intrigued," Thoma replied with a wince as he returned the salute.

"Please have a seat," Below said as he motioned to a chair by the desk. "Would you care for a drink, Herr Doctor?"

"Thank you, but if you don't mind, I would like to get right to the point." Jülicher was more than a little uncomfortable. He had been in a prison camp for months; now he found himself in the company of very senior officers in smart uniforms. He knew it was unusual for someone in his position to be granted such a meeting, and he felt the pressure to make it worth everyone's time.

"But, of course. Do tell us your idea," agreed Below.

"Gentlemen, I have been working in a prison hospital, a rather grand term for a hut with some beds and not much medical equipment, but it is the medical centre for a POW camp. We have thousands of mainly British prisoners, with troops from all over their empire, including India."

"India?" Thoma interrupted.

"Oh, yes. The British are using every resource their empire can provide. I have been told that there are, quite literally, tens of thousands of Indian troops in the trenches in Belgium. But I digress. Most of our prisoners accept their fate; a few try to continue the war behind barbed wire, but occasionally we get a prisoner who feels he has more in common with his captors than with his fellow soldiers. And just recently I have become aware of one of these very rare prisoners." Gerhard stopped; he was encouraged to see that he had their full attention.

"The soldier's name is Private Harold Woods; he is seventeen-years-old. He was wounded and captured on the first day of the spring offensive. After receiving treatment for a serious head injury in a field hospital, he was transferred to my POW camp. Due to the nature of his wound and the ongoing need for medical attention, I saw Private Woods on a regular basis and got to know him well. Sometime after he'd arrived in the camp, we experienced an attempted escape by a few of the prisoners. Woods was caught up in the violence in the medical centre, where his serious injury was made worse by a sergeant from his own side. As if that wasn't enough, the private had grown fond of one of our nurses, Sister Rumpel. I do not believe they were intimate, but she was one of the casualties in the final gun battle, and he was deeply affected by her death.

"In short, his fellow prisoners don't trust him, and his belief in the British cause has been shattered. We're keeping him in the medical centre for his own safety, and he is allowed no visitors. He is now, effectively, in solitary confinement. He understands that the only way out for him would be, in theory, to join the German army, which he is willing to do. His only condition is that he be sent somewhere he won't face British troops. He won't fight his fellow countrymen, but he has no similar reservations about the French or Americans."

Below leaned across the desk. "Think of the propaganda: we could turn this into a news story both in Germany and in Britain – maybe even get it across to the British trenches. It could cause dissent in the British ranks. At the very least it would be demoralising. But wait … you said he has a head injury, is that correct?"

"Yes."

"How bad is it? Is he so disfigured that a *Hausfrau* would faint? The newspapers won't print a picture of a man with half his face blown off," Below mused out loud.

"Oh no, the issue the first time around was the blunt-force trauma, which caused serious concussion and a swelling around the eye socket, resulting …"

"Yes, yes, thank you, but I don't need a medical report," interrupted Below. "I just want to know if he looks acceptable for a photograph."

"He has a broken nose and a still-healing scar on his left cheek, but I am sure he will be fine in a photograph. He's a little on the thin side, but even with his injuries he's a handsome young man."

"Excellent," exclaimed Below, clapping his hands together in a display reminiscent of childish delight. "Now, Colonel von Thoma, would you be willing to have him under your command?"

"How's his German?"

"It's not bad, getting better all the time. He understands more than he can say, and his accent is well … quite British."

"What does 'not bad' mean?" I don't want him staring blankly at one of my officers when he's ordered to give covering fire. And while we're at it, he's very young, not to mention that he was captured on the first day. How good a soldier is he? How's his marksmanship?"

"Funnily enough, Herr Colonel, we don't tend to allow the prisoners access to rifles."

"You know what I mean," Thoma snapped.

"I can only take his word for it, but he claims he was a good shot in training. He got to fire his rifle only once in combat before being taken prisoner," Gerhard explained.

"So we don't even know if he's capable of killing a man," said Thoma, voicing aloud just one of the many potential pitfalls.

"Also, Herr Doctor," continued Below, "how do we know he's not a spy?"

"Harry, a spy? You must be joking!" laughed Gerhard. "If the British spy masters have recruited him, then he is the greatest spy in history because I would say there's no chance in a million that he's anything other than what he says he is: a teenage Tommy, who has been captured by our soldiers."

"Look," Thoma continued, "we all know we're running out of men of fighting age, so if we can use the enemy's resources against them, as we've done with British tanks, then why not? I'll put him in an experienced platoon, and if he isn't any good … well then, he's a dead Brit rather than another dead German. And as for him being a spy, I'll give the sergeant the order that if he suspects anything – anything at all - he's to put a bullet in the back of his head without hesitation."

"That's pretty cold," observed Gerhard.

"Herr Doctor," Below interjected, "make no mistake: you may be getting Private Woods out of a prison camp, but he's not going to the beach for a holiday. He's going to the trenches on a front that has already seen millions of deaths. He will be lucky to get out of this alive, but the same can be said for all of us." A sombre silence descended on the group as Below's words sank in.

"General Below, despite certain reservations, I like this idea. It works for Private Woods, and it works for our army, and I am sure the politicians will be pleased with the favourable publicity it generates. So I would very much like to put Doctor Jülicher's proposition into effect. But, like Private Woods, I also have one condition," said Thoma, hoping to wrap up the meeting.

"What is that?" asked Below and Jülicher simultaneously.

"I would like to meet the new recruit before making a final decision."

***

"Remember," Gerhard was saying, "that this is your one and only chance to get this right. If Colonel von Thoma has any doubts, then you remain in this camp, and I'm not sure how much longer I can protect you."

Harry sat in Gerhard's tiny office, fidgeting nervously in his chair. "I understand, Gerhard; I won't let you down," Harry said, trying to speak unaccented German.

"Oh, Harry, don't worry about the accent. Germany has only recently become one nation, which means there are many accents and pronunciations around the country. What you need to show the colonel is that your vocabulary is adequate. It's ironic that under other circumstances I would have taught you the vocabulary for shopping in a market or finding the train station; instead, I've had to explain terms like 'covering fire' and 'flanking movement'."

"In the current circumstances, it's better to know the phrase 'fall back to our lines' than 'how much for four oranges'."

"True, true," said Gerhard with a wry smile. Before he could say anything else, there was a knock at the door. Gerhard called, "*Kommen*", and Private Schüler opened the door, admitting Colonel von Thoma. Both Harry and Gerhard stood and saluted the superior officer. Gerhard made the introductions, offered the colonel his chair and headed for the door. As he did so, he caught Harry's eye and gave him a subtle nod of the head and a smile to wish him luck. Harry responded with his own slight nod of thanks. Jülicher closed the door on his way out, leaving the German colonel and the British private to their own devices.

From behind the desk Colonel von Thoma looked Harry up and down with an impassive stare. Harry met the gaze of the older man and hoped he was successfully concealing his jangled nerves. He was going to switch sides and he felt queasy. The decision wasn't sudden; it was something he had been wrestling with for weeks, but he had come to the crossroads and the direction he took from here would determine everything about his future.

Gerhard had left a letter opener on the desk. Harry could grab the small blade and lunge at Thoma. Maybe his countrymen would treat him with respect if he cut the throat of a colonel. But then what? Face a firing squad? Besides, killing a man who had come only to speak to him seemed a cowardly thing to do.

"I'm not going to beat around the bush. You, Harold Woods, have been the topic of many recent conversations in high places. Do you understand what I'm saying?"

"Yes, Colonel von Thoma," replied Harry, holding himself as formally as he could in an attempt to match the older man's posture.

"Good," Thoma said and offered Harry a cigarette from his silver case. Harry nervously declined. Thoma took one for himself and lit up.

"I have been a soldier for many years. I have fought in numerous battles and have suffered several injuries. I love my country, and I am willing to sustain these injuries in order to keep my country safe. I respect the British; your countrymen have fought bravely, if a little foolishly, and we are unable to break the spirit of your army. It is my belief that the enemies I fight are instilled with the same patriotic feelings for their countries that I have for mine - that they, too, would willingly bleed and die for the safety and welfare of their fellow citizens. But then …" Thoma stopped abruptly. He looked down at the desk before raising his head with a sigh, " … but then, there's you."

Harry shifted uncomfortably in his chair.

"You are a British soldier. You have sworn a patriotic oath, and you have fought my fellow countrymen. Now you want to turn your back on that and join us. Can it really be so simple to betray your country?"

Harry had become impatient, waiting for a chance to rebut the colonel's comments; now it was his turn. "Herr Colonel, if I may, you accuse me of a serious character flaw, and I cannot let that pass!"

Thoma was taken aback by this sudden and unexpected outburst from the seemingly meek private sitting in front of him.

"I may be a British subject, but unlike you, I didn't choose to join the army; I was *forced* to join the army. I fought conscription because I wasn't eighteen, but they didn't care … called me a liar, and then it was too late. So there is a very big difference between your military career and mine. The stories we were told about German atrocities were meant to make us hate you, and along with almost everyone else, I called you 'Bosch bastards'. But all that changed during my time in the prison camp. I will be honest with you, colonel. I fell in love with Katarina Rumpel, a nurse shot by a terrible man who was a British soldier. Now everyone in the camp is calling him a hero, completely ignoring the fact that they all knew he was a thug even before the attempted escape. He and his gang were bullies before they became murderers. How can I defend that? The doctor outside this room has shown me nothing but kindness, and indeed, almost every German I have encountered since my capture has shown me compassion, which is more than I can say for my fellow countrymen."

The last words were spat out with sneer of sarcasm. In a flash Harry's mind filled, yet again, with his hatred of Hannigan. "The first two guards those British thugs attacked were murdered in cold blood, for no reason at all. And that was just the start. The guards here aren't any different to me, my brother or my friends in the camp. It's not true that 'the only good German is a dead one'. I have been lied to so that I will fight, but a lie is a lie, and I cannot excuse that, even if the lie was for 'king and country'."

"Tell me, Private Woods, does the British army allow the rank and file to interrupt superior officers?"

"No, sir. Sorry, sir."

For the first time in the meeting, Thoma smiled. "Good. It's nice to see that English manners aren't a thing of the past. However, while your manners may be intact, I have concerns about your soldiering skills. How many battles have you been in?"

"One, sir, and that didn't last very long for me."

"I see, and the doctor tells me you only managed to fire your rifle once in that battle?"

"That's correct, sir."

Harry's mind filled with images of the German soldier he had shot, images which kept replaying themselves: the startled look, the light fading from his eyes, his face disappearing as his head tilted forwards and he slumped to the ground. It was a sequence that came back often, mostly at night and sometimes in the quiet of the day.

"Why do you wish to kill other Englishmen? Surely, according to your logic, they are also just mere pawns who have been lied to?"

"I cannot fight against my fellow countrymen. I ask only to be put on a part of the front where I face the French. I don't know much history, but I do know we English have spent centuries fighting Frenchmen."

Thoma paused, taking his time. He brought his cigarette to his lips and took a long drag as he stared hard into Harry's eyes. "I have a dilemma, Private Woods. I need more men, and Germany needs some good news. The idea that enemy combatants are switching sides and joining us would be great for morale, but can I trust you, private? What if I put a gun in your hand and send you to the trenches with my men … will you send messages to the Allies? Will you grab some grenades and kill an entire platoon in an act of sabotage? What reassurances can you give me?"

"I can give you my word, which may not mean much coming from a man who wishes to change his allegiance in the middle of a war, but that's all I have."

Thoma sat pensively, mulling over his options. Then he stood up and saluted, "Welcome to the German Imperial Army, Private Woods."

Harry jumped up and mirrored the salute. The salutes turned into a hand shake.

***

Richard Barley read the German newspaper with a mixture of anxiety and bewilderment. He half-puffed, half-chewed his pipe as he did so. There on the front page was the photo of a young private, Harold Woods, first in a British uniform and then in a German one. Barley had asked for records, hoping that the whole story was clever disinformation, propaganda to bolster the morale of the German population, while spreading alarm amongst the Allies.

It turned out that he was half right: while that was clearly the intention of the article, sadly, Private Woods was all too real. He had been wounded on the first day of the spring offensive and, since then, held captive in southern Germany with other prisoners of war. Barley knew he'd never met Private Woods, but there was something familiar about him. He cast his mind back and tried to recall the connection. It wasn't easy. He sat in a large hall, surrounded mainly by women tapping away on typewriters. The background noise was incessant as sheets of paper were torn from their scrolls, telephones rang and people tried to speak over the din. It was the clamour of intelligence gathering, the worker ants moving purposefully around their nest to the arrhythmic racket from the tools of their trade.

The article in front of Barley was morale sapping, political dynamite and one more story that would never be allowed to appear in the British press. Private Wood's family would not be informed of the situation either. Their post would be intercepted to ensure there were no hints of Harry's defection and betrayal. On a story this big, the government could afford no leaks.

Then the connection dawned on him … the prison footage … the German news reel. He jumped away from the organised chaos of his desk and hurried down a corridor to the room where movie reels were stored. He stuck his head round the door and saw Malcolm, sitting there surrounded by metal canisters, pen in hand, a slave to routine and bureaucracy. The room was dark and gloomy, the only light coming from a small lamp on the desk where the grim little clerk was studiously filling out forms.

Happy to have a reason to break from the monotony of his routine, Malcolm loaded up the footage Barley had requested – and there they were. The walking wounded were at the front of the crowd of prisoners, and there was Private Woods, his face half-obscured by a bandage. Barley remembered thinking at the time that his face must have been shot off, but looking down at the newspaper photos, he could see that Woods had come away with only a scar on his left cheek.

"Private Harold Woods, I'm going to enjoy meeting you," Barley said to himself.

***

Just three candles in makeshift holders fashioned from ration tins broke through the murkiness in the bunker. Two had been placed in rough-hewn alcoves in the wall; the third sat in a puddle of its own wax on a crudely-made table.

Colonel von Thoma sat behind that table, his uniform smudged with the dirt that was everywhere in trench life. Opposite him sat Captain Schwartz and Sergeant Müller from B Company. Schwartz was in his mid-twenties, a tall, athletic soldier with closely-cropped auburn hair. He was a man who took pride in his grooming and, despite the dreadful conditions, still managed to convey the impression of a perfect Prussian officer. Müller was physically compact; his abundant whiskers were showing the first hint of grey but, in contrast to Schwartz, he looked rough: his clothes were crumpled and his equipment had seen better days. Everything about him was well-worn, but as a veteran with over a dozen years' experience, he had learned that it wasn't how things looked, but whether they worked and were close at hand that counted.

Schwartz and Müller listened intently to Thoma. The colonel was respected by all of his troops, so their obedience was guaranteed; but what he was now telling the two men seemed like a joke, except Thoma never joked about anything. "Of course, under normal circumstances, I wouldn't be involved with new recruits joining one of the companies, but today things are a little different. I don't know if you've been keeping up with the news from the home front, but there have been a few defections of Allied soldiers to our side. We've got one of them."

Müller sat in his chair, arms crossed, a blank look on his face. The fact that he was sitting in front of the colonel meant he was going to be the sergeant who had this British soldier dumped on him.

"I will not insult either of you. You are here because you are the most reliable and experienced team I have. Müller, you will be getting two replacements today ..." Thoma looked down at the sheet of paper in front of him, "… a Franz Hössler, who is eighteen and from Oberdorf, and a Harold Woods, just seventeen, from London … formerly of the British army."

Schwartz and Müller shot each other sideways glances.

"I have met Private Woods and, to be honest, I think he is young enough and eager enough to do a good job. But this is war, and war turns everyone from bakers to bankers into killers. So, Sergeant Müller, if you suspect any irregularities, any wavering of allegiance from this private, you are to shoot him without hesitation."

Schwartz raised an eyebrow in surprise. It was not like Thoma to be so ruthless where soldiers were concerned, but then again, everyone recognised this was not a normal situation.

Müller remained completely impassive.

***

For Harry, it wasn't the new uniform that felt odd, it was the rifle. He had gone for months without a soldier's key tool by his side; now, once again, he had one. The Gewehr 98 was longer than his old Lee Enfield, but it was a similar weight, and the bolt action was close enough to what he was used to. He was trying to absorb everything around him. Here he was, in a trench, the truest symbol of this war; but it was a German trench, full of German soldiers. His mind was screaming that this was wrong; fortunately this voice was drowned out by the incessant chatter of the friendly and extremely anxious new recruit walking along beside him.

Franz hadn't stopped talking to him all day, which was the entire amount of time they had known each other. While Franz was a year older than Harry, he had only just been conscripted into the army and, as such, Harry, technically, had more soldiering experience. Franz was so busy talking about everything and nothing that he hadn't yet realised that Harry wasn't German.

Harry's animated companion was about his height, but he had a slightly heavier build and a shock of sandy hair that was currently concealed under a steel-grey helmet. The number of topics Franz had covered in the hours they had known each other had been extensive. They had leapt from the future of aeroplanes to a bizarre book called *The Protocols of the Elders of Zion,* then to the implications of the Russian revolution for Germany and, finally, to Maria, the girl back home. Mention of Maria had inspired Franz to deliver a monologue on the attractions of his hometown, which, quite frankly, sounded distinctly parochial when compared to London.

The two of them were being led by a corporal to a bunker where they would meet their NCO and CO for the first time. While the trench formed a dirty scar across the countryside near the French town of Soissons, the sky was a vivid blue, and the sun was hot on their backs. Eventually they arrived at their destination. The corporal shot Franz a stern glance, clearly annoyed by the incessant chatter pouring from his mouth. Franz got the message. He looked down and started fiddling with his rifle strap to hide his embarrassment.

"In you go," ordered the corporal as the two new recruits approached the entrance to the gloomy bunker. Thoma, Schwartz and Müller all stared at the new arrivals.

"Private Harold Woods and Private Franz Hössler reporting for duty, sir," the corporal announced.

"Thank you, corporal. You are dismissed," said Thoma. "At ease, privates," he ordered, while giving a subtle nod and the hint of a smile to Harry.

"I am Colonel Wilhelm von Thoma, and these men are Captain Hans Schwartz and Sergeant Hermann Müller. They are the NCO and CO of your company. You arrive not a minute too soon. The French have been quiet of late, which invariably means they are planning a nasty surprise. Sergeant Müller will take you to your squad's position; what I need you to do is fight. Whatever comes at us, shoot it. We spilt a lot of blood to gain this ground in the spring offensive, and we are not going to lose it. Do you understand, men?"

"Yes, sir!" Harry and Franz replied in the same voice.

"Good. Now, Sergeant Müller, if you would take these replacements to your forward position, I have to speak to the captain about another matter."

Müller got up, saluted and led the two privates out of the cave-like bunker. All three men blinked in the bright July sunshine. Müller led the way past scores of soldiers, all enjoying both the quiet and the sun and all too aware of the necessity to keep themselves below the edge of the trench. French snipers were constantly scanning their positions, hoping to take out any soldiers careless enough to drift above their defensive cover. As they trudged along, Müller addressed them gruffly. "I've been in the army for twelve years. I've been to Africa, Russia and, now, here I am in France. I have survived men trying to shoot me, stab me and blow me to pieces with heavy artillery, but here I am, still standing. The demon of war has tried to tear my flesh and take my life, but I have escaped its jaws so far, and I intend to keep doing so. I advise you to do the same. There will be an Allied offensive soon enough, and you two are my greenest soldiers: a boy from Oberdorf and a British turncoat."

Müller chose the word deliberately. 'Traitor' was too strong and would lead to resentment; he couldn't risk anyone from his squad resenting his orders and wishing him dead. Instead, he hoped the term he used would embarrass Harry, get him to realise his choice was irrevocable and that he, Hermann Müller, was the one in charge. "My squad is a great squad, best I've ever had; but we lost two good men in our last offensive, so you have very big shoes to fill."

"Yes, sir. Don't worry, sir. I'm sure I can do it," said Franz, brimming with naive confidence.

"And the first thing you had better learn, private, is not to interrupt me unless you want to be on night watch until your hair is grey and your teeth have fallen out," Müller said, shooting a look at Hössler that could bore through steel plate.

Franz blushed and Harry marched along in silence. It amused him to see that all sergeants, irrespective of nationality, seemed to have honed their skills in the same school. Or maybe it was just that war turned everyone into the same man. Harry also noticed that the sergeant was armed with the same strange looking rifle, the short one with the angular metal box that had done so much damage in his only battle as a private in the British army.

"Excuse me, sergeant," said Harry, in as confident a voice as he could muster.

"What is it, private?"

"Most of us are equipped with Gewehr 98 rifles, but what is that rifle you have?"

"Ah, good question. This is a Maschinenpistole 18, a fully automatic rifle, better known as MP 18. Not many around but as we're a *Sturmtruppe* company, we got the best equipment for the offensive. Now though, it's back to defending the position and holding the line." Müller visibly puffed up with pride as he described his unit as *Sturmtruppe*. "Where do you recognise the gun from?" Müller asked out of genuine interest.

"Let's just say I have seen what it can do," Harry said, feeling hopelessly awkward.

Müller understood and they walked on in silence for a minute more before they approached a group of soldiers in the middle of a typical soldier story. A rotund private was saying, " … and then her little sister walked in on us and said 'Are you two wrestling?'" The men burst out laughing, but before the story could finish, one of the group saw the sergeant. The men stopped their banter and wiped the smirks from their faces.

"Another of your tall tales, S?" Müller asked, with a hint of amusement.

"No, sir. It really happened," replied the plump soldier with a large grin.

"Squad, meet the new recruits," Müller said, pointing to the two new arrivals. "This is Private Franz Hössler and Private Harold Woods."

A young man with smiling eyes picked up the introductions and continued. "I am Corporal Karl Wald. The fat one is Private Simon Sigurdsson, which is why we call him 'S', and the one looking through the trench periscope is Private Wilhelm Goldmann." Goldmann waved at the new recruits while never looking away from the periscope.

S looked the new recruits over and pointed to Harry. "You …" S began. Harry winced. He had been hoping the soldiers wouldn't recognise him from the papers, but obviously it was going to be the first thing he'd have to deal with. S continued, "You look like a little boy … a Bubi."

Wald smiled and added, "Yes, let's call him 'Bubi'!"

"Ah, but what you don't know is he's English!" Hössler blurted it out, desperate to be part of the group and more than willing to sacrifice Harry's dignity to do so.

"So, how about 'Brit Bubi'?" S laughed, keener to make a joke than to comment on the surprising news of Harry's nationality.

"Yes, Brit Bubi it is!" Wald chuckled.

Was there was a flicker of amusement on Müller's face, or was it only his moustache twitching? And with that, Harry was accepted into the group. A nickname was a small price to pay to be welcomed into the squad.

***

It was the dead of night when Harry was awakened by a whispered discussion between Müller and Goldmann. "I have been looking out across no man's land for hours, and I tell you there's a sniper in that crater just in front of the French position. I think he's acting as a spotter, and I think I can take him," Goldmann quietly explained.

"Here's my problem," said Müller. "If there really is a sniper, why hasn't he shot out your periscope? And if he's as good as you think, he must be certain he'll spot you before you can take him out."

"We'll wait until sunrise. When it's just beyond the trench line, he'll be blind for several minutes; that's when he's most vulnerable. If he's spotting, he can't move, and if he's hiding, he can't shoot at me anyway."

"You sure it's worth the risk?" Müller asked, concerned.

"I would rather ruin Frenchie's plans now than deal later with an assault that's being guided by a sniper who will then also take shots at targets of opportunity."

Müller shrugged and sighed. It was a solid argument. "Okay, let's get it done," Müller agreed, stroking his moustache thoughtfully.

Harry drifted back into exhausted oblivion.

***

There was a loud crack, which woke Harry with a start. Goldmann slipped down beside him, a grim look on his face. He looked at Müller and gave him a nod. Harry looked over at Müller, who smiled and gave an appreciative nod to Goldmann. "Good morning, Brit Bubi. Today we have one less Frenchman to worry about," Goldmann said as he looked down at the bleary-eyed Harry.

"For God's sake, Goldmann, it's bad enough being woken up by enemy shooting, but did you have to use your rifle as an alarm clock?" S asked, somewhere between a grumble and a yawn.

"You're a good shot for a Jew," Franz declared.

"What the hell is that supposed to mean?" snapped Goldmann.

"Er … nothing."

"Alright, you rabble, if we've got French snipers creeping out of their trenches, then we have to be close to the receiving end of an almighty assault. Corporal Wald, go tell the captain about Goldmann's early morning hunt, and the rest of you, I want an equipment check in five minutes," Müller ordered. Wald trudged off, keeping his head down in the instinctive hunch that all soldiers adopted during their time in the trenches.

***

The sun shone brightly, glancing off gun metal; summer was at its peak. Harry discovered that when the soldiers were tucked into the trenches, they felt safe enough to take off their cumbersome helmets, but they were always within arm's reach, as were their rifles. Corporal Wald was coughing into a handkerchief.

"Got a cold?" Harry asked, trying to pass the time.

"No, got gassed last spring. I recovered well enough to be put back into the ranks, but …" He waved at his throat, "… sometimes I still have to catch my breath. It's like asthma or something." Wald nodded towards Harry's face. "And you, how did you get that scar?"

Harry wondered how to describe the past four months' events. He caught Wald's eye and saw that he regretted asking. "Let's say it started with a German rifle butt and finished with a British fist."

Wald smiled wryly and nodded in appreciation.

"You're lucky, Brit Bubi," Franz said from nowhere. "Corporal Wald here may have a war wound, but it's one you can't see, but you … you have that scar, which will always show the world you are a warrior."

"What are you talking about?" S said, pulling up his sleeve to reveal his left forearm, covered in the scars of third-degree burns. "Eastern Front, eighteen months ago, a grenade ignites a can of paraffin and now look at me. Sure, when I'm walking around with my sleeves rolled up, the girls are going to rush over to the disfigured fat guy!"

"Franz, you're assuming all wounds are visible," said Goldmann. "Everyone wants me to take out that enemy soldier at long range, but it's not long range to me. The telescopic sight means I can see the enemy's face; I can watch his last breath escape from his mouth. I am as close to him in his final moment as he is to his comrades, and yet I'm the one who ends his life. Don't you think that stays with me? The Frenchman I shot this morning, do you know what he was doing just before I pulled the trigger? He was shielding his eyes from the rising sun. I shot a man blinded by the sun, at that instant as harmless and helpless as a newborn baby - and then my bullet tore through the bridge of his nose and blew his brains out."

Goldmann's story forced the unwanted image of the German soldier he'd shot into Harry's mind once more. He shut his eyes in an attempt to escape the man's dead eyes but found them still there, beneath his eyelids.

"Enough of this self-pitying shit. What are you all, French?" asked Müller, puffing on his pipe. "At least this war is soldier-against-soldier. My first posting was in Africa, where we got rid of the local Herero tribe. They were a nuisance to the German farmers, so the solution? Shoot the blacks or drive them into the desert. That's not soldiers' work. We were treated like pest control, and the Herero were treated like vermin. At least the men over in those trenches have a fighting chance. We are soldiers of the German Imperial Army, and our sworn duty is to shoot anyone who decides they're going to move in on this position. Anyone got a problem with that?"

There was silence.

Müller grunted that it was the end of the conversation, and the men went back to inspecting their equipment, checking the trench periscope or sitting lost in their thoughts.

Perhaps the only thing worse than being in battle, was waiting for it. The inevitability of further violence hung over the trenches; it thickened the air like a gas attack but was far more sinister.

***

A distant rumble of thunder made every man in the trench jerk into action. "Artillery!" bellowed Müller.

The men all piled into the concrete dugout. The small room was packed full of soldiers, huddled together as metal death rained down around them. The detonations, while fierce, were way off the German trench. "I thought the Frenchies were better shots than the Russians, but at least Ivan could hit our positions, back on the Eastern Front," commented Schwartz.

Harry was on the horns of a dilemma. He knew what was happening, but using his knowledge of Allied tactics felt like betrayal in a German trench. Too late to worry about that now; he had thrown in his lot with the Germans, and what he knew could save the lives of his squad mates. "It's called a 'creeping barrage'," Harry said, above the background rumble. "Their artillery starts up by hitting the wire just in front of their trenches, then it moves slowly away towards us. The guns tear up the barbed wire for the infantry, and by the time the artillery starts hitting us, the French soldiers and tanks have moved forwards and are that much closer to us. It means that by the time we're back into position on our firing steps, they are already on top of us!"

"Oh, ho! That's *very* smart. The Russians never did that," nodded Schwartz, approvingly, but with a grim look on his face.

"How about we start by throwing out grenades. If the French are close, we should get them with the grenades," Müller offered, looking in Schwartz's direction.

"Yes, that should work," Schwartz agreed and added, "Thank you, Brit Bubi, for that."

"For you new guys: never throw the grenades as soon as you've pulled the pin. Instead, pull the pin, count to two and then throw. That way they detonate in the air and not on the ground, always more effective," Müller said, looking at Harry and Franz, who both nodded that they understood.

The explosions were coming closer now. Dirt and dust drifted from the ceiling onto the preoccupied men below, but all they could do was wait. Harry was close to Karl. "Your surname – 'Wald' - it means 'forest', right?" asked Harry.

"Ye-es," said Karl, not sure where this was going.

"It just struck me as funny. You see, my surname is Woods; a 'wood' in English means a kind of small forest. My nickname is 'Brit Bubi', but maybe it should be 'Wenig Wald' - little forest."

Karl chuckled. "So, what you don't know, Brit Bubi, is that 'Wenig Wald' is what I call my thirteen-year-old little sister, Sophie. Do you want the same nickname as a girl from Hannover?" It was Harry's turn to laugh, but the sound was drowned out by the increasing intensity of the bombardment.

High explosives deafened them as the god of war returned in search of victims. It bellowed at the bunker door and screamed overhead in a rage of frustration, unable to get at them in the relative safety of a reinforced concrete bunker. As the shells thundered and whined, the bunker shuddered. And this was just the prelude. The artillery was a precursor, a hound from the hunt sent out to track down and kill the slow, the poorly hidden – or the unlucky. The real danger lay in what came next.

Harry felt a tug on his left shoulder. He turned to see Franz Hössler looking pale and sheepish. He leaned in to whisper in Harry's ear, "I've wet myself," Franz said, tears of shame welling up in his eyes. Harry pulled him closer. "Shhh … it's okay. Don't worry. I don't think anyone noticed, and judging by the smell in here, you're not the only one." Franz smiled in pitiful thanks as they broke apart.

Müller and S had taken out their small spades, standard issue to all soldiers, intended to be used as entrenchment tools. They seemed to be sharpening the edges as if they were knives. Franz took the opportunity to distract himself by shouting out to S, "Why are you sharpening your spades?"

"Well, if you can find a better weapon to use in close-quarters combat in a trench, let me know."

And then, just as suddenly as the barrage had started, it ended. There was a delay of seconds to make sure the French guns really had finished. As soon as that was clear, the men stumbled to their feet and began dashing out of the bunker, back along the trench lines. As Harry's company headed out and to the right, Müller reminded them to have their grenades ready. Even now they could hear barked orders in French wafting through the air, accompanied by a metallic clanking noise and the crack of rifle fire. Small detonations were going off all around Harry and his unit.

Once the squad was together, even before looking out beyond the lip of the trench, Müller ordered the men to toss out their grenades to stop any particularly eager French soldiers from coming at them. The men obeyed and threw their stick grenades out over the top. Shouts of warning were immediately followed by the sound of explosions. The French were close, very close.

Harry peeked carefully over the trench, rifle in hand. It was a scene from hell. The ground in front of him was a chewed up mass of earth and craters. Shards of wood stuck out in jarring contrast to the soft mounds of earth. Sinews of steel flecked the landscape, shattered remnants from the layers of barbed wire destroyed by the artillery assault. Then there were the men: some were already dead or injured; some were dashing forwards; others clustered in craters, partially obscured by wisps of smoke from the remains of shells. There were thousands of them, most of them coming in his direction, but none of this compared with the sheer terror triggered by dozens of small metal beasts bearing down on them. "What the hell *are* they?" Goldmann asked everyone and no one.

Müller glanced inquisitively over to Harry. "Don't look at me; I've never seen anything like it before!" The tanks were small, smaller than the British ones Harry had seen, but they were nimble and had revolving turrets on the top, allowing them to fire in any direction. Each turret appeared to have one gun, which seemed to be either a machine gun or a small cannon; they were already pouring their fire onto the German lines, but the German artillery had lost no time with their response. A couple of the French tanks had taken direct hits and were now nothing but twisted metal shells, still on fire.

"We don't have anything to stop tanks!" said a panicking Hössler.

"Let's worry about the infantry first," Müller ordered.

They were already firing at the oncoming Frenchmen. Harry was next to Müller and S. The rifle fire of the squad was broken up by the occasional snarl from Müller's MP 18. Harry could hear the company's heavy machine guns further along the line. Their withering rate of fire kept the French at bay but could not prevent the tanks from replying with their own machine guns and cannons.

Some of the French troops were, by now, just meters from the German position. Müller ordered everyone to use more grenades. More screams and cries followed. The next time Harry put his helmeted head above the trench line, the chatter of machine gun fire loosed a spray of soil in his face. A chip of stone caught his eye, and he was temporarily blinded. As he ducked down to wipe away the grit, a six-pound shell exploded a few metres from where he had peered out, sending a shower of dirt into the air and pushing Harry over with the concussive blast. The impact knocked S senseless. Harry moved over to him as he lay stunned on the floor. He wasn't physically injured, so Harry propped him up against the trench wall and returned to his position. S would recover soon enough, but the squad was a man down, with the French on top of them.

As Harry rose up again, he saw three Frenchmen in their curved steel helmets and dull blue uniforms charging towards him. The bark of Müller's gun tore out the throat of one man, and he crumpled to the ground. Goldmann's shot through the heart killed the one on the right as the man in the middle came straight for Harry. Without thinking, and in one fluid motion, Harry raised his rifle to his shoulder, stared down his sight and shot the man in the face, his bullet blowing out the man's left eye. His head kicked back with the impact, and he collapsed in a heap.

Harry didn't have time to reflect. Canon fire, rifle fire, tank fire, machine gun fire all whizzed by his head and blended into the cacophony of war. Artillery, mortars and grenades punctuated the din. Occasionally the sound of a human voice made it through the raging uproar, sneaking into Harry's ears. He didn't need to understand French to recognise cries of shock and agony, to imagine men pinned down in ditches, hugging the earth as if it could offer them both safety and escape.

The Germans fired relentlessly into the oncoming French forces, but the French tanks were unaffected by anything other than direct hits from artillery. There were dozens of them in Harry's vision, some providing cover for the French soldiers crouching behind them as they moved forwards.

"Well, this isn't looking very good," said S.

"We've been in worse," remarked Wald, reloading his rifle.

"When, Wald? When have we been in worse than this?" countered S, indignantly.

Wald responded by bringing his rifle to his shoulder and picking a target. Two Frenchmen were getting closer. One was ready to pull the pin from a grenade as the other scanned the trench line for someone to shoot. Wald fired at the rifleman, but the shot went wide, an inch past the man's left ear. It was enough to distract him and bought sufficient time for his partner to throw the grenade.

"You have a poi … GRENADE!" yelled Wald, ducking down.

The rest of the squad instinctively curled their bodies to become smaller targets for any flying shrapnel. The grenade detonated, sending out a shock wave that knocked everyone senseless for a few seconds. Nobody had been injured, but it had gone off closest to Wald, who now lay on the bottom of the trench, thrashing around, clutching his head, groaning.

Just five seconds, perhaps two breaths, had passed since the detonation, but it was enough time for the enemy to reach the trench. Wald's two Frenchmen jumped in and were quickly joined by two more. Müller raised his submachine gun and fired at point-blank range, tearing a bloody hole in the chest of the Frenchman who had landed next to him. S lunged at a second man with his sharpened spade, connecting it with the man's collar bone and driving it deep into the base of his throat. He buckled, gurgling and choking on his own blood as it spurted onto the ground, instantly turning it a muddy red. The weapon was yanked from S's hand by the dead soldier's fall.

In the meantime, a third Frenchman had jumped in and aimed his bayonet at Wald's prone body. Harry got there first and struck the Frenchman in his midriff using the butt of his rifle as a club. The enemy soldier fell next to Wald, doubled up in pain, his rifle lying temporarily forgotten on the ground. Harry was outraged that the man had tried to attack Wald as he lay concussed and shot the Frenchman in the chest. As he lay there, groaning on his back, Harry worked the bolt on his Gewehr and took a second shot. This one hit the French soldier in the temple, silencing him instantly.

Meanwhile, Hössler was dealing with a fourth man and had managed to deflect several swipes of a French rifle with his steel bayonet. This had given Goldmann sufficient time to recover; he took his bayonet and jammed it between the ribs and into the right lung of the Frenchman.

By now two more soldiers had appeared at the edge of the trench. They were about to fire on the squad when Müller fired off his MP 18 and brought down both men. Just then Schwartz came round the corner, out of breath and a little shaken. "We have the order to fall back. Müller, move your men back to the rallying point." Müller nodded in understanding and turned to the rest of the squad. "You heard the man! Grab your gear and follow me. Woods, take care of Wald. Hössler, take Wald's rifle; he's going to need it."

The men moved warily along the zigzagging trench, making their way back to the support and supply works. Harry grunted under the weight of the still groggy Wald. Behind him was Goldmann, who had passed his rifle up the line and now defended the back of the squad with a Mauser semi-automatic pistol in his right hand and another of those lethally sharp spades in his left. He also had several grenades tucked into his belt.

It took the squad half an hour to extract itself from immediate danger and return to the rear. Goldmann had managed to fend off two attacks from a handful of Frenchmen. By the time they reached the area where many of their fellow soldiers had already gathered, Wald had come back to his senses. Judging by the bedraggled state of most of the company, it was clear they had been lucky to escape serious casualties.

***

By the evening of the same day, Müller returned to the squad, having been briefed. "Alright, men, before I say anything else, I want to tell you how proud of you I am. I know some of you are new, but you did well today, particularly you, Woods." Müller nodded appreciatively towards Harry.

"Today has been bad. The French and Americans have conducted an all-out attack on our lines. We have no option but to pull back to prepared defensive positons. Casualties have been high and Colonel von Thoma is missing, possibly captured. It's not clear at this point." Müller gave them time to absorb this last piece of information. Everyone respected von Thoma and his loss would be keenly felt.

"I want you to get some food, check your equipment and, Hössler and S, see if you can get us some extra rations and spare ammunition: rifle rounds, grenades, anything. Let's be in a better position an hour from now. Woods and Goldmann: I'm going to recommend you both for a commendation, but right now I'm going to liaise with the captain."

Wald, Goldmann and Harry sat together. Goldmann was already stripping down the Mauser pistol, ensuring it was in full working order. Wald was going through his pockets and pack to check what equipment he still had, while Harry got out his entrenching tool and began sharpening the edge.

"What are you doing?" asked Wald.

"Well, after I saw how effectively it was used as a weapon today, I want to make sure I've got the same option if I need it."

Wald smiled in agreement and went back to rummaging but then stopped to look back at Harry. "Brit Bubi, Goldmann over there told me you saved me today. He said if you hadn't killed that Frenchie, I would have been skewered for sure. Thank you."

Harry nodded 'you're welcome' back at him. He looked down at his equipment and fell silent. He had saved a life, but he had taken another - two, in fact. Two French soldiers were now dead because of him. Two more mothers were bereaved, and two wives were widowed. Maybe they had children. He sighed audibly. A man could go crazy flipping all the 'what ifs' around in his head. He went back to sharpening his shovel, a conscious choice to save himself and create more widows if he must.

***

The barrage had finished, but hours of constant shelling had put a whistle in everyone's ears. The respite meant a new attack was heading their way, and there was a mad scramble to get back to the firing steps. At first Harry, like the others, thought the new noise was in his head, but as it persisted and grew louder, Harry looked up. Aeroplanes. French aeroplanes were zooming down towards their trench line.

As the little rectangle shapes of the biplanes grew larger, there was a new sound when bullets began strafing the trench. Harry crouched down, putting his arms over his head in an instinctive but completely ineffectual gesture. High velocity rounds slammed and buzzed their way into the wooden supports and dirt of the trench. He wasn't hit but more planes were coming. He looked out over the rim of the trench and saw French soldiers surging in his direction, supported once again by the small tanks with turrets. They were being attacked from land and air.

"Well, this is new," S said grimly.

"Everyone okay?" asked Wald. There was a general thumbs up; then Wald looked around, obviously puzzled. "Where's the sergeant?" he asked. Lying on his back, further along the trench, was Sergeant Müller. Several rounds fired from a biplane had gone through his helmet and into his head. He was dead. He was dead before he had hit the ground, and now blood was pouring freely from his wounds.

"Medic!" cried Hössler futilely.

"Shut up, Hössler!" spat S. "What's the point? He's already dead."

The men wanted to pause and pay their respects, but the insistence of war didn't allow for that. The enemy was on them, and they were in a fight for their lives. Bullets cracked near their heads; explosions rumbled and shook the earth, while overhead, aircraft poured down their rounds of ammunition with a rat-a-tat-tat. The German line and its artillery support were putting up a furious defence. The French advance was slow. Every minute hundreds of men were killed or wounded, some calling for help, some crying out for their mothers, some asking forgiveness from Jesus.

Harry was the first to snap back, perhaps because he hadn't been through long days of warfare with Müller, or perhaps because he had the strongest drive for self-preservation. "Wald, Hössler, S, start laying down suppressive fire. Wald, take Müller's MP 18; it'll be needed." The squad struggled back to reality and obediently followed Harry's lead. Harry turned to Goldmann, "Can you hit one of those planes where it could do some damage?"

Goldmann looked up and thought out loud: "There's a light breeze coming from the northwest. I estimate they are about 300 meters above us and travelling at approximately 100 to 110 kilometres per hour. Their engine block, I would assume, is roughly the same size as a man's torso …"

"Can you make the shot?" asked Harry anxiously.

Goldmann grinned, "Of course, the trick is to shoot where the plane will be, not where it is."

Harry pointed to a lone biplane, which was turning to make a run on their trench. "Okay, Wilhelm Goldmann, that's your target; hit it or we end up like Müller."

Harry watched as Goldmann put his rifle to his shoulder and looked through the telescopic sight. He steadied himself, took aim at the blue sky in front of the plane and, as he slowly breathed out, squeezed the trigger. The bullet passed harmlessly through the canvass of the lower wing of the plane. Goldmann worked the bolt on his rifle and brought it up to his shoulder again. He paused, making the calculations in his head - speed, velocity, bullet arc, wind - all the factors that needed to be taken into account with a long-range shot. Harry glanced over to the others; they were on the firing step and clearly in control of their situation. Harry stood just behind Goldmann, not daring to interrupt the sniper as he assessed the target.

The plane was starting to dive down now, ready to rake the front trench with its twin machine guns. Goldmann fired again, and the plane visibly wobbled. He must have hit the propeller and damaged it, forcing the pilot to adjust his course, but it wasn't enough to take out the aircraft.

Goldmann reloaded and, with a steely look in his eye, returned to assessing the target and the shot. Harry could barely breathe. The pilot had wrestled back control of his aircraft and was continuing his strafing run on the German line. Goldmann readjusted the formulae in his head and stared down the sight. He could see the gentle wobble of the aircraft as it was lightly buffeted by the momentary breeze above the battlefield. He saw sunlight glint off the goggles of the pilot, who had returned to firing his guns at the German soldiers below. Goldman breathed out and again, slowly and deliberately, squeezed the trigger. The bullet ripped into the engine block of the plane. The rhythmic cycle of pistons, firing just behind the propeller, was shattered by a high velocity round. The plane lurched violently and smoke could be seen rising from the engine. The whine of the plane could be heard as it dived, full speed, towards the ground and smashed into the dark earth. All was quiet as a small fire started to spread from the engine to the canvass covering the skeleton of the aircraft.

Harry hugged Goldmann, who had a satisfied smile on his face. "You're a genius!" Harry shouted with relief. "That should stop any immediate threat from the air. Let's join the others."

Goldmann raised a finger to show there was one more thing to do. He quickly bent down and tended to Müller's body, positioning him fully on his back and placing his arms by his side, legs together. He put Müller's helmet over his face and then nodded. Under the circumstances, it was the best he could do.

***

The war had fallen into a new pattern. The French and now some American forces would attack the lines with full force, and if the momentum was carried, they would keep pushing; otherwise, days went by while the enemy regrouped and reformed once more. After weeks of gruelling combat, Harry's squad was rotated off the front line and given leave, much needed time to go home and rest their exhausted bodies. Before they headed off, Captain Schwartz had come by to inform Harry that he was being promoted to sergeant and that he and Wilhelm were both to receive the Iron Cross, second class, for their bravery. Harry had acquitted himself with honour in his first battle for the German army.

While the squad waited for transport in a café near the train station, S entertained everyone with his elaborate stories. It seemed his home town near the Danish border was unusually blessed with a large population of well-endowed and amorous women … or then again, they could all be the product of a fevered imagination, the result of being surrounded only by other men for too long. This time the story ended with a literal roll in the hay.

Goldmann had gone to make a telephone call to his family in Aachen, which left Hössler, Wald and Harry at their table. The café was busy, bustling with a mixture of civilians and German military personnel. A table with three soldiers was nothing unusual these days.

"I can't believe you got an Iron Cross and were made sergeant," Hössler said to Harry.

"It's propaganda again, isn't it? The Brit who fought so bravely for Germany that he gets the medal and a promotion. It's all noise and smoke," Harry replied, feeling a little sheepish in front of Karl, who had been his superior but was now his subordinate.

"No, I won't accept that," Karl said, putting down his coffee cup with a clatter. When Müller died, we all just froze; you got us working as a squad again. And your belief in Goldmann making that shot and saving probably a dozen lives - I couldn't have done that."

"Yes, you could," replied Harry, trying to deflect the attention.

"No, I couldn't, and I'll tell you why: because I didn't. The amount of time I hear people saying, 'I could have done this' or 'I could have done that' … Whenever I hear that I always think, 'Well, why didn't you then?' No, Harry, you deserve those stripes."

Harry shrugged as Hössler stubbed out his cigarette and said simply, "I need to take a piss." And with that, he got up and left.

Karl looked over at Harry, "What are you doing with your leave?"

Harry shrugged again, "Not sure, really."

"I thought so," said Karl, leaning forwards. "Everyone in the squad is so excited about going home, they forget you can't. You can hardly take a ship back to England, can you?"

Harry smiled and sipped his tea. For some reason he had yet to find any tea that tasted as good as the one he remembered from home.

"Just as I thought. You've had a tough time; we've all had a tough time. Come with me. Come back with me to Hannover. Meet the family and check out our little empire of shops."

"Empire of shops?"

"Yes, the family business. We have two shoe shops called Perle and a cobbler's shop. We have workshops in the basements where we make our own designs. What did you do before the war?"

"To be honest, I wasn't that long out of school. I mainly did odd jobs - sold eggs on a market stall, swept a few floors. I did actually work in a cobbler's cutting leather for a while."

"Ha! Already you have the necessary skills to help us expand the empire!" Karl laughed, but as his laughter faded, his voice took on a serious tone. "Harry, you're a good man. It would be my pleasure to introduce you to the family."

"Okay. I'd be honoured," Harry nodded as Hössler came back to the table.

"Ah, that's better! Corporal Wald, Sergeant Brit Bubi, I'm off to catch my train." He grabbed his things, gave them a mock salute and headed for the door.

Harry waited until Hössler was gone, then turned to Karl, "Is it me or do you find Hössler as annoying as I do?"

***

Harry followed Karl up the steps to a large apartment above one of the family shops in Hannover. Karl knocked on the door and waited. The sound of footsteps clipping along a wooden floor got louder until the door opened to reveal an attractive middle-aged *Hausfrau* in a smart, navy blue dress. Her salt-and-pepper hair had been pulled into a bun; she was a woman who took pride in her appearance. Her first curious gaze melted away into a smile, and her face beamed as she pulled Karl into her arms with a cry of happiness. "Karl!" she sobbed. "Oh, my boy! It's so good to see you! Are you alright? Are you hurt?"

Karl extracted himself from the vice-like grip of his exuberant mother. "I'm fine, Mother, fine. I've got some leave so I've come home, that's all." Karl pointed to Harry, who had been keeping a polite distance from the emotional reunion between mother and son. "And this, Mother, is Harry Woods."

Harry removed his army cap.

"Harry Woods, but that's a strange name for a German boy. It's almost like he's English."

"That's because he *is* English. Didn't you read about the Tommy who switched sides?"

"Yes …" Frau Wald hesitated, "… and this is that young man?"

"Yes. Harry, it is my honour to introduce you to my mother, Anke Wald."

She beckoned to Harry. "Come here, Herr Voods. You are a long way from home, so please consider our home yours too."

"Thank you, Frau Wald."

The two men dropped their packs in the entry hall and followed Karl's mother towards the drawing room. The Walds were clearly doing very well.

Just then a voice rang out, "Karl! Karl! Karl!" A blur of legs and a blaze of red dress hurtled itself straight at Karl who, with a soldier's reflexes, caught his would-be attacker and bundled her into his arms. "Oh, Karl, I've missed you so!" Karl gave his little sister a brotherly hug and set her down on the floor.

Seeing Sophie and Karl together reminded Harry of just how much he missed his own little sister; he remembered that Karl had said his sister was thirteen, not far off Nancy's age. Sophie was a sweet-looking kid, with a smattering of freckles and blue-grey eyes in a head framed by honey blonde curls, not so very different from his own hair at the same age. Her hair and clothes had probably been neat and clean in the morning, but both were now decidedly unkempt. She stopped in her tracks when she spotted Harry.

"Sophie, this is my good friend, Sergeant Harry Woods. Harry, this is my little sister Sophie - or Wenig Wald as we like to call her."

Sophie turned on her heels and glared at Karl. "Stop it! Not in front of guests!" she said, clearly annoyed. Then she pivoted back to Harry. The anger had evaporated from her face, and she presented him with an expression of angelic purity as she held out her hand. "Sergeant Harry Woods, it is a pleasure to meet you." Harry understood a handshake was in order and took her hand with a smile.

As they entered the drawing room, Karl asked, "Where is father?"

"I think he's at the cobbler's just now. We didn't know you were coming or he would certainly have been here to welcome you," replied Frau Wald.

"You know how the trains have been ever since the war started. I didn't want to worry you if I didn't arrive as planned," Karl explained, sitting down on the sofa, relishing the room's comforts.

"I understand that, but you could have warned us you were bringing company," his mother scolded. Frau Wald was still talking as she went into the kitchen to prepare coffee for the men. Harry sat awkwardly at the other end of the sofa. Sophie kept staring at him, which made him feel uncomfortable. What was she thinking? He had no idea.

Almost an hour later, Karl's father arrived, and once again, there were exclamations of happy surprise and an enveloping hug, and Harry was given a second enthusiastic welcome to the family home.

Walter Wald was a distinguished looking man with neatly parted hair that was losing its struggle with the grey of older age. He was heavy, with a large beer belly, kept in check by the waistcoat of his dark business suit. His eyes sparkled behind horn-rimmed glasses, and a genial smile could be seen below his bushy grey moustache. He gave every impression of a man who was the head of his business and his family.

When it was time for the evening meal, the family - and Harry – moved to the stylishly decorated dining room where they sat around a mahogany table covered in a hand-embroidered cloth with matching serviettes. Crystal glasses, silver cutlery and porcelain plates spoke of sophisticated dinner parties, but the dinner that night was a stew composed mainly of root vegetables and bits of beef so tiny that they might have been missed. Rationing had clearly forced a change in eating habits.

Sophie carefully made her way around the table, pouring red wine for each of the adults. Harry had only ever drunk beer and that, not for long. His first reaction was that wine was for a better class of person; wine was for real grown-ups, not young fools like Harry Woods. Taken aback, Harry realised that everyone here saw him as just another adult. Had he really changed so much in six months? His hands had become calloused, and he had that scar on his face, but had he been so busy fighting and surviving he hadn't realised he had become a man?

As the conversation flowed, Harry sat looking at his wine in its elegant goblet. It reminded him of the promise he'd made to Katarina about the bottle of wine they would now never share. Here in front of him was a poignant reminder of Katarina, and the realisation that they would never have more time together, a life together, stabbed him anew. Sometimes he thought he couldn't bear it. Before he knew it, tears had filled his eyes and began to spill down his cheeks.

The conversational chatter came to a halt when Frau Wald looked over and realised Harry was weeping. "Oh, my dear boy, whatever is the matter?" she asked kindly, her face a picture of maternal concern.

"Mother, let's give Harry a few minutes, shall we?" Karl said, leaping in to protect his friend.

Harry wiped the tears from his eyes and felt humiliated. What a guest he was, turning up unannounced and then ruining the family's reunion. "I am terribly sorry," Harry said, getting up from the table. "Excuse me, please."

As Harry left the room to regain his composure, he heard Sophie say, "Mother, did I do something wrong?"

"Hush, Sophie," chided Herr Wald.

Harry hurried to the lavatory where he caught his reflection in the mirror. Of course he regularly saw his face as he went through the routine of shaving, but this was the first time in a long time he had really looked at himself. As he assessed his hardened jaw, his slightly crooked nose and his scar, it seemed to him that a stranger stared back at him. The catastrophic events of the last six months were reflected there in the mirror. He sighed and turned the tap to splash water on his face, then found a towel and dried himself. He felt foolish, but he wouldn't allow this incident to mar the evening.

Harry re-joined the others, who were now busy making polite conversation to spare him further embarrassment. Grateful for their consideration, he sat back down and ate heartily, mopping up the juice from the stew with the coarse pumpernickel bread. The family listened eagerly to Karl's news from the front and the story of how Harry had saved his life. Harry was once again the centre of attention, but this time he had no reason to feel embarrassed.

Over the course of the evening, Harry learned that Karl had a younger brother, Max, just turned twenty, who was safe from the front, at least for the time being. Max's bunker had collapsed, breaking his arm and a leg, which meant he would miss the war for eight weeks.

"Where was he fighting?" asked Harry, genuinely interested.

"He was in Belgium, fighting those British bastar …" Herr Wald caught himself as he remembered who he was talking to.

"My apologies," Herr Wald finished quietly.

"No need to apologise, sir. I bet I know more British bastards than you do," Harry said with a smile, and they all laughed with relief.

***

Harry had his uniform rolled up under his arm as he walked down the street with Karl. It had seemed sensible to invest in something other than a uniform to wear, and he had just bought some civilian clothing. They ambled along, taking their time. It felt like a luxury to be out in the open and not have worry about incoming artillery fire. Even so, they were still on edge. A horse cart had come apart and crashed noisily to the ground behind them, making them both jump and dive for cover. These instincts had saved their lives on the front, but here in Hannover, they just got strange looks.

The autumn sun beat down on them, generating a sensation not just of warmth, but of languor as well. Except for the stop to get Harry some new clothes, Karl had been giving him a grand tour of the family empire. Harry had been impressed by both the upmarket shoe stores and the cobbler's shop. It seemed the Wald family had both old and new covered.

The business of the day completed, Karl took Harry to a favourite *Bierkeller*. It was busy, with a buzz of conversation drifting around the smoky room. He ordered two steins, and they sat at a table in the corner. It felt safer to have their backs to the wall, where they could see everything that was happening around them. A youthful woman in a low-cut top revealing an ample bosom returned with the steins.

"They look like a couple of grenades I wouldn't mind getting my hands on," smirked Karl as she turned away. Harry laughed and stared at the enormous drink in front of him. "Does everyone in Germany drink beers this size?" asked a bemused Harry.

"Oh, yes! We Hannoverians may not be too keen on the boys from Bavaria, but even we have to admire the way they can hold their drink."

Harry started to work on his stein.

"So what are your plans after the war?" Karl asked, wiping some foam from his mouth.

Harry ran his hand through his hair as he stared into the middle distance. "I have no idea. I don't think I can go back to England, but I like it here. In any case, trying to make a plan while we're still fighting a war … well, what's the point? We could both be dead within the week."

Karl smiled grimly. "That's true; a soldier cannot count on much, but we *can* count on each other. We *are* friends, aren't we, Harry?"

"Yes, of course."

"Thank you, and after the war, I want us to continue being friends - and I want to work with friends. Besides, there aren't as many able-bodied men as there used to be, so we need all the good workers we can find. Why do you think I showed you the family shops? I want us to work together after the war; we can make some money and have some fun. I think we deserve some fun."

Harry was mid-swig at Karl's last suggestion, but he nodded in agreement as he swallowed hard. "That would be great, but I have to be honest: I have never done shop work. I think I'd be better in the cobbler's."

"Fine, then. Rudi could do with some help, so the cobbler's it is," Karl said enthusiastically, slapping Harry on his back, making him spill some of his drink.

***

The chatter was lively as the soldiers congregated near the mustering point. Their uniforms were freshly laundered and had yet to be spoiled by the ubiquitous dust and dirt of the trenches. The men still had a few hours to go before heading west, and everyone wanted to talk about what had happened on leave.

"Hössler has found us a place we can go for a drink. He says he's got something special lined up for us," S reported with a wry smile.

"Any idea what it is?" Wilhelm asked.

"None," said S with a shrug.

Hössler came dashing round the corner with a big grin on his face. "Come! Come! Follow me!" he ordered, summoning them with his arms. Harry looked at Karl, and they both shook their heads in resignation. What on earth had the irksome Hössler gotten them into? They walked briskly for five minutes before arriving at a parade of shops and bars, where Hössler opened an inconspicuous door and ushered them up the stairs. "Funny place for a bar," commented Wilhelm.

Hössler led them impatiently along the hallway and knocked on a door. It was opened by a blowsy blonde of indeterminate age, wearing a flimsy chemise.

"Ah!" blurted Harry, who began to blush.

"You're a genius!" S enthused, clapping his hands together as he walked purposefully through the door. The soldiers moved into a large room occupied by a number of women in various states of undress, lounging around in the dim light.

"Um, should we be doing this?" Harry asked pointlessly. Karl shrugged and said, "Well, it's not what I'd usually do, but then again, I wouldn't usually be hours away from going to the front line in bloody war either."

"Come, come my circumcised friend! They'll take money from Jews as well as gentiles,"Hössler beckoned to Wilhelm. Goldmann rolled his eyes at Hössler's casual anti-Semitism.

Some of the men sidled up to a group of women and began chatting uneasily; others hung back until the women came over to them. Hössler turned to Harry. "Herr Sergeant," he said, smiling, "I'm guessing that as you've been either in a prison camp or on the front line, you haven't exactly had many women recently." In reality, I've never had a woman, Harry thought to himself. "So I have made sure they kept their most popular girl for you, and I have paid for her myself. It's the least I can do for our sergeant."

"Hössler, you shouldn't have," Harry said, more than slightly irritated.

"Oh, it's quite alright!" Hössler smirked.

"No, I really mean you shouldn't have. I can show you no special favours as your sergeant."

Hössler's face fell. "No, no Brit Bubi, you misunderstand; I didn't mean ..."

Harry sighed, waving Hössler away. "Where is my ... um ... companion?" he said, addressing the woman who had let them in and who seemed to be in charge. She pointed to a door in the corner. Anxious to cover his inexperience and eager to escape from the limelight, Harry made a beeline for the far room and stepped inside to see a corpulent brunette with a bad complexion. She was sitting on the side of the bed in a silky pink dressing gown, which did little to cover her nakedness. She smiled, gesturing for him to come closer.

"Hello, my name is Harry," Harry said in nervous German.

"Alors, je suis Belgique. Je parle francais seulement," she replied.

Great. I can speak English and German, and she can only speak French. This will be awkward, he thought, failing to grasp that little in the way of conversation would be required. The room had been perfumed with the sweet smell of lavender, but the scent of human sweat clung to the musty air. Harry instinctively undid the buttons on his tunic. The girl, in turn, slipped the dressing gown from her shoulders to reveal an impressive pair of breasts, each one a plump pillow. Harry began tugging at his shirt, animal desires taking control of the inexperienced young man in his body.

As the girl lay back on the bed, her gown parted. *"Allons,"* the girl instructed impatiently, her breath reeking of alcohol. Drink probably got her through a day of being screwed by soldier-after-soldier, Harry thought, somewhere in the back of his mind. He hadn't a clue what *'allons'* meant, but he got the idea. As he wriggled free from his trousers, he noticed the girl had tilted her head and closed her eyes. He was just another customer, and he had no idea what number he was today. She probably didn't either.

The logical area of Harry's brain was not enjoying this weirdly intimate encounter, but his burning lust consumed all reason. Harry knew he had taken only a minute or two, but it had felt wonderful. She nodded politely at him, and Harry smiled back. They stayed together in the room for nearly an hour, giving each other sidelong glances and amiable smiles. Then his time was up.

Harry and his squad returned to the mustering area – and then to the front.

***

Along with thousands of other soldiers, Harry and his squad marched to a position just north of the Argonne Forest. It had once been lush and verdant, but autumn had stolen whatever foliage had not been destroyed by the war. The few remaining trees stood in silent condemnation of the carnage around them, naked skeletons and shattered sentinels looking down on the killing and dying at their roots.

As soon as the soldiers reached the area, the order came to dig in. For weeks now, the Allies had been steadily pushing forwards, and while Harry and his fellow soldiers were miles behind the front line, they were there to defend every step back to the German border. Harry's squad was located near an artillery battalion, which had been positioned to cover any potential Allied advance through the forest.

While the *Siegfriedstellung* (which Harry had heard referred to as the Hindenburg Line, back in his days in England) was seen as an unbreachable defensive position, Harry and his men were in front of this line of concrete fortifications, where they spent the afternoon digging and setting up slit-trenches. By evening their clothes were heavy with dirt, and they were all tired and hungry. The men hurriedly collected the vegetable stew and black bread of their evening meal and then settled down as best they could for a night's sleep in the trenches. Normal army life had resumed within hours of returning from leave.

Before dawn the men were shaken awake by the rumbling and vibrations of a thunderstorm in the distance. As light flashed across the sky, Harry came to his senses and realised it was not a thunderstorm but an artillery bombardment taking place on the front lines. He leapt out of the trench, ducked down and sprinted to the artillery that sat huge but silent. "Why aren't you firing back?" demanded Harry to a gunner, who was propped up by the side of the giant gun. He lay there, half asleep under a blanket.

"What are you talking about?" he asked tetchily.

"Well in case you hadn't noticed, there's an Allied assault going on. Shouldn't you be getting your ass out from under that blanket and firing back?"

The gunner snorted in contempt. "At what? The artillery barrage is only meant to soften up our troops. There are no Allied soldiers out from their trenches yet. Don't worry, when they finish, we'll start. Oh and a bit of advice: if you haven't been next to a sFH 13 when it fires, best to keep your mouth open as the shock waves can rattle your teeth. You could lose a few if you clench your jaw. We may not have the longest range, but we can hit targets up to 8,500 metres away." Harry was dumbstruck. The artillery man clearly knew more about the situation than he did. He had no option but to nod in thanks at the advice.

The gunner was true to his word. As soon as the Allied artillery died down, the giant guns near Harry and his squad exploded in anger and hurled their fire down on the attacking soldiers, now so far away and obscured by the woods that Harry could only guess at the carnage being wrought by the cannons spewing out their high-explosive death.

Hours turned into days. Intelligence coming in from the front reported that the Americans had arrived in force and were fighting alongside the French. However, the hard-won lessons the French had learned had not been passed on to the Americans, who were using tactics that had become out-dated in the summer of 1914. The Yankees were poor at finding cover and were suffering thousands of casualties. Some German soldiers said it was like shooting fish in a barrel and refused to fire anymore. But while the Americans were laying down their lives in their thousands and getting nowhere, the French pushed on.

"It's almost as if the plan is to make us run out of ammunition killing Americans so the French can advance," mused S, making his observation during a lull in the artillery fire.

"Better them than us," said Wilhem grimly.

"Well, if we're winning, why can't we get more regular meals?" complained Hössler.

"Because, my dear Hössler, we're not winning. We may be holding back the Americans for now, but the French and the Brits seem to be advancing all the time," Karl said bluntly.

***

It was a week into the assault when Captain Schwartz scrabbled over the muddy field and down into the slit-trench where Harry was sitting. "Enemy troops are almost on us, but they seem to have no support. We're attempting to surround them, but I need you and your men to come forward with the rest of the company – now!"

"Yes, sir!" barked Harry as Schwartz disappeared into the next foxhole.

It seemed to Harry and the squad that the entire division was being sent to try and hold back the Allies while enveloping this pocket of men. As they approached the area with hostile forces, an artillery barrage crashed through the remnants of the forest canopy and exploded on the Allied troops. "Look, those gunners are giving us a helping hand!" Hössler shouted excitedly as he pointed to the rising smoke.

"Actually, Hössler, the sounds of firing came from the south; the Allied artillery is doing our job for us," corrected Karl.

"Poor bastards," muttered Harry to himself. The squad mustered next to a heavy machine gun, which had set itself up to cover a clearing in the forest.

"More heavy equipment on our flank," observed Wilhelm.

"How did we get so lucky?" asked S sarcastically.

"Don't point it out or you know we'll be 'volunteered' for the first wave of attacks," Karl sagely observed.

Suddenly a figure burst out of the undergrowth, startling everyone. As the soldier ran around the edge of the clearing, the machine gun crew began firing; but the runner, with no rifle or pack, was lightning fast, and the slightly cumbersome heavy machine gun found it hard to track him as he dodged and scampered. Wilhelm raised his rifle to the soldier and was about to fire when Harry called out, "Wait! If he's got no rifle, he must be a messenger! Don't kill him; we need him alive!"

Then the figure did something very odd: maybe it was concussion from the artillery barrage or the intensity of the machine gun fire, but rather than run south towards his own lines, he seemed to be running towards S, who looked at Harry as if to ask what to do. Harry made a motion to grab him. The runner leapt from one little bush to another and pivoted around a tree, knowing this would take him out of the firing ark of the machine gun. He was about to break free when he came face-to-face with S, who efficiently jammed his rifle butt into the man's gut, winding him. The soldier instantly crumpled over on pain. Harry and Karl hurried over to S and the prone runner. Karl manhandled the soldier around and took his pistol from its holster. He observed that the man's uniform was clearly not French and checked his insignia and regimental badges. "We have a cowboy! A Yankee from the 77th Division!" Karl announced animatedly.

The soldier looked utterly terrified. He had no idea what Karl was saying. Harry put his hand on his shoulder and looked him in the eye. Then for the first time in months he spoke in English. "Don't worry; we're not going to hurt you unless you do something stupid. You're our prisoner, under our protection. I am going to have to search you, but after that we'll get you to the rear for questioning."

The American now looked confused. He didn't understand why a German soldier was speaking English. "How … how do you know such good English?" he stammered.

"Long story. What's your name and where are you from?"

"Bill, Bill O'Keefe. I come from New York City," he said as he was being frisked. Karl pulled a piece of paper out of his pocket and handed it to Harry. The note said:

"WE ARE ALONG THE ROAD PARALLEL 276.4. OUR ARTILLERY IS DROPPING A BARRAGE DIRECTLY ON US. FOR HEAVENS SAKE STOP IT"

Harry was reflecting on the fact that this man had come from another continent to fight a war that had nothing to do with him, and now he was under attack from his own side. The situation reminded him of the words of his father who had described how his ancestors had fought on other continents for 'king and country'. Maybe this was the story of war. Maybe he was not that different from O'Keefe.

"You're a brave man to survive an attack by your own artillery and then try to outrun a machine gun," Harry said, shaking O'Keefe's hand. He turned to S and said in German, "You stopped him; you get the honour of delivering him to HQ. While you're there, see if you can scrounge us some food." S Saluted and led O'Keefe away.

Harry's head was in turmoil. For the first time as a German soldier, he could understand what the enemy was saying, and his squad knew it. As the days passed, the shouts of the American soldiers became less ordered as they begged for water and food. There were cries for assistance and the screams of the wounded and dying; it was heart-breaking. Every time an American called out, Harry's troops wanted to know what he was saying. This meant he felt the impact of natural empathy for a fellow human, reduced to begging for water, and then felt it again as he translated the torment for his men.

On the afternoon of 8 October, Harry and his squad heard a furious firefight to the south and discovered, hours later, that the Americans had managed to evacuate themselves from the area. It was estimated that 500 men had walked into the woods, but less than 200 made it back out again.

***

Herr Wald sat at the dining room table, smoking and reading his newspaper. In the kitchen Frau Wald and Sophie stood by the stove. Winter was starting to bite, and the kitchen was always the warmest room in the apartment. Warmth and food, what was there not to like about a kitchen? And it was for these two reasons that, during cold weather, Sophie almost lived in this one room - except, of course, when she went to school.

"You see, Sophie, when times are hard, you can always make things go a little further with water. You can dilute the milk a little bit; you can cover meat with it and it retains more of its own weight and, of course, soups and broths may be thin, but they have nourishment." As her mother was telling her these things, Sophie was stirring a pot of soup, which would be lunch for all of them. Her mother had some dried beans, which they had soaked and vigorously boiled in an attempt to make them passably edible.

Herr Wald made a loud noise of disgust in the dining room. His wife sighed. It seemed to her that as the war came to its bloody conclusion, her husband almost relished the bad news coming daily from the front lines. The newspapers gave as positive an account as possible, but troops were forever falling back to 'prepared positions', and they could not hide the fact that it always seemed to be the German forces who were doing the falling back.

"What is it, Walter?" Frau Wald called, not moving from the cooker.

"The whole damn navy is in revolt!"

"What!" Frau Wald said, locking eyes with Sophie, who gave her a concerned look. Frau Wald wiped her hands on her apron and hurried into the dining room with Sophie just behind her.

Walter waited for both his wife and daughter to join him before he continued. "It seems that when Admiral Franz von Hipper ordered the fleet in Kiel to break out into the North Sea for one last offensive against the Royal Navy, they refused. They mutinied! They've been sitting in port for two years since the Battle of Jutland, just watching the army get slaughtered, and when, finally, they were asked to put their asses on the line, they refused to fight!"

"Language, dear," Frau Wald chided automatically.

"What? Oh, sorry, Sophie. They mutinied! Can you believe it?"

"So what does this mean?"

Walter put the paper down as he replied, "I don't know, but nothing good. The paper doesn't say the rebellion has been stopped. Maybe it's gaining support."

"Papa, this must mean that the war will soon be over!" Sophie said, hopefully, not fully understanding the implications of what she was saying.

"My child, you may very well be right," Walter said, and returned to devouring the news.

***

Captain Schwartz dropped down into the entrenchment that Harry and his squad had only just finished digging. Everyone was cold and hungry, and the continual pressure from the Allies was taking its toll. Sunken and sallow eyes stared back at the captain; no one had had either the time or the inclination to shave for over a week, and stubble was developing into beards. Their once fresh uniform coats were now frayed and covered in mud. Harry's men had gone from being modern, twentieth-century soldiers to cavemen scratching out an existence beneath the ground. Schwartz was still trying to process the information he had been given, but as Harry's was the third group he approached, he had had time to practice.

"Captain," Harry said with a nod.

"Sergeant," Schwartz replied.

"Any activity at the moment?" Schwartz enquired, trying to distance himself from the real reason he was in the trench.

"It's all quiet today, sir. Seems the French and Americans have forgotten there's a war on," Harry said with a thin smile. His eyes were still shiny and alert, but his jaw was heavy with whiskers that poked through grime.

Schwartz signalled to the rest of the squad. "Gather round, all of you." The squad huddled in, surrounding their captain. "As of yesterday, we are no longer a German empire, but a German republic. The uprising that started in Kiel has led to the Kaiser's abdication, and an interim republic has been declared." Schwartz paused to allow the men to absorb the shock of the news. The first reactions came as expressions of denial, then cries of outrage, followed by anger aimed at the Kaiser. Once they had died down, Schwartz continued. "There is more. It has been agreed that an armistice will be declared at 11:00 a.m. tomorrow." More shock, followed by shouts of disbelief.

"Does that mean we won the war?" Hössler asked, giving Schwartz a hard look.

"Look around you, private. Does it feel like we won?" Schwartz asked bluntly.

"But we're still in France! We get to keep the bits of France and Belgium we're sitting on, don't we?" an incredulous Hössler half asked, half demanded.

"Private, I think you have me confused with General Marwitz. I have no idea what our leaders and politicians will decide. The most important thing is we are now just hours away from the end of this war, so keep your heads down and stay out of trouble for twenty-five-and-a-half hours."

The men all nodded, still in a state of incredulity.

"Oh, and Sergeant Woods ..." Schwartz began, just as he was about to leave.

"Yes, Herr Captain?"

"You're now the lieutenant of second platoon."

Caught by the surprise at the announcement, Harry was speechless. Then, "Th-thank you, sir," Harry faltered as he tried to take in yet another piece of news.

Schwartz turned and put his hand on Harry's shoulder. "Well done, Harry; you've earned it, but I am pleased to say you won't be using that rank for much longer." And with that, Schwartz boosted himself up and out of the trench to move on to the next group. No sooner was he over the top when they saw his head kick to one side and his body fall back. Only then did they hear the crack of rifle fire. The captain was dead as he fell.

"Sniper!" S called out in vain.

Hössler went to pull Schwartz's body back into the trench.

"No!" cried Wilhelm, who threw himself at Hössler and dragged him down.

"Why did you do that?" grumbled Hössler , stumbling to his feet as he brushed himself off.

"Because that sniper has this trench in his sights. If you so much as stick your arm out, a high velocity bullet will hit it - and probably tear it off!"

"Hössler, what Wilhelm's saying is that the captain is already dead. There's no need for anyone else to die today," Harry added.

"The delay between the impact and the sound of the shot means he's probably a kilometre away, which means he's an exceptional shot. Nobody take any risks," Wilhelm instructed. "We can get the captain's body tomorrow when the armistice starts."

"What if nobody tells the sniper about the armistice?" asked a chastened Hössler.

"Then you get to be the first person to die in the peace," S replied with a smile.

***

The men sat quietly and patiently, willing away the minutes. There had been a light mist at dawn, but by ten o'clock, that had been burned away by the winter sun. The men gnawed on their thick dark bread, made somewhat more edible by dipping it in hot water. The rough texture reinforced the general belief that the flour was bulked out with sawdust. It was so hard that a man could cut the soft tissue of his mouth if he had a particularly gritty chunk. As it was, the bread barely kept hunger pangs away.

The weather was cold and, even in winter coats, the men shivered. Ten-thirty came and went. The men didn't dare so much as peek over the trench's edge in case the captain's fate should become theirs.

Quarter to eleven and the front line was eerily quiet: no sounds of gunfire, no shouts, no background thunder. Instead, for the first time in longer than anyone could remember, there was birdsong coming from the skeletal trees. The men continued to glance at their watches.

Five to eleven; nobody said anything, but the men began to fidget. A few stretched their cramped limbs, while others exchanged anxious glances. Then they began to lay their rifles down, a terrible error in war, but always the first step in peace.

Eleven o'clock. No great gong sounded; no last shot or soaring siren marked the passing of war into peace. The men looked up. Could they stand up? *Should* they stand up? What of the sniper? Seconds turned into minutes, but then their bewilderment was interrupted by a call.

"*Bonjour!*"

The men looked at each other and began to smile.

"*Allô?*" came another voice.

An air of tension and stifled hope hung over the trench and stopped the men from getting up.

"Well, if you're not getting up, I am," Harry said as much to himself as to his men. He rose slowly, hoping no sudden movement was the best way to proceed. There, in front of him, no more than twenty-five metres away, stood a group of French soldiers. Their rifles were all shouldered, and one of them was holding out an open cigarette case. Harry beckoned to the rest of his squad. One-by-one they stood up to their full height as if rising from the grave.

The men all congregated a few paces from the trench. Everyone had scrounged whatever they could to swap and share; some men even swapped helmets. A few of the Germans who had come forward could speak French, and a few of the French soldiers could speak German. The talk was fast and jocular, the mood was festive.

It was during all this that S noticed a Frenchman's rifle: it was a high-velocity, high-precision rifle with a telescopic sight. The smile drained from S's face. "Hey, you!" he shouted, pointing at the sniper, who was chatting and smoking a cigarette. The soldier turned to look at S. "Yes, you! Are you the one who shot our captain?" S asked, walking aggressively towards the Frenchman, who turned to a friend to translate. His eyes widened. The rest of the squad stopped their conversation to watch the developing situation. All eyes followed S as he gestured to their captain, still lying by the side of the trench. "Why did you shoot him? He was only there to tell us the war was nearly over. You murdering bastard!" S lunged at the Frenchman, who took a step back while Harry and the rest of the squad grabbed S.

"Easy, S. The captain died in war. Do you really want to start another one so soon after the last one ended?" Karl said in an attempt to smooth the situation.

Someone on the French side translated for the sniper and then relayed his answer to S. "I shot an enemy officer in a time of war. That is not murder; that is called 'doing your duty'. He wasn't the first man I ever shot, but I am glad to say he was the last. I have no wish to kill again. I am going to return to my farm in Provence, find a wife, have lots of children and never speak of this war to anyone ever again."

"That's easy for him to say," muttered S, still in the grip of his squad mates.

"Hey, private!" Harry called. "Yesterday was war; today it is peace. Let's not get into who killed who. There are millions of dead because of this war. Let's not linger on a war that is over; instead, let's enjoy the peace." When the sniper heard the translation, he came over and shook Harry's hand.

S was still angry but had calmed down and drifted away from the group. Drama over, the rest of the men took up where they had left off and mingled for hours until senior officers came to talk about what everyone wanted to hear – going home.

Part 2: Weimar

The young girl ran into her room and dived under her bed. She pulled out a glass jar with a screw-top lid. In it was all the money she had in the world. A few notes and several fists of coins were poured out on the carpet. She stopped to catch her breath, then wiped the hair from her face and set about carefully counting the cash in front of her.

When she had finished, she came to the conclusion that it would be enough; it *had* to be enough. She scooped up the coins and put them back in the jar where they clattered to the bottom with a satisfying ring. Then she placed the two paper notes on top of the pile as if they were the garnish on a strange metallic cake.

She opened the door and looked around. What she was doing wasn't wrong, but she didn't want to be stopped and questioned. She put on her coat and picked up her jar, cradling it like a baby to make sure it made no noise that could give her away. She slipped silently out the door and sprinted down the front steps. As she burst onto the busy pavement, she bumped into a man who had changed direction and crossed her path. Her legs wobbled but she clung onto the glass jar, holding it tightly against her stomach.

"Watch where you're going!" shouted the irritated man.

"Excuse me!" She walked off quickly but didn't run. As much as she wanted to hurry to her destination, what had just happened was her own fault. She couldn't afford to drop her precious cargo and lose even one coin. She had enough but nothing more. As she weaved her way along the crowded streets, horse-drawn carts rumbled by, and the occasional automobile hooted and passed. She knew exactly where she was going and, after a ten-minute journey, she arrived at the book shop.

This particular book shop specialised in foreign language titles. The proprietor sat quietly behind the counter, intent on his hardback, his half-moon wire spectacles perched on the end of his nose. He looked up at the sound of the opening door and nodded his welcome; she smiled in return. As she walked towards a specific section, his curious eyes followed the slightly flustered girl, clutching a jar of money.

The shop was empty of customers, but like all book shops, there was an unmistakable smell of paper and ink and a pleasant calmness to the atmosphere. The silence was punctuated by the ticking of a wall-mounted clock and street sounds intruding from the outside. "We don't have much in stock. That's not exactly a popular language what with the war only just finished," he offered.

"Thank you. I'm buying a Christmas present." The girl quickly discovered that the owner was right; the section she wanted was largely empty. But now there was another problem: she realised that while she was good at reading, she didn't know foreign languages. She clutched the heavy jar in her left hand and ran her right index finger along the spines of the books as if hoping to understand what might be inside from the way they felt. She couldn't read the title of an impressive leather-bound volume, but she guessed from the cross on the front that it was a foreign language edition of the Bible. Perhaps a little too religious, she thought. She continued to search and opened a less formal looking book full of diagrams of what looked like geological features. Too technical, she concluded. She flicked through a few others, which were obviously novels, but it occurred to her she had no idea what the stories were about, and she didn't recognise the names of any of the authors.

A small book on the end of the shelf caught her eye. Flicking through the pages, she could tell it was not a novel but a series of short stories. Closer examination revealed that some of the stories were very short. As she tried to mouth the unfamiliar words, she realised that they seemed to rhyme. It must be a book of poetry. There were pages and pages of poems, so the recipient of the present wouldn't necessarily like all of them, but surely there would be some here that they would find funny or thoughtful. Yes, this was the one. This was to be the Christmas present.

She walked up to the counter and presented the book. The shop keeper looked at the title, then at the girl's smiling face – then he looked quizzically back at the title again. "Are you sure you want this one?" he queried.

Her mind was made up. "Yes, thank you," she replied politely. She placed her jar on the varnished wood counter and began to pour out its contents. The coins spilled onto the hard surface, some skipping across to the edge. The man looked at the random coins and notes and sighed before gathering them up and counting them under his breath. "You're a little short."

The girl looked back at him, lost for words. She wanted this book; she *needed* it. What could she do?

The owner could see the rising tide of panic on his young customer's face, but before she could say anything, the man smiled. "But it's close enough," he said with a wink.

She nodded her appreciation and beamed at him. Then she picked up the empty jar with her right hand and held the book close to her chest with her left.

"Merry Christmas!" he called out as she left.

"Thank you, sir, and a Merry Christmas to you too."

She ran all the way home, her heart full to the brim.

***

November 1918

Dear Harry

I am writing to tell you some bad news. The Spanish Flu has taken Nancy. Dad also caught it and with his weak heart we thought he would go too but he's a tough old soldier. He's recovering as best he can, but we are all missing Nancy so much. It was such a shock and our hearts are breaking. Mum is taking it very bad. The funeral is on Friday so I guess you'll miss that.

I know the war must have been terrible for you and I'm sorry to tell you this news to add to your burdens but we're hoping to see you soon. After the war and all we count our blessings that you're still with us.

Write to let us know when you're coming home.

Your loving brother

Alfred

***

Harry was standing with the rest of his squad at the train station. The atmosphere was both joyous that they were finally going home and downhearted as it gradually dawned on them that they were also saying farewell, perhaps forever, to the best friends they would ever have. Along with their release papers, everyone had just been handed their final letters and packets from home. Miraculously, Harry's letters had been redirected from the prison camp to his army unit, so his family was oblivious to his situation. Now the news of his beloved little sister's death hit Harry like a blow to the stomach. He staggered as he read the short note from his brother and let out a sob.

"Oh, God, what's wrong!" Karl said, turning to the stunned Harry.

The letter creased in his hand as he clenched his fist, tears filling his eyes. "It can't be true!" he cried.

Karl put his arm around Harry's shoulders as his friend buried his face in his hands. The rest of the unit looked on anxiously, unable to guess the cause of Harry's distress. After a few minutes, Harry pulled himself together. He moved away from Karl, nodding his thanks, and approached the rest of his group. "The Spanish flu got my fourteen-year-old sister."

There were general mutterings of sympathy and compassion. "I hear there are a lot of men shipping home with it, especially the ones coming from the north. It seems this influenza is killing the young and healthy, not the old and weak, as usually happens," S said, reporting the current rumours.

"I didn't want to say anything, but I recently found out my cousin, who has been on the Western Front since 1914, died a couple of weeks ago from this," Wilhelm volunteered.

"Seems like we're just going from one way to die to another," sighed Karl.

Harry's sad news changed the atmosphere and made everyone reflective. Three of the men had fought together for years, but even Harry and Hössler had now become part of a unit where the only excuse for not being present was death itself. Reluctant to leave each other in a sombre frame of mind, the teasing and back slapping resumed as they endeavoured to lighten the mood and make each other laugh.

Harry couldn't join in; his heart wasn't in it. It was S, with his perennially saucy stories about buxom girls, who eventually succeeded in making Harry smile.

The greatly anticipated train arrived and they boarded, heading off to their different destinations. Harry was going to meet up with Karl in a few days, but first he had something to do.

***

Insofar as their various circumstances allowed, Harry had corresponded over recent months with Doctor Jülicher, who encouraged him to visit once the war was over. Because of all they had experienced together, a special bond had developed between the two men, and Harry was anxious to see the man who had become his first German friend. He hadn't sent a message ahead as he was hoping to surprise Gerard, and in any case post-war travel was so uncertain he couldn't be sure when he'd arrive. The train and tram journey had taken hours, but along the way he had been able to buy some *Weißwurst*, the strange sounding sausage Gerhard had mentioned the first time they met.

As Harry walked along Gerhard's road, he noticed how affluent the area was. Clearly doctors in Germany are as well paid as the ones in Britain, he thought to himself, the brown paper pack of sausages under his arm. He knew that Gerhard had a wife and a young child, a girl, if he remembered correctly. He easily found the doctor's house where he hesitated on the front steps. The door had been freshly painted black and displayed the number '27' and a polished brass knocker. He playfully rapped the knocker and heard the sound echo down the hall behind the substantial wooden door.

"One minute, please," a woman called out and Harry smiled. He was going to meet Frau Jülicher for the first time. He hurriedly removed his flat cap and tucked it under his arm along with the packet of *Weißwurst*. He smoothed down his hair to look as respectable as possible.

A striking young woman appeared as the door opened. She was wearing a white blouse and a long black skirt, her dark hair tied back with a ribbon. A chubby baby perched on her right hip. "Can I help you?"

"Yes, I hope so. Is this the Jülicher residence?"

"Yes, it is. I am Frau Jülicher."

"It's a pleasure to meet you," Harry said with a slight bow. He continued, "I am, I guess, an ex-patient of your husband's. I didn't tell him I was coming. Is he at home?"

The woman's face fell. "I'm sorry to tell you that my husband is dead."

Harry was speechless. "But that can't be. We were writing to each other. He survived the war!"

The woman's eyes were filling with tears. "That's true, but he came home with the influenza, and it took him two weeks ago. His funeral was last Thursday. Your accent … are you the British man? Are you Harry?"

Harry was taken aback by the question. "Yes, yes I am."

"Please, come in! You must have travelled a long way."

Harry stood frozen to the step. After everything he and Gerhard had been through, it wasn't bullets or bombs that had killed him but a microscopic virus. It was the second time in a week he'd learned that this insidious illness had taken someone dear to him. He could hardly believe it. "I'm dreadfully sorry, but I don't want to intrude."

"No, please, I insist. It's just my daughter and me now, and I could do with some adult conversation." The baby was taking in all this while trying to force her fist into her mouth. "Besides, you and Gerhard were obviously good friends. You'll bring him close to me again."

Harry stepped through the doorway and followed her to the sitting room. The house was tasteful but comfortable, a family home. He laid the *Weißwurst* on a side table and looked at the brown paper packaging. It felt like such a stupid gift now.

Frau Jülicher had gone off to prepare refreshments and came back with a tray of coffee and sandwiches. She went off again and this time returned with her daughter, who gurgled and babbled on her mother's lap while the adults talked. The conversation was tinged with melancholy for both of them, but there was laughter too.

After a pleasant afternoon of chatting and exchanging stories, Harry thanked Frau Jülicher for her hospitality. It would be a long journey back to Hannover, and it was time for Harry to take his leave. She made it clear that he was welcome anytime, but they both knew this was a bittersweet meeting that would never be repeated.

^^^

Back in Hannover, Harry settled into civilian life in a new country. His German was good and getting better, especially now that he was rapidly adding everyday words to his vocabulary. He had found a role in the Wald family business looking after the cobbler's shop and mending shoes with the middle-aged and introverted Rudi, who, like Harry, had a room above the shop. At the Walds' insistence, Harry ate his evening meals with the family, and he was grateful for their friendship, for a place where he felt at home.

Harry didn't know what awaited him in Britain – whether anyone even knew that he had fought for the Germans in the closing days of the war - but any thoughts he might have had about returning to London were fading. He missed his mother, a pillar of stability, and Alf, who must be growing up fast. It had been good to hear that his father had survived influenza. As irritable and as distant as he could be, he was still the family's provider; he did his best. But it broke Harry's heart to think of returning home and not seeing Nancy. He had always felt responsible for her, believed that he was her protector. Could he have done anything to save her? He didn't know, but now she was gone, leaving a gaping hole behind her. Nancy and Katarina: two innocent women taken by the harsh realities of life. 'What might have been' was too painful to think about. It was better to stay in Hannover, where he was making friends and taking a keen interest in his new occupation.

Christmas was in the air, and with the lifting of wartime embargoes, Hannover's Christmas market was full of stalls displaying all manner of festive food and drink, cards, decorations and presents. Harry ambled around, selecting gifts for the Wald family, while enjoying some spiced schnapps, which warmed his blood, and iced gingerbread, which filled his stomach. He was truly happy for the first time in a long time. Was it right that he should feel so content? Were there feelings of guilt lurking just beneath the surface? He had earned this happiness, hadn't he? He wasn't sure, but just now, he didn't care.

On Christmas Day Harry and the Wald family sat down to a dining table that struggled to hold the abundance of dishes. The years of belt tightening and rationing were over, and besides, it was time for a celebration. Karl and his little brother Max were together for the first time in four years, and the whole family said a prayer of grateful thanks that the young men had returned safely from the war. Walter Wald had bought the largest goose he could find, and he took great delight in ostentatiously carving the huge bird. Frau Wald served up a banquet, and Sophie made sure the adults' glasses were always filled with beer or wine. When she sneaked a little wine for herself, she was disappointed to find it tasted like cough medicine.

After the meal everyone sat around, rubbing their stomachs, happily complaining that they had eaten too much. Then it was time for the gifts. This was a year when they could all say that the best gift was having everyone in the same room, safe from harm; equally, everyone wanted to make it a memorable Christmas by giving special presents. The exchange took some time as the packages were opened one-by-one and everyone exclaimed their delight at the contents.

Sophie insisted that she distribute her gifts last. She had knitted scarves for every family member; these were greeted with loving thanks and warm hugs as each was unwrapped. Then she pulled out her present for Harry. It was a small package, wrapped in green tissue paper and tied with string. She blushed as she handed the present over to him.

Harry carefully undid the wrapping and pulled back the paper to reveal a book. It was upside down, so he quickly turned it around to see that it was in English. It took him by surprise to see something in his mother tongue, and he needed a few seconds to switch the language gear in his brain. He hadn't read any English in more than six months: "*Anthology of Melancholy Poetry* by E.E. Fowler."

Harry stared blankly at the title. Why had she bought him a collection of gloomy poems in English? He had never willingly read a poem in his life, and the last thing he wanted was to wade through a bunch of miserable poems about war and death after he'd just experienced it all first hand. Then it dawned on him: Sophie couldn't read English, but she had tried to buy him a book he could read in his own language. Books were expensive, English books more so; she had spent her money on what she had obviously hoped would be a special gift for him. He was touched.

Sophie looked at him anxiously. After staring at the book for some time and flicking through it in what he hoped would come across as considered interest, he looked up at her. "It's such a thoughtful gift, Sophie," he said honestly. "Thank you very much."

The family gathered around. No one could read English, and they all wanted to know what it was about. "It's a book of poetry," Sophie said cockily.

"Is that right?" Frau Wald asked.

"Yes, yes, Sophie has cleverly worked out it's a collection of poems," replied Harry.

"What are they about?" Max asked.

"Ah ... they are about travel," Harry said, hoping to keep the pretence of interest going.

"Read one out!" Sophie begged.

"What's the point? None of you understand English, and if I translate them, they won't rhyme," Harry said, smiling, still trying to avoid the truth about Sophie's purchase. The family roared with laughter at this. Sophie hugged Harry and said, "I hope you really like it."

"I know it must have been hard for you to find," Harry replied, neatly dodging an outright lie. He tucked the book into his jacket pocket. It was the strangest gift he'd ever received, but it was worth keeping for curiosity's sake – and for the warmth of the thought behind it.

ᴧᴧᴧ

The January air in Berlin was icy cold, and Harry shrank into his winter coat for maximum warmth. "Remind me again why the hell we're out here, freezing our asses off," muttered S.

"Because," Hössler began, "when Colonel Siller asks for a favour, you don't say '*nein*'."

"No, I realise that," replied S tetchily. "I mean, why are we freezing our asses off in Berlin, taking orders from a colonel, when we're all civilians now? After the Christmas feast I've had I could barely get into my uniform again."

"You always were a fat bastard," Wilhelm quipped.

"I, for one, didn't spend long years fighting a foreign war only to come home to watch my country descend into anarchy. I'm here to stop these communist bastards before a revolution takes hold. I think you'll find, Private Sigurdsson, that behind those barricades, there are hundreds of angry socialist workers who want to bring down the government and join the Ruskies," Karl said with feeling.

"Then let 'em join! You and I have been to Russia, and we know how shit it is," replied S.

"Come on, S," Harry said, stepping into the midst of the soldierly griping, "You know they want to bring down the government and set up a kind of German 'soviet union', and I don't think any of us would agree that's a good idea. So we are now *Freikorp* volunteers."

"Yes, the *Freikorp*: those brave veterans of the war, who defended Germany's borders from her enemies, and who are now keeping Germany safe from the enemies within," Hössler said, meaning every word. The rest of the squad looked at each other and rolled their eyes at Hössler's effortless spouting of propaganda.

"But S makes a good point. For heaven's sake, why couldn't they have picked a warmer month?" Wilhelm said, with a moan.

"That's the thing about a 'January Uprising' - it tends to happen in January," retorted Harry wryly.

"No kidding! I was reading the paper and thought we were trying to put down the 'Spartacist Uprising'," Karl added, deliberately unhelpfully.

"So what name do we use?" Hössler enquired.

"Let's leave that one for the historians to worry about and, in the meantime, we'll concentrate on resolving this situation, while trying to stay alive. Here comes trouble," S said, nodding in the direction of an approaching figure. A man in a German military uniform darted towards them, stooping low as if avoiding heavy fire. Not a single shot rang out.

"Who's that idiot?" Wilhelm asked contemptuously.

"Lieutenant!" the man called out.

Everyone in the group looked at Harry, who in turn, looked around for the superior officer. Karl elbowed Harry in the ribs. "He's shouting at you, Brit Bubi," he whispered under his breath. Harry had not had time to get used to his new rank, but the *Freikorps* insisted that when he had left the army as a lieutenant, he was a lieutenant in the *Freikorps* too. The running sergeant caught up with Harry and his group and, breathing hard, came to a stop.

"Sergeant, why did you feel the need to run as if under fire?" enquired S.

"Standard orders while near enemy positions. There could be snipers anywhere in that building," the man said, pointing towards the corner.

"True," Wilhelm said, picking up from S. "The building we have cordoned off and surrounded does, indeed, have some excellent elevated positions, which could be used as snipers' nests; but tell me, sergeant, how are they planning to shoot from around a corner?"

The sergeant looked crestfallen.

"How long were you in the army during the war?" asked Harry.

"Two years."

Harry's squad looked sceptical; a veteran with two years' experience wouldn't have made such an amateur mistake. "And what did you do during the war?" Harry followed up.

"Perimeter guard at an airstrip."

"So, you've never been in combat, have you?" Harry asked, waiting for confirmation.

"No, sir," said the sergeant meekly.

"What's the message, sergeant?" Harry asked curtly.

"Colonel Siller says we are to attack from all directions in one hour."

"Thank you, sergeant. Is that all?"

"Yes, sir," the sergeant replied, then turned around and tried to saunter nonchalantly back down the street.

The hour passed uneventfully before the men peered around the street corner towards the barricade, which had been erected next to an imposing building. "Where do you think they have their armed men?" Harry asked Wilhelm.

"If I was them, I'd be on the third floor; but then again, I think these guys are workers, not soldiers, so who knows?"

Harry looked back at the rest of the squad, huddled together for warmth. "Okay, who wants to head over to that empty *Bierkeller*, the one with the yellow sign on the left?"

The men looked at each other and Hössler shrugged, "Fine, I'll go." He turned to Wilhelm and pointed a threatening finger at him. "Don't miss!" he said with a glare. Wilhelm nodded in response.

The streets were deserted. Following days of skirmishes and the occasional rifle shot, the citizens of Berlin had got the message to stay well away from this explosive situation. After years of intentionally avoiding any of the violence of the war, it was as if the war had turned up for an epilogue in Germany's capital, a final bookend to all the years of bloodshed.

Hössler leapt around the corner and started zig-zagging a crazy route towards the *Bierkeller*. Twenty meters down the street, a shot rang out and kicked up a chip from a cobble; the shot was well wide of its mark. Wilhelm raised his rifle and in its telescopic sight saw a man in a dark coat and grey hat chewing on the end of a cigarette as he worked the bolt of his rifle. The man brought the rifle up to his shoulder but never got to fire a second round as Wilhelm's shot passed through the man's skull a split second later.

Several more shots buzzed angrily at Hössler, revealing several more marksmen. By now Harry and the rest of the squad were working their way towards the barricade, moving along the street underneath the rebel-held building. The shooters were preoccupied with trying to hit Hössler, who was just disappearing into the safety of the *Bierkeller*.

Karl, Wilhelm, S and Harry popped up right beside the barricade and caught a number of socialist guerrillas by surprise. Only one of them had a rifle; another had a pistol; the rest were armed with bats and makeshift weapons. Harry and his squad fired, taking down four men in one go. However, an unseen rebel had ducked down and was lighting a petrol bomb. He hurled it at the closest *Freikorps* soldier. S felt the hard glass bottle smash against his temple. The concussion was instantly followed by searing pain as the petrol began to cook through his skin. S let out a gut-wrenching shriek.

"No!" cried out Hössler, who ran towards his comrades when he saw the chubby S engulfed in the oily flames of the bomb.

S thrashed wildly, screaming in agony, as the petroleum roasted him alive. Wilhelm tore off his coat, wrapping S in it and pushing him to the ground as he tried to stifle the flames. Everyone stopped to watch the horrific sight as the smell of petrol and burning flesh filled the street. After frantic seconds, the inferno was out. The stillness that followed brought everyone back to their senses. In a brutally efficient reflex reaction, Harry, Karl, Wilhelm and Hössler shot dead every man on the other side of the barricade, then turned to the horrifically burnt S, lying on the cold ground, tendrils of smoke drifting upwards from the charred remnants of his coat.

Harry looked at Wilhelm, "Get a medic, now!" he ordered.

Without pausing to acknowledge the order, Wilhelm ran off in the direction of the *Freikorps* headquarters, screaming, "Medic! Medic!" The rest of the squad knelt beside their fallen comrade. S wheezed, his laboured breathing a sign of his seared lungs.

"He's alive!" Karl exclaimed.

"Can't see," S said, barely audible to his friends. S's face was a mess of burnt flesh, and it was unclear if skin was in the way of his eyes or if his eyes had been burnt out by the blaze.

"It's okay, S. Wilhelm has gone to get a medic. Stay with me. Help is coming," Harry said, his eyes filling with tears. It was so unfair! His friend had fought on both the Eastern and Western Fronts and had walked away only with burns on one arm. He couldn't die two months after the end of the war!

After a few ragged breaths, S said, "Hold my hand," his voice, the tiniest whisper. Harry looked down at the charred left hand visibly protruding from under the coat and gently placed his hand over what remained. Then the wheezing stopped.

***

After the newspaper arrived, Max and his father spent the morning arguing about Germany's future. Both agreed that the socialist uprising was doomed, but what would be the outcome of the peace talks scheduled in Paris? Max hadn't joined the *Freikorps* as his leg had never healed properly since he'd suffered a compound fracture during the war. He had a cane and walked with a limp.

Sophie could hear Max and her father in heated debate as she prepared for school, glad to have a reason to get out of the house. As much as she loved her brothers, she wasn't used to them being at home and, although she would never admit it, she resented sharing her parents once again. During the war she had had her mother and father to herself, but now, with the family reunited, she was at the bottom of the pecking order. These were selfish thoughts, and she knew she should be ashamed, but she wasn't a little girl anymore, and she felt aggrieved at being treated like a child. The nickname Wenig Wald was no longer amusing – not to her, anyway.

Karl was away, serving with Harry in the *Freikorp*, but his letters came thick and fast, much to her parents' delight. The *Deutschpost* service was more frequent and more reliable than the military post had been. While her parents poured over each letter, all she needed to know was that both Harry and Karl were safe.

Since Harry had started in the cobbler's shop, Sophie had taken an interest in visiting after school and helping out with customers until it was time for supper, when they walked together to her home. But with Harry gone and the near-silent, but ever-reliable Rudi sitting quietly at work behind the counter, the shop seemed empty. She missed the amiable and handsome puzzle that was Harry Woods.

She could barely remember Hannover before the war, but she recognised that the influx of young men going about their daily work was a welcome return to a more normal way of life. The only advantage to having her brothers around was that her parents were now so distracted by their sons, she could slip off on her own to explore the city.

Everything was changing. One war seemed to have turned into another, and a deadly sickness lurked in the shadows. It was reassuring to visit the magnificent Herrenhausen Gardens or the imposing *Rathaus*, the city hall, places that seemed to defy the shifting world around her. Sophie was lucky enough to pass the *Aegidienkirche*, the medieval church, every day on her way to school. Having survived for centuries, its ancient stone walls exuded stability, seemingly immune to the violence of man and the invisible plague that had seeped across Europe.

Still, onwards to school. Wars might come and go; deadly viruses might sweep the continent, but there was always school, which was reassuring in its own way.

***

Summer 1919

Harry

What have you done? Why are you living in Hannover? What did the Hun do to you in prison to make you want to stay in the Kaisers own country? You haven't even seen Nancy's grave. We feel like you turned your back on us. But then you turned your back on your countrymen and the men you fought with too. Do not bother replying to this. You are dead to me Harry. I lost a sister to flu and I lost my brother to the Germans.

Alfred

***

The early summer sun shone down on the troops as they swayed together in the back of a truck that trundled through yet another small Bavarian town. They had travelled to numerous similar villages and, where necessary, had stopped to guard the government buildings until any imminent threats had dissipated. Harry's mind was filled with the angry words of his brother. He was being accused of betrayal. Was he a traitor? Because he had not returned to them after the war, it must seem that way, and he knew he could never explain all that had happened. Alfred couldn't understand that he didn't want to see his little sister's grave, that it would be too panful for him, that he could somehow keep Nancy alive in his mind if he didn't have to face that reality.

Harry looked around at the troops in the truck, his brothers-in-arms. They didn't care that he was British. Just now they were tired and, like all soldiers, grabbed every opportunity to rest. The men were dozing or lost in their daydreams, all except for one who was reading a newspaper. "Treason!" shouted Hössler as he scrunched the paper in his hand. Everyone woke with a start.

"What are you shouting about?" grumbled Karl, annoyed that his nap had been so rudely interrupted.

"The peace agreement at Versailles," explained Hössler. "We have to say not only that the war was our fault, but we have to pay for *all* the damage caused by the war!"

"What!" blurted Wilhelm in disbelief.

"Exactly," Hössler said, pointing to Wilhelm. "Didn't Ebert say to the army, 'No enemy has vanquished you'? When the armistice was agreed in November, weren't we on French territory? How are we the losers?"

"Give me that," Karl said irritably as he reached for the paper. He started to read as the other soldiers looked on.

"Yes, Hössler is right! They're calling it the 'Versailles Treaty', but it's not much of a treaty, more a dictate. Our government was barely involved. We have to admit the war is our fault and … wait … what? We have to pay reparations of one hundred and thirty-two billion gold Marks!"

"How much?" Harry asked, finally joining in the conversation.

"One hundred and thirty-two billion, not million, *billion* gold Marks," Karl repeated slowly, to make sure everyone understood.

"How many zeroes is that?" asked another soldier in the truck.

"Ah, it's one hundred and thirty-two, followed by nine zeroes," Wilhelm replied.

"Nine zeroes! Does Germany even have that much money?" Hössler asked, echoing what everyone else was wondering.

"The new army is going to be tiny," Karl continued, reading more of the points listed in the newspaper.

"So that'll be us out of a job," another soldier said gloomily.

Harry stared down the quiet street, trying to understand the implications of this new information, when he saw a face he thought he recognised. He stood up and banged on the top of the truck.

"Stop the truck! Stop the truck!" he shouted.

The driver popped his head out of the open window. "What's the matter, lieutenant?"

"Nothing. Just let me off and pull over by the church. You've been driving for four hours, so stretch your legs, and I'll be back in ten minutes." Harry dropped down from the rear of the truck and dashed up the street. He ran towards the tall, thin man who turned to see why army boots were pounding up behind him. It was Colonel von Thoma. "Colonel!" Harry exclaimed. "I heard you were missing, probably captured!"

Von Thoma smiled, instantly recognising Harry. "Well, clearly, I'm not dead. I *was* captured at one of our machine gun posts during what I think was your first battle … for the German army. Your scar is looking better, Private Woods."

"Thank you, sir, and it's Lieutenant Woods now."

"Lieutenant! Well I must congratulate myself on spotting your natural talents as a soldier," he said with a smile and a wink. Then he noticed the Iron Cross pinned to Harry's uniform. "And an Iron Cross second class. So you have been putting yourself in harm's way for me!"

"Now you're back, may I ask why you aren't in the *Freikorps*?" Harry asked, modestly sidestepping the comment about his medal.

"The army has decided I need to rest before my next adventure. They seem to want me for the long haul and that suits me."

"So you're staying in the army even though you must have heard the news about the Versailles Treaty."

"Well, the treaty allows for an army, and even if it is a small one, it will still need officers. Listen Harry, I was impressed with you; that's why I took the risk of letting you join my company rather than let you rot in a POW camp. The fact that you've made it to lieutenant is testament to your natural ability. I would be honoured to have you serving under me."

Harry hesitated. Thoma had treated him with respect at a time when he was getting little from anyone else. He had found a place in the army and the offer was tempting. But he was putting down roots in Hannover, and no matter how tentative they were, they were being established in peace, not war. He had only been a soldier for a year, and yet he had already fought in two armies and was on his second war. The German soldier he had shot in the barn, just before he was knocked unconscious, still came to him in the night. Müller, Schwartz, S and many others came too … but most of all it was Katarina he saw. Her face was a dream, but his longing to hear her voice and feel her warm breath on his skin was real enough. It was time to put pain and death behind him. It was time to put war behind him. "Colonel, you flatter me, but soon I hope to be able to put my rifle down and take up the life of an ordinary civilian."

Thoma nodded in understanding. "Who is your commanding officer?"

"Colonel Siller, sir."

"Ah, a good man; I'm sure he will release you from your duties as soon as it is possible to do so." Thoma reached in his pocket to pull out a pencil and a small notebook; he wrote on the first page and tore it out. "Harry, this is my address and a telephone number where I can usually be reached. If you ever change your mind about a career in the army, let me know. I'm serious."

"But why? You have served with hundreds of troops, why me?" Harry couldn't help but ask.

"Oh, come now, Harry. How many Englishmen do you think I have I served with? You are quite the unique specimen. You could have betrayed my men, in which case I would have had Müller shoot you. Or you could have tried to escape, or you could have given it minimum effort. Instead, I see an officer before me who has fought not once, but twice for a country that isn't even his by birth. You've been promoted and decorated. That's incredible! And it all goes to prove that you are a remarkable soldier and a remarkable man. I would consider it an honour if that remarkable man would stay in touch with his old CO."

"Thank you, sir," Harry said, accepting the piece of paper.

"No, lieutenant, thank *you*. Remember, I am only a letter or a telephone call away."

They shook hands and Harry ran back to the parked truck.

***

Frau Wald opened the door to two weary soldiers. One was her elder son; the other, his best friend, a young man she had come to think of as her third son. "Welcome home!" she cried, just had she had done so many times before. No matter how often her men went off to fight, she would never get used to it, and they, for their part, would just have to put up with her tears of joy – and all that went with them. The other family members rushed into the hall to pull Karl and Harry into rib-crushing embraces. Harry didn't know whether to wince or laugh, so he did both.

Sophie caught Karls' eye. She must have grown by five or six centimetres in the last eight months, and she had filled out. With her womanly curves, she was no longer the child he remembered; she was becoming a beautiful young woman - but no brother would ever say that. "You got big and fat!" he said with a grin as he enveloped her in a bear hug.

In what had become a happy routine of celebration, the return of the men triggered preparations for a feast. Harry had difficulty keeping up with the platters of food that were passed to him. Army rations had been frugal, and this was the richest food he'd had since Christmas. Besides, the August heat dampened his appetite.

The dinnertime conversation moved from light-hearted trivia to heated discussions about the current political situation. Herr Wald was furious about the post-war treaty humiliation Germany was being forced to endure, while Karl, Max and Harry tried to temper his indignation with the reality of what they had witnessed on the front.

If the men thought they could dominate the conversation, Sophie had other ideas. One advantage of being left to her own devices was that she could read what she liked and that included the news. She had come to an age where she was developing a political awareness, and she cared about the world around her. After the aggressive militarism of the Kaiser, she had high hopes for the new Weimar Republic. True, it had nearly been throttled in its cradle by the socialist uprising earlier in the year, but thanks to brave men like Karl and Harry, that had been stopped and a democratic election had taken place. Sophie stood up and waved her hands to get the attention of the men. Karl stopped mid-sentence as they all turned to look at her.

"Friedrich Ebert is now our *Reichspräsident*," she started confidently. He is Germany's first elected leader; he is also the first leader of Germany who wasn't a general or an aristocrat. After all the millions of deaths we have just suffered, isn't it time for a man of the people to lead us into a new era?"

There was silence at the table. Frau Wald was stunned to hear her daughter so assertively voicing opinions that belonged, she believed, to the very male world of politics. Sophie's father looked a little dumbfounded. While he had never before heard his teen-age daughter speak about politics, he had to acknowledge that she had made her point eloquently.

Max started clapping. "Well done, Wenig Wald!" he said with no hint of irony in his voice.

"After a comment like that, nobody should call you 'Wenig Wald' ever again," said the slightly bemused Harry, who was looking at Sophie as if seeing her through new eyes.

"Thank you, Harry," Sophie said with a smile.

The meal continued, but now Sophie had earned a place in the conversation.

***

Harry sat at his workbench in his grubby apron, carefully scraping a few loose slivers from a shoe he was mending. The smells of glue, polish and leather filled the room, a reassuring aroma that reeked of honest work and satisfaction in a job well done. Harry enjoyed the routine of waking up in his bed above the cobbler's, making some tea and toast and then opening up the shop at 9:00 a.m. sharp. He greeted the taciturn Rudi, who had already taken up his position behind the counter to spend the rest of the day scraping, cutting and polishing through a thick cloud of tobacco smoke, lost in a world of his own.

With his first earnings, Harry had bought a wristwatch, his most prized possession, apart from Sophie's book of poetry, which he had a habit of carrying in his jacket pocket. Since that Christmas Day, he had never opened it, but it had become a kind of good luck charm and a reminder of the love and support he received from the Walds.

The years since the war had been kind to Harry. His wiry frame had filled out, but he had avoided the paunch that so many Hannoverians seemed to develop, if not cultivate. His nose would always be a little crooked, but his scar had turned white and was fading to a patch on his cheek. The strange thing about a routine is how it eats through the weeks. What seemed like days were actually months passing, and those months peeled away to reveal that years had gone by. Harry didn't mind; he was happy. He had found his niche in life.

Harry snapped out of his thoughts when he heard the shop's doorbell. He glanced up and saw Sophie, who was wearing a brimless yellow hat and a fashionable dress in the same colour. Harry noticed that the hem was at her knee. "Good morning, Sophie," Harry called out as he laid down the shoe he was working on and hastily rubbed his hands on his apron.

Sophie beamed at him, but said, "Oh, Harry … you're too good to be working as a cobbler."

"Thank you, but I am very happy being a cobbler."

There was a slightly awkward pause that Sophie broke with her news. "Well, I'm off to university now. My bags are packed and I'm heading to the station."

"That's great! You'll be the first woman in your family to get a degree. We're all so proud of you."

"Well, you know how I love politics. Now that women are gaining the right to vote, I think everyone is willing to listen to our thoughts on political theory … but listen to me! I already sound like I'm spouting lectures. Come here!" Sophie signalled for a hug, "Just wish me luck."

"Good luck," he said, his face buried in her hair. They clung together for a moment too long. Harry smelled the citrus of her perfume, while Sophie crushed herself against the dashing young Englishman who had stolen her heart and didn't know it. It slowly dawned on Harry that there was something different about this hug; something wonderful was happening. She held him for as long as she dared then planted a kiss on his lips and broke away. "I will miss you, Harry Woods," Sophie said and left the shop.

Harry was thunderstruck. Little Sophie has definitely grown into a woman, he thought as he wiped her lipstick from his mouth. He looked over at Rudi whose moustache twitched in a noncommittal way. Harry grinned sheepishly at him.

***

"But prices have been high since 1921," Max said, trying to minimise his father's concern. Max and Karl were with their father in his office in the flagship Perle building.

"It's these blasted war reparations! There was never anything good about them, but now the French want their payments in hard currency, so the damned government keeps printing money like it's toilet paper!" Herr Wald exploded.

"But Father, what can we do? This is out of our hands, and everyone is sailing in the same ship," Karl sighed.

"Yes, except the ship is the 'Titanic'!" Max added grimly.

"Look, I set up a shoe business because everyone buys shoes. We might as well put our luxury range in storage, but standard work shoes will still be needed," Herr Wald said thoughtfully.

"And Harry and Rudi should be fine at the cobbler's. If people can't buy shoes, they'll still need to repair them, right?" Karl asked rhetorically.

"I agree," said Herr Wald, reaching for a cigarette. "It's why we opened that shop, a sort of insurance policy against hard times. Little did I realise then that things could get so bad that a cobbler's would turn over more than two shoe shops."

"Still, prices seemed to have stabilised throughout '22," Karl added, trying to be optimistic.

"Who knows what's going to happen, but the pressure is on Germany to keep paying. Ebert avoided an election because the government thought the economic situation was so serious!" Max said, slamming the table.

"What do we need to tell Harry?" asked Karl.

"Nothing just now," Herr Wald said, thoughtfully puffing on his cigarette. There was a brief silence before he added, "Harry is a smart boy and conscientious. He and Rudi both work hard, but it's Harry who keeps that side of the business running smoothly. He couldn't do more for us and, let's face it, he's hardly there because it's glamorous. You end up smelling like oil paint, but he never complains. Leave him alone, but we need to keep an eye on all outgoings. And boys, push the cheaper shoes; people can still afford those."

"Do you think Sophie is alright at university?" Karl wondered out loud.

Herr Wald laughed. "My dear boy, this is what she wanted. I'm sure she's having the time of her life … as long as I keep paying the bills."

***

Sophie's roommate, Eva, was an overly serious philosophy student. Although the two girls were very different, they were both thoroughly enjoying the freedom that a life without parental restrictions allowed them, and both had taken the opportunity to reinvent themselves. Recognising that it was a brave new world they lived in, Sophie had turned her long blonde locks into an achingly fashionable bob. Germany was a democracy now; women had the vote, and the economy would be growing … except that inflation had stifled the predicted growth. She recognised that the situation was serious, but not insurmountable. If only the government would stop printing money as the means to dig itself out of the hole of war reparations.

"What do you think will happen?" Eva asked, looking at the stack of bank notes on the table in their dormitory room. Under normal circumstances the pile, as thick as two bricks, would have made them rich, but this week or to be more specific, today, it was about enough to buy a few days' worth of food.

"My dear Eva, if I could answer that, Ebert himself would ask me to become currency commissioner. I don't know, but it's safe to say nothing good can come of it."

"You can say that again. But the one thing I know we need now is some economic common sense." Eva sighed. "Well, I guess it's my turn to go shopping." She put on her coat and grabbed her copious handbag, then picked up the two bricks of notes and stuffed them inside. She muttered irritably to herself as she realised they were sticking out, but after a careful rearrangement of the bag's contents, she managed to fit them in. "All this money makes me feel a bit like a gangster. You know, like the ones we keep reading about in America."

Sophie laughed, "Oh, I know what you mean. The situation is unreal."

"This country ..." said Eva, the sentence hanging in the air as she left the room, shutting the door behind her.

Sophie sat on a chair looking at the table that only seconds earlier had the pile of bank notes on it. What had happened to the new start the Weimar Republic had promised? Why did Ebert and his cabinet seem intent on destroying the currency? Couldn't they see that this was the path to madness? She wasn't cold, but she wrapped herself in her shawl, a vain attempt to protect herself from the harsh realities that existed outside her dormitory.

***

Harry looked up from his work when he heard the doorbell jangle as a customer entered. Rudi was downstairs sorting through their meagre supplies. "Good morning, Mrs Zentz," Harry said with a pleasant smile.

Mrs Zentz nodded politely in reply. She was hefting a shoulder bag brimming with piles of notes. Her other hand held a toddler who seemed surgically attached to it. That was little Erik, who would be fine unless his mother let go of his hand, at which point he would cry floods of tears and shriek uncontrollably. Harry had seen the tantrum once and had no wish to see it again. Normally Mrs Zentz would carry Erik, but the weight of the bag meant that she had no option but to plod down the street with the toddler fiercely clinging on. Erik was a needy child.

"Your husband's shoes are ready." Harry put them on the counter.

"How much is it?" she enquired anxiously.

Harry looked down at the day's price list. He turned red.

"That will be fifty million Marks," he said, not looking at his customer. How could anything cost fifty million Marks? The amount sounded like the annual budget for Lower Saxony, let alone a simple shoe repair.

"But I thought you said it would be twenty million," complained Mrs Zentz.

"Well, unfortunately, that was on Monday, and it's Friday now. We all know prices are going up," Harry explained, embarrassed by the ridiculousness of the conversation.

Mrs Zentz sighed and lifted the bag off her shoulder. "Here," she said bluntly, "and when you've finished counting it, can you put the shoes in the bag."

Harry fumbled with the stacks of bank notes. There was no point using the cash register anymore. Instead, he had taken to stacking the money up against his side of the counter; it wasn't very safe, but no one was going to steal the worthless piles of paper. He had read somewhere that the currency was so devalued it was now cheaper to wallpaper your house with bank notes than with actual wallpaper. Harry added Mrs Zentz's notes to the top of the paper wall he was building. There was no point in counting it … even if he had the time or the inclination to do so. He placed the shoes in the bag and handed it back to his customer, who had picked up Erik.

"Let's go," she sighed wearily to the toddler, who was now sitting triumphantly on his mother's hip. Looking at Erik, Harry wondered what the future had in store for him and his whole generation. What chance did they have in this broken world? This can't go on, he thought to himself.

***

Herr Wald came home in a daze and hung up his coat without remembering to shut the door behind him. His wife peered out from the kitchen. "Ah, there you are; I thought I heard the door." She understood immediately that something was wrong. "Whatever is the matter?"

"Hmmm?" Herr Wald said from a daydream, not yet present in the apartment.

"Husband, what's wrong?" Anke snapped.

"Come. Come with me to the dining room. I need to sit down and I need a brandy."

Anke walked over and shut the front door, then followed her husband to the dining room, where she quickly poured him a drink. It was just the two of them at the big family table.

"I remember hearing about our victory in the Franco-Prussian War when I was still a boy. Our nation besieged Paris and made Napoleon III abdicate. Then, as I grew up, all I could see was growth and industry around me. Germany was going places. Germany was a force to be reckoned with. True, we were beaten in the last war, but we were not broken as a nation. After all the ceasefire happened while we were still on French soil. But now, somewhat ironically, it's the peace that's killing us."

"I know things are spiralling out of control with the money, but we'll survive," Anke replied, rubbing his arm, trying to reassure herself as well as her husband.

Herr Wald turned to look at his wife. "I went to the bank today, and on the way I stopped to buy a stamp for my letter." He said this as he searched through his jacket for his wallet, which he found and pulled out, saying, "As a place to keep bank notes, this old wallet has become inadequate to the task. But it can still hold stamps. Look," Walter said, holding a single stamp in the palm of his hand. Anke leaned over to better see the small print.

"Goodness, that's a lot of zeroes."

"This, my love, is a five billion Mark stamp. How can a country survive when a postage stamp costs five billion Marks? People are now using wheelbarrows of money to buy a day's food."

"I know," was all Anke could say in response.

"Then I went to the bank to discuss the loan we took out to buy our second Perle shop. The manager said, 'Herr Wald, I don't think there's a name for the number you owe us in the present currency crisis.' We talked about the various options, but the reality is that I can't sell it because nobody can afford to buy it. Meanwhile, the bank is finding it hard to keep up with the ever-increasing prices, so they don't even know what I owe, which means they can't foreclose on us ... yet."

"Will we lose the store?" enquired Anke anxiously.

"I don't know. But - and this is the hard part - we are going to have to bring Sophie back from university. We can't afford the expense of having her in another city."

"Oh, no, Walter!"

"I know, I know, but once this crisis has passed and we've picked up the pieces, she can go back."

"But you will break Sophie's heart!"

"Please, Anke, don't you think I know that? There's nothing I want more than to make my children happy, but we have to face facts, and right now we live in a country where a stamp costs five billion Marks."

***

Sophie was devastated. The letter from home had hit her hard, but when she saw the price of the postage stamp and then the cost of the train ticket back to Hannover, she knew her father had no choice. In a way she had been expecting it; Eva had gone home a month earlier but, even after taking all these factors into account, there was still a part of Sophie that felt aggrieved. She was more than half-way through her degree, and now, after all the hard work, she would have nothing to show for it.

Winter was setting in, and the fug in the train was pleasantly warm compared to the biting wind outside. She had a long journey ahead of her, so she bought a newspaper, more out of habit than necessity as her university course had required her to read two every day. The headlines screamed the news of the *Bierkeller Putsch* and those now on trial after the plot had failed. While its actual execution sounded comically amateurish, at least someone was willing – finally - to challenge the insanity of the current situation.

The story went that there had been a small rally in a Munich *Bierkeller*, which had been interrupted by an organisation Sophie had never heard of, the NSDAP, the National Socialist German Workers' Party. One of their leaders was the famous wartime general, Erich Ludendorff, and another was called Adolf Hitler. The group had interrupted a second rally, but that one was so loud Adolf Hitler had fired a shot into the ceiling to get everyone's attention. Apparently the interlopers had demanded – at gun point - that those attending the rallies should support the NSDAP, after which they settled into the *Bürgerbräukeller,* where they set about trying to dismantle the Bavarian regional authority and even the Weimar Republic itself. The group was quickly surrounded by the army, and in the ensuing shootout, some members of the NSDAP were killed. Ludendorff was on trial, but as a war hero, it was expected that he would be acquitted. The other ringleader, Adolf Hitler, was now on trial for treason, for which, no doubt, he would be found guilty.

It occurred to Sophie that while this *Bierkeller* revolution was based on a flawed plan, it was a sign that people had had enough. It was long past time that Ebert fixed the country's problems, or there would be nothing left of Germany. Sophie had had high hopes for the Weimar Republic, and there was a part of her that now felt betrayed.

As her train clattered along, her head swirled with conflicting emotions and impossible questions. The uprising was a scary omen. Was there to be yet another civil war in Germany? The Allies had won the war, so why did they now seem determined to destroy Germany? It was so unfair that she had had to abandon her studies and return home. She had done everything right, and yet she felt she was being punished for something that was not her fault. Just at this moment she hated the Allies, the government and the politicians - and anyone else who had a role in this whole sorry mess!

Sophie's new-found freedom was being taken away, and her future degree was being stolen from her, but she had to admit it wasn't all bad. She had missed the love of her family, the familiarity of Hannover and of course, Harry, her dear Harry.

***

Harry, Max and Karl sat at a table in a jazz bar called the *Schwartz Katze*. It was the place where every young Hannoverian wanted to be seen on a Saturday night, and with times so bleak, it was the perfect escape from grim reality. The animated chatter of all the twenty-somethings was loud, but the band was even louder, pouring out music like an unstoppable machine, as if determined to overwhelm the gloom of daily life.

"Look at all the girls!" Max exclaimed, excitedly, his eyes almost popping out of his head as yet more young women walked past in their fashionable outfits.

"Yes, I'm sure they're all very nice," Karl commented in a non-committal tone.

"What?" bellowed Max.

"I said, 'I'm sure they're all very nice'!" shouted Karl, trying to be heard above the din.

"You're just jealous because you're practically married, and Harry and I get the pick of the bunch," Max yelled, slurring slightly.

"We all know that if it wasn't for the economic crisis, I would already be married to Frieda, but as it is, we have to wait for the storm to pass," Karl muttered, not caring if he was heard.

"Oh, stop being so glum. The night is young and so are we!" Harry roared, raising his glass triumphantly, his confidence emboldened by the drinks he had been knocking back all evening.

"Hey, Harry," shouted Max, pulling at the sleeve of his jacket, "check out those two beauties standing by the edge of the dance floor." Max was pointing blatantly at a blonde and a brunette, both fashionably dressed, each with the latest bobbed hairstyle. They were sipping drinks behind the bright lights on the dance floor, where the shadows made the girls seem mysterious and alluring. Max turned to Karl, "*We* are going to speak to those lovely ladies, and *you* are going to sit here and watch us have some fun."

Karl waved his hand as if to shoo them away, and the two men strode towards the women with an air of assurance that belied their underlying nervousness. Doing his best to hide his slight limp, Max walked up to the brunette. "Good evening, Fraulein, would you care to dance?" he asked with all the false confidence he could muster.

"I think I'm free," the girl replied demurely.

Harry was planning much the same direct approach with the blonde. "Good evening, Fraulein, would you … oh, my God … Sophie?"

Sophie looked at Harry in surprise. "Harry! Hello!" she said, throwing one arm around him. It was an awkward embrace as both of them were holding drinks that sloshed out of their glasses. They were both a little tipsy.

Harry broke away from the embrace. It was good – so good - to see her, and she looked stunning, but he was no longer certain about asking Sophie to dance. "What are you doing here?" he asked, his mind clearing fast.

"Father can't afford the bills anymore, so he told me to come home … and here I am," Sophie said with a shrug.

"But what are you doing *here*?" Harry asked again, hoping he made more sense this time.

"I dropped my cases off at home and met up with my friend Klara, who is currently dancing with my brother," she said, gesturing to Max and Klara on the dance floor. . "You know, I just didn't expect Max to be such a good dancer … because of his limp," Sophie said, not meaning to articulate her thought out loud. She turned and looked at Harry. "So, Harry, do you want to dance, or do you want to take me home?"

"I will happily escort you to your home," Harry said, not daring to think she meant anything else by the comment.

Sophie shoulders slumped. Why was it always so hard with Harry? But she didn't dare push things, not here, not now, not after she had only just returned. "Aren't you the knight in shining armour," she said with an edge in her voice. "Come, Sir Harry, take this damsel back to her castle," she sighed. They slipped past the dancing couples, collected their coats and walked out into the cold, a thin layer of snow giving brightness to the night. Their breaths poured out like steam.

"Are you angry with your father for making you come home?"

"Yes and no. How can I not be angry that I've had this chance taken away from me? But it's not his fault. Look at the state we're in. Who can blame him? Everything is such a mess." As she said this, she moved closer to Harry who, without thinking, put his arm around her. "And right now, there's nowhere else I'd rather be," she said, trying but failing to catch his eye. As they walked along the dimly lit street, snowflakes began to fall, giving the night an air of calm.

"It's beautiful," Harry said, looking up at the sky.

"Yes, it is," Sophie agreed. Right now, right at this very minute, she felt as happy as she could ever remember feeling.

"Are you happy, Harry?"

"Yes … yes, I don't think I've ever been happier, politics and economic crises to one side. I love my job and your family has been so kind to me. I feel … blessed."

"Let me make you feel even happier," Sophie said, leaning in. Their warm lips met in a lingering kiss.

Harry pulled away. "Sophie, we can't do this. *I* can't do this."

"Why not?"

"Because you're a Wald. Your family has done everything for me, and while I know they like me, they won't exactly be pleased if their only daughter ends up with a cobbler."

"You were more than happy to come up to me in the club."

"That's when I thought you were just one of the girls at the club."

"I *am* one of the girls at the club!"

"You know what I mean." Harry started walking in long, determined strides.

"No, Harry, I really don't," Sophie said, running to keep up with him. When he did not reply, they continued in silence until they arrived at the door to her parents' apartment.

"Thank you, Herr Woods, for escorting me home," Sophie said, formally and curtly.

"My pleasure, Fraulein Wald," Harry replied in a similarly short manner, his head in turmoil. He needed to get away, to think about that kiss and what it might mean. He watched her open her door, then turned and fled back to his refuge at the cobbler's.

***

Max and Karl were smoking and daydreaming, trying to pass the time in a completely empty Perle, when their father exploded through the door, nearly taking it off its hinges. The bell was still ringing wildly as Herr Wald rushed towards them, waving something in his hand. "Karl, Max! Tell me, what was the exchange rate for the dollar and our Mark yesterday?" he asked eagerly.

"Ah, it was a little over four trillion," came Karl's bewildered reply. Checking the laughable exchange rate had become part necessity, part obsession with the Wald men. It was their way of measuring how terrible things were – and they were always getting worse.

Their father slammed the piece of paper onto the counter. "Not anymore!" he thundered.

"What's that?" asked Max.

"This," said Herr Wald, picking up the paper and brandishing it under his sons' noses," is called a *Rentenmark*, a currency the banks have been trading for a couple of months. This one *Rentenmark* note is worth a trillion of the old Marks. My boys, don't you see? This is the best Christmas present we could ever have! Hans Luther, that fat, bald genius of a finance minister has fixed the system!"

"Shit!" said Max, staring at the note in his father's hand as if it was a gift from the gods. Both he and Karl broke into huge grins.

"Language, Max," Herr Wald chided automatically, having been long under the steadying influence of his wife … and then added, "But, yes, 'shit' indeed! My God, after losing the war, then the civil unrest and finally the economic collapse, I think we can finally say the worst is behind us."

"But we lost the other Perle shop, and we had to let Rudi go, and Sophie had to come back from university."

"Yes, yes, we've had some setbacks, but don't you see? This fixes everything in time for Christmas! People will have money in their pockets again, money that's actually worth something - and that means that after all these years of cutting back and sacrificing, people will want to indulge a little. Boys, take the work shoes out of the window! I want all the stylish ladies' footwear on display. Women will want to pamper themselves; men will want to buy their wives nice Christmas presents!"

Herr Wald grabbed his sons and crushed them together in a great bear hug. "I am so proud of you. We made it!"

***

Harry was bent under the counter, sorting through a random collection of nails, when he heard someone come through the door. "Sorry, we're closed," Harry barked, not bothering to look up.

"It's okay; it's just me," a familiar female voice called out.

Harry jerked up in surprise, clipping the side of his head on the corner of the counter. He swore under his breath and clutched his head. Sophie! He'd hardly thought about anything else since that kiss.

"Oh, sorry, I didn't mean to startle you," Sophie said, cocking her head sympathetically.

"No, no, my own stupid fault," Harry said through gritted teeth.

"Have you heard about the new currency?" Sophie asked.

"Yes, your father was here first thing this morning, explaining all about the *Rentenmark*. It's good news."

"Honestly, you'd think he'd invented it himself, the way he goes on about it," Sophie said, rolling her eyes. "Anyway, Father asked me to pick up something from the basement. Is that okay?"

"Sure, fine, help yourself," said Harry, still rubbing his head. "I'd best lock up and tidy away here," he said as casually as he could, his heart racing.

Sophie went downstairs to a cellar that served as both a workshop and storage for Perle, while Harry went about gathering up the detritus that always accumulated over the course of a working day. After a few minutes, Sophie called out, "Harry, could you help me, please?"

Harry removed his cumbersome apron and made his way down the steps where he saw that Sophie had taken off her coat and was standing beside the work table.

"How can I … " Harry stopped mid-sentence as Sophie walked forward and kissed him, then paused to look at him. She correctly judged that he needed just one final push of encouragement and placed her arms around him. Harry's arms wavered and then moved to embrace her. They took their time at first, but gradually the tender kisses became more passionate and more urgent. Harry lifted Sophie onto the work table where she sat on the edge, Harry between her legs, their two bodies crushed together as they explored each other's mouths. They were both in the grip of lust as Harry moved from her lips to plant passionate kisses on her neck. Nothing could be heard but the sound of heavy breathing as it slowly faded into the stillness.

"Well, I guess this means I have overcome your concerns," Sophie whispered in his ear.

***

Karl and Frieda were married at the *Aegidienkirche* that Sophie had passed every day on her way to school. It felt right to her that Karl, who had always been part of her life, was getting married in this familiar church. Surprisingly, Max had married Paula first. They'd met when Max was visiting friends in Heidelberg, and a whirlwind romance followed. When Max found work in the city, they decided to remain near her family, but they had returned for Karl's happy day.

The wedding reception was being held at a nearby hotel. Over a hundred guests and family members ate, drank and toasted the new bride and groom. A little band had been hired but struggled to be heard above the cheery clamour of the day. "Frieda and Karl look so happy together," Sophie said to Harry, looking over at her brother and new sister-in-law on the dance floor. Their father adored Frieda and was applauding vigorously as everyone looked on.

"Yes, they do," said Harry, leaning over to whisper in Sophie's ear. "Have I said how beautiful you look today?"

"Oh, stop it," Sophie said with a smile, not really meaning it.

Frau Wald came over to the table where they were sitting with Max and Paula. "You have stolen Max away from us, Paula. I hope you are making him happy," she said with a smile, only half joking.

"Oh, I am," replied Paula, "but surely, you should be asking if *he* is making *me* happy."

"True! True!" Frau Wald laughed. Then she turned to Harry and Sophie. "It's all been such a whirlwind these last few years: 1925 was Max's November wedding in Heidelberg, and here we are, less than a year later, celebrating Karl's in Hannover. And Harry, I'm sure there have been some changes back home in London too."

Harry forced a smile and nodded without saying anything, but he felt a pang as he remembered the loss of his sister and the anger in the last letter he had received from his brother. He was cut off from his old life, and the mention of London as his 'home' sounded strange. It all seemed so distant now.

"Mother, how do you remember all these things?" asked Sophie, fully intending to divert attention from Harry. She knew his family felt betrayed and were no longer in contact. "Well, as for me," Sophie said, turning to Harry, "this is the church where I want to be married … if I get married. In fact I'm a little cross that Karl got here first."

"I think, my dear," interjected Anke Wald, "you'll find that your father and I got married here first."

"I'm sorry. Did you say 'if'?" Harry murmured to Sophie.

"Well, I'm keeping my options open," Sophie responded quietly in his ear, smiling as she touched Harry's arm to reassure him it was a joke.

"How are things at Perle?" Paula asked Sophie.

"Good." She pointed down to her shoes. "I designed these."

"Very nice," said Paula with an approving nod. "I didn't know you were interested in design. Don't you wish you had continued your political studies?"

"Of course, that would have been great, but as it is, I feel I can make a genuine contribution to the family business with my ideas. It's about time they had female involvement."

"Good for you," said Paula.

"Besides, as Jung says, 'Even a happy life cannot be without a measure of darkness, and the happiness would lose its meaning if it were not balanced by sadness.' But I can truly say I'm happy," Sophie said, picking up her drink.

"To Jung!" Paula said, raising her glass in a toast.

"And happiness," Sophie added with a smirk.

Max beckoned to his mother. "Come, Mama, sit next to your youngest son. My wife has something to tell you."

When Anke was sitting comfortably, Paula leaned towards her mother-in-law. "I'm pregnant, three months."

Anke Wald's jaw dropped and then melted into a huge grin. "Oh, that's wonderful!" she said, grabbing Paula in a huge hug. Then she turned to Max and gave him one too.

"They do this a lot," Harry said to Paula.

"I've noticed," she replied with a smile and a wink.

***

Harry and Sophie left the cinema, giddy over what they had just seen. "Wow, Lang is a genius!" Harry enthused, walking arm-in-arm with Sophie.

"I know. Where did he get all those ideas?" Sophie wondered aloud.

"Do you think the future will really look like that?"

"I hope not, because we could be one of the underclass, working in synchronised mechanical movements."

"That would be a shame. I hoped one day I might become that seductive female robot."

They walked down the street talking animatedly about *Metropolis,* when the conversation about the future turned into a conversation about the past. "Harry, you never mention your time in the war."

"No," Harry said neutrally.

"You've told me about your childhood in London and about your family, but you don't talk about your time in the army."

"Which army?" Harry asked dryly.

"I'm serious. That scar, for example … you said you got it 'during the war', but not how or which side did it. I asked Karl about your time … "

"You did what?" snapped Harry.

"I'm sorry. Did I do something wrong?" Sophie asked, taken aback by Harry's sudden outburst.

"Why would you go behind my back like that!"

"I spoke to my brother about the war, and you are part of that story," Sophie said, defensively.

"There are some things not worth sharing."

"Harry, you ended up fighting with the 'enemy' and you were good at it too. You got an Iron Cross and several promotions up to the rank of lieutenant. I'd like to understand what happened."

Harry rubbed his eyes with the tips of his fingers and sighed. The images he had locked away for so long came flooding back: Katarina's smiling face, Hannigan's snarl, the dead eyes of the German soldier he had shot, the first of too many deaths on his hands. Sergeant Müller at the bottom of a trench, Captain Schwartz's body on top of one, the burnt husk of his friend S, smouldering under a coat on a cold Berlin street – it all came back to him, including the rifle butt to his face. "There are things I've tried to forget, things that are too painful to remember. What you're asking me is as personal as it gets."

"My dearest Harry, we are lovers. It doesn't get any more personal."

"That's my point. There are some burdens I have to carry by myself, and there are some times that are so awful and ugly that I never want to share them with anyone."

"But I want to know about your past, what's happened to you ... to help if I can."

"There's nothing you can do about the past. It's a part of my life I've tried to put behind me. I just want to love you and look to the future, to be a good cobbler and have a normal life that doesn't involve anything more dangerous than the occasional cut finger."

"Everyone thinks you're doing a magnificent job at the shop. You've brought in a machine to cut keys, and you've introduced lots of new lines to increase the turnover. It's become a real 'fix-it shop', not just a cobbler's, but is it enough for you? You showed leadership and ability in the army ... did you ever think about making it a career?"

"Oh, God, no! Maybe a peacetime army is all parade ground drills and canteen camaraderie, but my time in the army was hardship, fear and death. I never want to go through that again!" Harry hesitated as a thought formed in his head. "Come to think of it, I don't want *anyone* to go through that kind of savagery ever again!"

***

Harry checked and straightened his already straight tie before knocking. Frau Wald opened the door and began to smile but changed her mind when she saw the serious look on Harry's face. "Good morning, Frau Wald. Is your husband at home this morning?" Harry said, trying to keep his nerves in check.

"Why, yes, Harry. Whatever is the matter?"

"May I?" Harry said, pointing to the hat stand.

"Of course," replied Frau Wald as she turned her head and called out, "Harry is here to see you, Walter."

After hanging up his hat, Harry gave a slight bow of his head to Frau Wald and made his way to the dining room where Herr Wald was sitting in his usual place at the head of the otherwise empty table, drinking coffee.

"Ah, Harry, always good to see you. Come in. Sit down, sit down. Would you like a cup?"

"No, thank you."

"Tea, perhaps, or something a little stronger?"

"No, no, thank you; I'm fine," Harry said, anxious to get to the purpose of his visit.

Herr Wald wondered about Harry's oddly formal manner and the fact that he was standing in their dining room in his best suit at 9:00 on a Saturday morning.

"What is it, Harry?"

Harry took a deep breath. The room was a pleasant temperature, but he could feel beads of sweat rolling down his face onto his collar, and his heart was thrashing at his ribcage, trying to get out. "Herr Wald, I have come here to ask for your daughter's ... that is, Sophie's hand in marriage."

Walter Wald stared blankly at Harry.

"Anke, would you come to the dining room, please?" Herr Wald called out, never taking his eyes away from Harry's pale face. Frau Wald appeared with indecent speed, suggesting she had been loitering in the hallway, listening to the exchange. "Ah, there you are. Harold Woods, the Englishman who runs our cobbler's shop, has just asked for our only daughter's hand in marriage."

His wife and Harry both stared at Herr Wald's completely expressionless face. He paused, savouring the tension. "And I am going to say 'yes'!" Walter's face broke into a beaming smile, and Frau Wald threw her arms around Harry as she burst into tears.

"Thank God!" said Harry, almost collapsing with relief. "I thought you were going to say 'no'!"

"Why, for heaven's sake? We've been waiting for you to get on with it for weeks."

"Yes, but all those things you said are true. I'm just a poor Englishman who speaks your language with a strange accent. I owe pretty much everything, including my job, to your family, and I'm sure Sophie could do better."

"Sophie picked you and whoever our children pick, we will bring them into the family. We want our children to be happy, and you make Sophie very happy," Anke said, still holding onto Harry.

"I don't think we've said this enough, but you have always impressed us, right from the start. You kept Karl safe in the war, and now you work hard for the family business. Don't underestimate yourself; you've done a lot for our family and for the business. Why wouldn't we want you to marry our daughter?"

"Thank you, thank you very much," replied Harry, who had recovered sufficiently to return Anke's embrace.

***

Sophie was mystified. Why had Harry asked her to meet him at the Herrenhausen Gardens? At this time of year the trees were bare and the flowers had yet to bloom; it was a cold and muddy and inconvenient place to meet in late February. When she finally spotted Harry walking purposefully towards her, she wasn't feeling particularly affectionate and responded without enthusiasm as he greeted her with a quick kiss. He was ten minutes late and she was cold; her feet were freezing, and she had no idea why she was standing in a dead garden. "Why have you dragged me here?" Sophie sighed, showing great forbearance.

"Come, come," Harry said with a mischievous smile as he headed towards one of the water features. "We've known each other for a long time now, right?" Harry asked.

"It's getting on for nine years now, yes, why?"

"And you're happy with our relationship?"

"No!" Sophie snapped.

Harry's face dropped. "No? Why not?"

"Because I'm cold, Harry, and whatever you want to say could be said somewhere warm and dry!" Sophie said, stamping her foot to emphasise her lack of enthusiasm for whatever he had in mind.

"Oh, right," Harry said, his hand slipping into his coat pocket. He dropped to one knee and produced a small box. "Sophie Wald, will you do me the honour of becoming my wife?" Harry said, opening the box to reveal a small diamond engagement ring.

Sophie had been wondering when Harry would get around to a proposal, but she had not been expecting it this morning. Taken completely by surprise, she was overwhelmed with emotions. In an instant she went from being cross and cold, to feeling shock and shame, before giving in to joy and happiness. She understood now why he had brought her here. How many picnics, how many hand-in-hand walks, how many hushed words of love had they shared in these gardens? It was their place, the perfect place for his proposal. But her thoughts were taking too long, and Harry was looking questioningly at her.

"Well?" said Harry, breaking into Sophie's thoughts.

"Yes, of course!" she said and tried on the ring with trembling hands. It was a bit loose.

"I can get that fixed," Harry said, pulling her into an embrace and kissing her deeply.

***

Sophie had just finished doing up the buttons on her blouse when she heard a scream coming from her parents' room. Her mother's cry made her heart lurch. She burst out of her room and ran down the hall, her skirt flapping as she went. She raced into the bedroom to see her mother sobbing and pointing at the motionless body of her father. He had been dressing for the day when he had collapsed and was now lying, face up, on the bed in his trousers and shirt. His open eyes stared unflinchingly at the ceiling, and his skin had already lost that lustre of life.

Sophie took her mother in her arms as they both stood weeping. It was a devastating loss, but a mercifully quick way for a great man to go. Sophie sat her mother on the bedroom chair and approached her father's body to feel for a pulse. He looked smaller than usual, and it was clear that his strength and vitality were now gone forever. Whatever the cause, he had died instantly. Sophie rushed to call Doctor Apfelbaum, knowing there was nothing to be done.

The next few days were a blur as people came and went, everyone wanting to know how she was. Mainly she was numb. "He's in a better place now", they said. Though she called herself a Christian, Sophie didn't often go to church. She wondered if her father really was in a better place and why a loving God would take him away without warning.

When the day of the funeral arrived, Sophie stood with Harry and the rest of her family at the graveside. Hymns had been sung, readings had been read, prayers had been said, but it had all seemed hollow to her. A part of her was missing. Her life was less vibrant, but she found comfort in an overheard conversation between Harry and her two brothers. After all the death they had witnessed, after all the lives of friends cut so brutally short, this was the first funeral any of them had attended. In a way this period of mourning for Walter Wald gave them a chance to reflect on all the men they should have had time to bury but didn't. Maybe that was a gift that God and her father had given them: a chance for these three men, all physically and emotionally scarred by war, to finally lay their ghosts to rest. She didn't know whether this was true or not, or if God had a grand plan, but Sophie clung to the idea that her father's funeral had, in some way, healed the men she loved.

***

While her wedding at the *Aegidienkirche* was everything Sophie had hoped, there was no disguising the fact that her father's absence meant there was an unfillable emptiness in the day. Karl had stepped in to give her away at the altar. He was also the Best Man, so the traditional speech by the father of the bride went to Max. Harry followed him with a short, rather hesitant address, and Karl finished off with a perfectly pitched talk that acknowledged the loss of their father but was full of joy too.

As Karl spoke, Max's Paula played with their three-month daughter Adele, who was bald, drooled copiously and took in the proceedings with curious little smiles. Frieda, Karl's wife, sat nearby, stroking her pregnant tummy. Sophie looked at her two sisters-in-law and wondered how long it would be before she became a mother.

In the absence of any of his own family, the Walds had spread themselves out to sit on Harry's side of the church as well. He had just two guests: a young man of angular features with wiry black hair, wearing a dark blue suit, and a tall, thin army officer wearing the uniform of a major general. During the reception, Sophie made sure she was introduced to both.

Karl warmly hugged the man in the blue suit and introduced him as Wilhelm Goldmann, who Sophie felt was a key part of the puzzle that was her husband's war story. Goldmann was a dignified man who was keen to offer his congratulations rather than talk about the war. Sophie recognised the name and knew he had served with Karl and Harry both in the Great War and the civil war, but she sensed she couldn't push this rather modest and reserved man. Later in the evening Karl told her that Goldmann was the best shot he'd ever seen, and that he and Harry wouldn't be alive if it wasn't for his skills as a sniper.

Sophie found it amusing that both of Harry's two wedding guests were called Wilhelm. Major General von Thoma was, however, very different to the introverted Goldmann. Thoma was the epitome of the courteous, if slightly too earnest officer frequently found in Germany's military, but he was not without charm. He spoke of Harry in the most glowing of terms, which took her aback, but she was disappointed to learn that Harry had not long served under him before he had been captured during Harry's first engagement in a German uniform. Her time with the proud officer was over too quickly as she was whisked away to greet a distant cousin from Frankfurt.

Karl, Goldmann and Harry stood together, each with a glass of champagne. "So nobody could find Franz?" Goldmann asked.

"No, we had an address, but either it's old or he's off being Hössler somewhere," Harry explained.

"My God, Hössler could be irritating!" Karl said with feeling. They all chuckled at his candid observation.

"Oh, just call it youthful inexperience," Goldmann said with a shrug.

"How can you be so dismissive, when he was positively racist about Jews? Why excuse him?" Harry asked.

"My dear, Harry, *who* is nice about the Jews? It's our lot in life. We're individually befriended but collectively despised."

Karl and Harry nodded, accepting Goldmann's observation as Thoma approached, cigarette in hand. "Lieutenant Woods," Thoma said with a hint of irony.

"Major General," Harry replied with a nod. Karl and Goldmann did the same.

"Congratulations! You have a beautiful and intelligent wife, who spent most of our conversation pushing me for details about your war record. Haven't you spoken to her about such matters?"

"Why would I want to upset the woman I love? But tell me, how is peacetime service suiting you?" Harry said, changing the subject.

"Oh, it's pretty dull. Do you remember that *Bierkeller Putsch* in Munich a few years back?" Thoma asked, addressing all of them.

"Yes, at the height of the currency inflation," Goldmann replied.

"That's the one. I was one of the officers in the shootout with Ludendorff and the thugs he'd gotten involved with. I had the pleasure of marching their leaders into the back of a prison truck. Hess, Hitler and that fighter pilot hero, Göring … they were all war veterans who should have known better. I really don't know what they were thinking, but that's about as exciting as it's been for me in the last eight years."

"So, it's all high command gossip, drinking coffee and carrying out drills," Karl said with a wink.

"Yes, it's all pretty much routine stuff; it's the scientific advances that are amazing. Automation and motorisation are the future. What that ultimately means, however, is that every army is getting better at killing, if you can believe it after the carnage of the last war. But it's peacetime now and it's an easy life … and I'm sure the army pays better than a cobbler's," Thoma said, looking at Harry. "Ever thought of coming back? We could always do with a man like you. You're exactly what I'm looking for to put some iron-hard discipline in the men under my command."

"You've come a long way to be disappointed if that was your plan," Harry said defensively.

"Oh, not at all! I wouldn't have missed the wedding, but you can't blame an old soldier for trying. Anyone can see that you've made a good life for yourself here, but my offer stands. You never know what might happen, and if you ever change your mind, if ever you wanted to come back, just say the word. I trust you still have my contact details. I'm in a pretty good position to twist a few arms and get you anything you want - within reason."

"Well, I must say, it's nice to have a major general up my sleeve if ever I need one."

***

The rest of the day was a blur for Sophie and Harry, who saw little of each other until well into the evening, when the newlyweds were delivered to Harry's quarters above the cobbler's shop. When the Walds had had to let Rudi go, he moved in with his brother's family in a suburb of Hannover, so Harry had enlarged his upstairs room into a small apartment.

Over the course of the day, they both had had quite a lot to drink, but Harry managed to carry Sophie over the threshold and make his way to the bedroom, where he dropped her on the bed. In keeping with tradition, they had been careful not to consummate their love before marriage, but now it was their wedding night, something they both had been eagerly anticipating. Harry drunkenly wrestled his way out of his clothes until he stood in the middle of the bedroom wearing nothing but his right sock and a sheepish smile. "Well, *hel-lo*, Harry!" Sophie said, grinning as she looked pointedly at his growing erection.

Beaming back at her, Harry swayed towards his bride who was, herself, reeling from too much champagne. Harry knelt on the bed and began to fumble with the tiny buttons on the back of her ivory wedding gown. They felt like an impossible puzzle to his fingers which had, inexplicably, become thumbs.

"Can't you go any faster?" Sophie complained through a yawn, while Harry continued to grapple with the mysterious fastenings. "What's taking so long?" slurred Sophie, full of longing, lust and alcohol. Harry finally managed to undo just enough to help the tipsy Sophie manoeuvre out of the dress. One final tug and she was free, just as she lost her balance and collapsed back on the bed. Still grinning and giggling, she wriggled out of her undergarments; she was naked except for her veil.

Harry crawled along the bed to Sophie's open arms. In spite of all the alcohol, Harry's animal lust overcame the chemical obstacles. He was hard and eager for the promised soft embrace between Sophie's thighs, while Sophie longed to feel him inside her. There was no lengthy foreplay; they had waited too long; they had both ached for this consummation. The lovemaking was brief but intense. They remained in each other's arms and feel asleep instantly. It had been a long but perfect day.

***

They honeymooned deep in the Bavarian Alps. The sun was hot on their backs, but a welcome alpine breeze rolled down from the mountains, refreshing them as they hiked and climbed. Harry had never experienced anything like it; he was a city boy who had rarely been to any countryside that was not war torn, but he was certain England had nothing to compare with this. He loved to stand on a mountain ledge, drinking in the scenery: a lush forest valley below, a single bird of prey in silhouette against a sharp blue sky and distant snow-capped mountains bearing silent witness. By his side was the most beautiful woman in the world: strong, intelligent, fiercely independent - and sexy. He couldn't believe his luck.

They spent their days exploring the foothills of the mountains and their nights, exploring each other, making passionate love in the *Berchtesgadener Hof Hotel*. It was an idyllic ten days. Everyone knew they were on their honeymoon, and people went out of their way to make sure the handsome young couple enjoyed a perfect stay.

One afternoon they were caught in torrential rain, which disappeared as quickly as it had arrived but left them drenched. They had been walking around a glassy mountain lake, so they decided to dry their clothes on the nearby rocks while they went skinny dipping. The clear mountain water was invigorating but bearable, and the warm sun had done its job on their clothes by the time they were ready to get out. They shared a towel from the back pack and rubbed each other down, enjoying the frisson of adventure and the fact that there was no one to see them. They simply couldn't get enough of each other. But as the afternoon drew to a close, they dressed and hiked back to their hotel, more than ready for a fine evening meal in the dining room.

On their last morning they woke with heavy hearts and made languid love in the huge four-poster bed. Then they packed their bags and made their way downstairs where Johannes, the receptionist and concierge, sat behind the counter quietly reading a newspaper and smoking his ostentatious pipe. They were sorry to be leaving the lovely old hotel, and they thanked him profusely for their wonderful stay. Johannes reached under the counter and produced a twelve-year-old bottle of brandy, which he insisted they take, declaring them to be the most charming guests the hotel had ever had. Harry and Sophie laughingly thanked him again and walked out into the sun, still getting used to being addressed as Herr and Frau Voods, as the Germans called them.

With every passing kilometre on the trip back to Hannover, reality set in. The train became more crowded, and no one cared about the newlyweds holding hands. Harry was thinking about work and what would need to be done on his return; Sophie was thinking about how she would balance helping her husband in the shop, while also cooking and cleaning. Was it what she thought she'd be doing when she was younger? No. But was she happy? Yes.

***

Karl and Harry were sitting in the corner of a *Bierkeller*; the atmosphere was tense and subdued. The Wall Street stock market crash had happened just a few weeks earlier, and the ripples from this great financial disaster were already being felt on another continent. The stories on the news reels and in the newspapers were getting bleaker by the day. It was likely that 1930 would see record unemployment in the Weimar Republic. Another devastating economic crisis was looming only a few years after the last. "So, what are we going to do?" Harry asked Karl.

"How should I know?" snapped Karl.

"Sorry, it's just that your father always seemed to have the answers."

"And I'm not my father," retorted Karl.

"No, of course not; I said that badly."

"It's just … why is this always happening to us?"

"Well, it's not just us; it's the entire country."

"You know what I mean. We fought the biggest war in our country's history, and we lost our empire and some of our homelands. We can't travel to East Prussia now without having to cross a foreign border … *and* there are French troops in the Ruhr Valley - still - a decade on from the war. We've had a civil war with communists and inflation that destroyed the economy - and now, this shit! Is life always this difficult? Is Germany cursed as a nation?"

"Don't ask me; I'm just a cobbler," Harry said into his beer. "Besides, isn't next week's referendum supposed to throw out the Young Plan and the Versailles Treaty? Won't that help the economy?"

"Referendum. Ha! It's just a chance for the left-wing extremists to make Germany part of the Soviet Union and a blatant attempt to stop the right-wing nationalists from getting power. It won't help the economy, but it might just start another civil war!" Karl was almost shouting in frustration.

"Shhh, calm down," said Harry, aware that Karl's agitation was starting to turn a few heads.

"Sorry." It was Karl's turn to apologise. "It's just … what kind of mess will we be leaving for our children? Sonia is nearly two; Frieda is pregnant with our second, and now you and Sophie are going to be parents. You know how happy we are for you, but what future do these children have?"

"What about savings and assets? Won't they see the family through?"

"Papa did a great job of getting us over the bad years after the war, and he managed to start building the surpluses again, but he had three children, all of whom got married and started families of their own in recent years. It pretty much wiped things out."

"So, there's nothing?"

"The good news is that both shops are debt-free and have good stock levels, but that's it; that's all there is … no safety net, no money hidden under the mattress."

"Then all we can do is ride out another storm," Harry sighed and drained his stein.

"I'll drink to that," Karl said, raising his own stein in agreement.

***

Anke Wald looked down at the bed where her exhausted daughter's hair was plastered to her head and neck with sweat. Sophie was utterly spent, faint from the physical effort of childbirth, but she was smiling weakly and looking down at her tiny newborn daughter, wrapped in a white towel.

"I am so proud of you," Anke said, gently pushing the tangled strands of hair from her daughter's face. Sophie was only vaguely aware of her mother's attention as she stared into the screwed up face of her baby. It was incredible to think that she had made this little girl. She had given birth to a living, breathing human being, perfect in every way.

Harry was still waiting to come in. Anke had been insistent that he wash before meeting his daughter; she wanted him - and everyone else – to be as clean as possible. Harry had reluctantly complied, annoyed at the further delay before meeting his daughter.

The midwife had received a call about another woman in protracted labour and was leaving as the doctor arrived, taking a few minutes to fill him in on the difficult birth. After making a thorough examination of the newborn, Doctor Apfelbaum pronounced her to be fit and healthy, but he had concerns about the mother's pale face and listless demeanour. When he pulled back the sheets, he saw they were drenched in Sophie's blood. He called immediately for an ambulance, and Sophie was hurried off to the hospital, accompanied by her husband. Shaken but capable, Anke stayed behind to care for the baby.

The unexpected events had left Harry sober and silent as he waited for news from the operating theatre, where Sophie was having urgent surgery to repair the damage caused in the course of the delivery. He couldn't lose Sophie now, he couldn't! It was unthinkable, so he paced and sat and paced some more, anything to distract himself from his worst fears. After a century of anxious waiting, a surgeon appeared and informed him that the operation had been successful and the bleeding had been stopped, but his wife had lost a substantial amount of blood. Sophie was stable but weak and her fight for life continued. The damage to her birth canal and womb was extensive, and she was unlikely to have any more children.

It wasn't over yet, but the news was better than Harry had feared. He shook with relief and choked back a sob as he thanked the surgeon, practically hugging him in the process. It was late and Sophie would not wake for hours; she needed time to rest and recover. Under the circumstances it was best for Harry to go home, see to his daughter and return to the hospital in the morning.

***

Anke cried with relief when Harry arrived at her door with the news. Sophie was in the best possible place, receiving the care she needed; it was up to him to look after their baby. Anke wanted the newborn to remain with her, while Harry was insistent that she should go home with him. Since there was no way Sophie's mother was going to abandon her granddaughter to the care of her inexperienced father, they reached a compromise when he agreed that it made sense for the two of them to remain with Anke.

As long as Sophie was in hospital, they would have to substitute boiled cow's milk with a touch of honey for mother's milk, and when the baby needed a new nappy,

Anke showed Harry how to exchange one full of a thick, treacly paste for a clean one. Harry panicked when he saw something that looked nothing like a normal bowel movement. Was his daughter sick? Anke explained that this was quite normal for a newborn, as was the umbilical cord still protruding from his daughter's tummy.

Harry was not a religious man. He had attended church with his parents when he was made to do so and, while he considered himself to be a Christian, as soon as he was able to get out of Sunday church, he did so. But on his way to the hospital the next morning, Harry stopped off at the *Aegidienkirche*, where he and Sophie had married. He said a prayer of thanks that he had a healthy daughter and another that pleaded for Sophie's life. Harry prayed, his daughter slept and Sophie continued her fight for life.

When Harry arrived at Sophie's beside, she was just waking up. She was pale from the blood loss and groggy from the anaesthetic, but she signalled for a hug. Harry was only too happy to oblige, but his embrace was gentle as he whispered loving words in her ear. When she looked around for her baby, Harry explained what had happened and that their daughter was safe at home with Anke. He would bring her on his next visit.

Following his visit to the hospital, Harry had plenty to keep him busy, tending to the needs of the tiny infant, while Anke hovered over him, making sure he did everything in the approved manner. His daughter was just the distraction he needed to keep from worrying about his wife. He had never before realised just how much attention a newborn required – and this was just the first few days!

Amidst his constant anxiety and deep concerns for Sophie, Harry had instantly fallen in love with the wrinkly little girl, so small and helpless. His daughter was oblivious to the world, while Harry was overwhelmed by a sense of awe at the prodigious responsibilities of parenthood. This child was everything to him, and this child needed her parents, both of them!

That afternoon, the three of them set off to see Sophie, who was overjoyed to be reunited with the daughter she had barely seen. "Harry, you said if we had a girl, you wanted to name her after your sister."

"That's right," Harry replied, looking lovingly at his wife and daughter.

"I think 'Nancy' is the perfect name," Sophie said, holding her daughter a little closer.

Anke, fearing for the fragility of both her daughter and granddaughter, leaned over and gave Harry a hug of relief and joy.

***

It was August and the economic mood remained gloomy. Chancellor Brüning's policy of deflation meant everyone was tightening their belts … again. Both wages and prices were going down as the government tried to unravel the Gordian knot of war reparations and economic recovery. The new emergency measures had triggered a fresh election, and the extremes on both the left and right were ready to pounce on the centrist politicians. Most people hoped only that cooler heads would prevail.

Harry and Sophie had decided an afternoon away from their business worries would do them good. The Herrenhausen Gardens were busy with the town's citizenry trying to escape the summer heat, and when times were tough, the local park was convenient, beautiful and free. The young couple sat on a gingham picnic blanket with a bottle of lemonade and a ham sandwich each. Between them lay Nancy, now five months old. She was lying on her stomach, one fat hand clutching a wooden rattle with a bell, which jingled randomly as she tried to put it in her mouth. The proud parents were focused on their daughter as they chatted about everything and nothing, but they stopped when they heard a band approaching. Everyone looked up as the music came closer.

A band of six musicians, with a selection of brass instruments and a drum, was marching towards the nearby central bandstand. They were led by a man carrying a red banner with a white circle and a bent black cross, a swastika, in the middle. Harry recognised it as the emblem of the NSDAP, now commonly referred to as the Nazis, a political group whose posters had begun to appear in the streets of Hannover. Dressed in their Sunday best, both the standard bearer and the band members all wore red armbands with the same symbol.

The band played on until it had most people's attention. Harry and Sophie tried to ignore it, but as it was no more than fifty metres from their family picnic, they had no choice but to listen in. When the music stopped, the leader placed the standard in his left hand and rested it on the ground. Then he thrust out his raised right arm with his palm facing down. It was an awkward salute that looked out of place on a sunny Sunday afternoon in the public gardens.

"Fellow countrymen of Hannover," shouted the standard bearer, attempting to smile while projecting his voice as loudly as he could. "We of the Nazi party ask you to look at Adolf Hitler not as a potential leader, but as a potential saviour. For too long have we suffered under the oppression of the French, British and American economic burden. For too long have we lurched from one leftist liberal disaster to another. For too long this great nation has been forced to submit to lesser nations." Some of the picnickers began to walk towards the speaker; others listened where they sat; many studiously ignored the new arrivals, while a few packed up their things and left.

"If you want change, if you feel the same way we do, then vote Nazi this September 14th." There was a smattering of applause, but the vast majority remained silent. The speaker signalled the band, which struck up a new tune, and the little ensemble marched and played its way back out of the gardens. Harry noticed one young boy imitate the awkward salute with a laugh. He thought it was funny, but his parents told him off, and he received a clip around the ear for his joke.

Sophie and Harry glanced at each other, but before either could speak, Nancy burst into tears. Frustrated at losing her battle with the rattle, she now demanded the attention of her parents.

***

Sophie was visiting her mother and Frieda at the family apartment they now shared. She was staring sullenly at the headlines of her newspaper, while Nancy sat in a playpen, absorbed in the novelty of different toys. Apparently Hitler and his party had received only nineteen percent of the vote, but it was enough to stop a new coalition from being formed. The result also meant that for the first time, Hitler, a failed Austrian artist and a fascist, had a say in the German Reichstag. Sophie wasn't sure what it all meant, but it made her uneasy. Sophie's mother came into the room and saw her daughter scowling over the newspaper.

"Oh, for heaven's sake, Sophie, whatever is the matter?" she sighed, tired of the constant political talk that was everywhere these days.

"It seems to me that the basis of Nazi policy is fear, and nothing good can come from that."

"Oh, nonsense! Hitler is the only one who is willing to take on the challenge of making Germany great again. That's why I voted for him."

"You did what!" blurted Sophie, appalled at her mother's words.

"I voted for him. Don't you think this country has been through enough? Don't you think it's time to make the men who fought the last war, men like your husband and brothers, heroes and not criminals?"

"Yes, but ..."

"Your Ebert and Brüning," interrupted Anke, "have had their chance and look at the mess they've made. Inflation, deflation ... I'd never heard those words when I was your age. Did you know that, right now, the army is out with trucks of food to feed the poor and unemployed? It seems to me that Herr Hitler is the only one who has the guts to tackle this mess, once and for all."

"Hitler is a great orator, I will give you that, but too many of his speeches are about heaping blame on others. And his SA members are nothing but a bunch of thugs who take their cues from him. Have you read his book *Mein Kampf*?"

"No, have you?"

"Well, not the whole way through. Lord knows I tried, but it's a poorly written rambling diatribe against the Jews, communists and Freemasons he believes are the cause of all the evils in the world. That's not a political point of view; that's a conspiracy theory."

"He wrote that years ago, when he was in prison. People change, and if they don't, we've got Hindenburg to keep an eye on him."

"Well, I'm not so sure people do change, and if all our hopes lie with a fat, geriatric Prussian general, then we really *are* in trouble."

Both women were shouting at each other when Frieda stormed into the room and put her finger to her lips. "Mother, Sophie, could you please keep your voices down! I have only just got the baby off to sleep, and you are scaring Nancy and Sonia!" she hissed in exasperation, Sonia clinging to her legs.

Stunned, Anke and Sophie stopped immediately. Nancy was wide-eyed, looking in alarm at her mother, her lips trembling. Sophie rushed over to her little girl and scooped her up, making soothing noses in her ear. When she looked back at her mother, Sophie had the final word: "We'll see, Mother, but I hope, for everyone's sake, you're right."

***

Sophie tucked Nancy back into her cot for the third time that night and then slipped into bed beside Harry with a sigh. He held out his arms, and they snuggled up together. Harry was about to turn out the light, when Sophie reached over to stop him. He looked back at her, his face a question mark.

"Harry, why are you here?"

"Um, because this is our bed; it's where I usually sleep?" Harry replied, bewildered.

"No, Harry, I mean, unlike the rest of us, you have options. We are blessed with a beautiful daughter, but you have a wife who can have no more children. And now you have to struggle through Germany's third crisis in just over a decade. You must know that when Brüning visited London, he told Prime Minister MacDonald that the entire German banking system is on the verge of collapse. You could easily escape all this and go back to England. You are just one ticket away from finding financial security and another woman who could bear you more children."

"Where did this all come from?"

"Nowhere."

"Has this been playing on your mind?"

"Yes, of course it has!" Sophie said in exasperation. Men could be so obtuse.

"But why? I've never said anything to make you think like this."

"That's what I mean! All this time, all these problems, and you just accept your fate."

Harry leaned over his wife and looking into her eyes said, "In all my life I never thought I'd be this lucky. I have a gorgeous wife, who is, let's be honest, smarter and better educated than I am, and who has given birth to the most perfect daughter in the world. Your family has supported me for years, and if the price for all this is that I have to live with a succession of politicians who insist on ruining the country, well that's a price I'm willing to pay." Harry stopped, then said simply, "You are my life," and leaned over to kiss Sophie on the lips. They held each other for several minutes before Sophie reached across him to switch off the light and whisper in Harry's ear, "I love you so much."

***

Karl had travelled to Altona, a small city to the north of Hannover, in an attempt to source some cheaper materials. Tough times called for drastic measures, and this was an opportunity worth investigating. The Wald businesses were hanging on, but barely. Every day Karl woke up feeling anxious, and by mid-morning, the anxiety had produced a splitting headache. Everyone was relying on him to keep things going, to keep the good name of Wald solvent. The responsibility rested squarely on his shoulders, and the responsibility threatened to crush him.

It was Sunday, so the business district was quiet as Karl walked through the empty streets on his way to the nearby Jewish quarter. The Jews were open for business on a Sunday and, while they had a formidable reputation for negotiation, Karl felt that, given the present state of the economy, everyone was willing to do a deal. He had telephoned ahead and meetings with suppliers had been arranged. In the current political climate a new, non-Jewish buyer could mean trouble, and they had been hesitant, but Karl had persuaded them he only wanted leather; there was no political agenda to the proposed meetings.

After a few hours spent talking to various tanners, Karl had agreed the price he was hoping for and was now heading for his train in a buoyant frame of mind. He walked along, lost in his thoughts, when he heard noise coming from the manufacturing district just ahead. Something was wrong. Karl wasn't familiar with the area and felt he had no choice but to continue on the path he knew towards the train station. As he rounded a corner, he saw a long procession of Nazi *Sturmabteilung* and *Schutzstaffel*, whose rally was being disrupted by large groups of German communists, screaming and shouting obscenities at them. The police presence was insufficient to keep the groups apart. The situation was dynamite.

Karl's route would take him straight through the throng, so he took a side street, hoping the detour would still get him to his destination. He walked parallel to the march for a while and then tried cutting back again. He came to what appeared to be the tail end of the protest, but even here the crowd was agitated and ugly. It was a short distance to the other side of the street, where he would be able to leave the mob behind and head towards the safety of the station. He stepped into the jeering crowd of communist supporters, remembering grimly that it was this party he had fought in Berlin, but the brown shirts marching down the centre of the street under their swastika banners were no better. As Karl squeezed his way through the angry men, he saw one of the policemen lose his hat in the crush of the crowd. The atmosphere was becoming more heated by the minute.

A shot rang out, followed by a sudden eerie stillness. Karl used the opportunity to edge quickly past more protesters. He had been in enough combat situations to recognise the quiet before the storm; he needed to get away and quickly. The silent pause turned into a roar as communists, Nazis and police descended into a frenzy of thrashing fists, hurled bricks and raised batons. The fighting was accompanied by the occasional sound of more gunshots. Some men recoiled from the violence; others gleefully leapt in, eager to do harm. Karl put a hand on his fedora and hunched down as he aimed for the quickest route to a side street.

Cries went up and bodies hit the ground. Windows were smashed. It was as if a man-made hurricane was tearing its way through the streets of Altona. Karl kept his head down and made it to an alleyway, where he ran for his life. He was wheezing and breathing heavily by the time he got to the other end. Not as fit as I was all those years ago in the army, he thought to himself. Or was it that he was getting older? Either way, he had escaped the riot.

As he made his roundabout way via backstreets to the station, a series of grim thoughts occurred to him. During the times of inflation there had been no fighting on the streets. Now, during this new economic crisis, Germany was descending into the internecine violence he had seen just after the war. Had the German people simply had enough, or was it that there were too many radical parties fighting over the fate of the nation? How long could civilised society last with all these pressures? Could Germany tear itself to pieces, a return to the warring factions before unification, or was there someone who could hold it all together? Karl felt the familiar gnaw of anxiety returning. His few hours away ended with only more worries to add to his burden.

***

The radio crackled into life: "Over fourteen years have passed since that unhappy day when the German people, blinded by promises made by those at home and abroad, forgot the highest values of our past, of the Reich, of its honour and its freedom, and thereby lost everything. Since those days of treason, the Almighty has withdrawn his blessing from our nation. Discord and hatred have moved in. Filled with the deepest distress, millions of the best German men and women from all walks of life see the unity of the nation disintegrating in a welter of egoistical political opinions, economic interests and ideological conflicts.

"As so often in our history, Germany, since the day the revolution broke out, presents a picture of heart breaking disunity. We did not receive the equality and fraternity which was promised us; instead we lost our freedom. The breakdown of the unity of mind and will of our nation at home was followed by the collapse of its political position abroad.

"We have a burning conviction that the German people in 1914 went into the great battle without any thought of personal guilt and weighed down only by the burden of having to defend the Reich from attack, to defend the freedom and material existence of the German people. In the appalling fate that has dogged us since November 1918, we see only the consequence of our inward collapse. But the rest of the world is no less shaken by great crises. The historical balance of power, which at one time contributed not a little to the understanding of the necessity for solidarity among the nations, with all the economic advantages resulting therefrom, has been destroyed."

The Walds listened intently as the speech continued. After some ten minutes, it finished: "With resolution and fidelity to our oath, seeing the powerlessness of the present Reichstag to shoulder the task we advocate, we wish to commit it to the whole German people. We therefore appeal now to the German people to sign this act of mutual reconciliation.

"The Government of the National Uprising wishes to set to work, and it will work. It has not for fourteen years brought ruin to the German nation; it wants to lead it to the summit. It is determined to make amends in four years for the liabilities of fourteen years. But it cannot subject the work of reconstruction to the will of those who were responsible for the breakdown. The Marxist parties and their followers had fourteen years to prove their abilities. The result is a heap of ruins.

"Now, German people, give us four years and then judge us. Let us begin, loyal to the command of the Field Marshal. May Almighty God favour our work, shape our will in the right way, bless our vision and bless us with the trust of our people. We have no desire to fight for ourselves, only for Germany."

It was 31 January 1933, and Adolf Hitler was now Chancellor of Germany.

***

The economy was turning around. Hope was returning to the streets of Hannover, hope and something else, something intangible but more sinister than many recognised. The late May sun was setting behind the *Rathaus*, the great monolithic town hall casting its shadow across the square in front. Nazi party members and local National Socialist students had spent the week promoting a special event, and the Walds had come with their children to see what all the fuss was about.

A stack of wooden pallets had been planted in the centre of the square, and a marching band stood on the *Rathaus* steps playing some jaunty music. Dusk was turning to night as a large crowd gathered, and uniformed members of the *Schutzstaffel*, now generally referred to as the SS for the sake of brevity, encouraged everyone to move closer to the centre.

One of the SS made a short speech about the dangers of 'corrupting political views' and 'decadent liberal attitudes', but most people didn't really understand what he was talking about. When he'd finished, he looked towards the *Rathaus* and gave a signal. Students began bringing out stacks of books and placing them around the wooden pallets. Then the SS men set fire to the wooden pallets and began hurling the books into the flames. Gasps could be heard, but except for the cracking fire, there was silence. Some of the authors' names were shouted out in disgust: "Kafka! Marx! Brecht!" These were German philosophical writers whose views were not in step with Nazi ideology. At this point, the SS started to offer books to the crowd, encouraging them to join in. Non-German names were also spat out: "Hemingway! H.G. Wells! Tolstoy!"

"What a shame. I loved reading Wells when I was growing up," Harry said to Sophie, trying to put a brave face on this casual act of barbarism.

"So did I," Sophie said, her face eerie in the light of the rising flames.

Nancy started pulling at her mother's hand. "Mama! Mama! I want throw a book," Nancy said excitedly.

Sophie looked down at Nancy's pleading face. "No, dear, nothing good has ever come from burning books," Sophie made clear to her daughter.

Harry felt the weight in his left jacket pocket, the book of poetry that he'd never bothered to read, but always carried with him. Was his *Anthology of Melancholy Poetry* on the list of banned books? Was he inadvertently carrying around contraband?

Sophie looked at Anke Wald. "Happy now, Mother?" Sophie's asked, her tone dripping with sarcasm.

Anke stared in horror at the roaring fire, refusing to answer her daughter.

"I think we've seen enough," Karl said.

And with that, the family edged its way out of the crowd, relieved to get away from what felt like the scene of a crime.

***

Harry was just handing over a pair of newly heeled shoes to his customer, when he heard the sound of tiny feet coming down the staircase. The customer nodded approvingly at Harry's work, paid and left the shop. The footsteps were getting closer and louder as hard shoes hit the wooden floor. Harry smiled; it was Nancy coming down to see what Papa was doing.

Harry quickly became very interested in lacing a pair of shoes. As she approached, Harry continued to appear utterly absorbed in his work. He could hear her little breaths as she waited for her father to acknowledge her. Harry continued, smiling to himself. Would she wait until he had finished, or would her childish impatience get the better of her? Five seconds later he felt a tug on his trousers, and a little voice asked, "Papa, what are you doing?"

Harry spun around, and in one swift move, picked up his daughter and tickled her under the arms in what she called her 'tickle spots'. "Never you mind, young lady!" Harry said to the rosy-cheeked Nancy, who was shrieking with excitement. They were almost nose-to-nose when Nancy stopped laughing and lifted her right hand to run a finger along Harry's old wound.

"Papa, is that an ouch?"

"Not any more, my dear," Harry said, allowing her to explore the white scar. She was being very gentle.

"Did it hurt when you had the bump?"

Harry was not sure that being savagely beaten in the face with the stock of a rifle and getting a fist in the same place was, technically speaking, just a 'bump', but he put himself in the shoes of his four-year-old daughter. "Yes," said Harry with a wry smile, which was completely lost on Nancy.

"Did you cry?"

"I guess I did," Harry said honestly, putting Nancy down on the floor.

"But it's better now," she said, to reassure herself.

"Yes, it's all better."

Then, "Papa?"

"Yes," said Harry, intrigued to see where his daughter's mind would take them next.

"I like our secret language."

"Darling girl, I keep telling you, it's not a secret language; it's called English. It's the language I spoke when I was your age."

"Yes, but Mama doesn't know it."

"That's true."

"And Uncle Karl doesn't know it."

"Right again and, Nancy, before you say it, I know that no one you know can speak English."

"So it *is* a secret language!" Nancy said with impeccable logic.

"Except that if I were to take you to the place where I was born, everyone would speak that language."

"Will you take me there some day?"

It was a reasonable question, but one that Harry hadn't previously considered. "Of course."

"Can we go there now?" Nancy asked, taking her father by the hand.

"It's a long way away from our house, but one day I'll take you to England."

"And can we have a dog?" continued Nancy, taking advantage of her father's good will with deft negotiating skills.

"I'll have to think about that."

***

Anke Wald was celebrating her 65th birthday. Sophie and Frieda had prepared the usual Wald celebration spread, and Max and his family had arrived for the occasion. Harry and Karl were crawling around on the floor, playing with the children. Periodically, a mother would appear from the kitchen to see what all the noise was about, only to discover someone being dangled upside down or both men play wrestling in a pile of children. Harry and Karl were admonished for their childish behaviour, looked suitably contrite and then returned to the excited children, who begged for more.

Times were good again, at least financially, and the meal was a banquet, with far more food than could possibly be eaten even by the hungry horde around the table. As if more noise were needed, someone had turned on the radio, and the children danced around the dining room to the music as the adults cleaned up and washed dishes.

It was Max's idea that as the whole family was together, they should have a professional photograph taken. This was greeted with whoops and cheers from the children, who were quickly wiped clean by their mothers before they all made their way into town. It was agreed that as well as Anke, Max, Karl and Sophie would each have a copy so everyone could have a keepsake of their mother's special birthday and a record of their ever-expanding family.

Photograph taken, the air of frivolity continued as Harry bought everyone ice cream on the way back. Nancy agonised over the choice of flavours, finally picking chocolate over vanilla and strawberry. Everyone was enjoying the day and no one wanted to go home, so on impulse, they decided to go to the cinema. Everyone was talking about *Triumph des Willens,* Triumph of the Will, so they bought their tickets and took their seats. The boisterous children had finally tired themselves out, the older ones ready to sit quietly, the younger ones eager to curl up on a mother's lap.

The film was an epic work, and the nearly two-hour long message hit the grown-ups hard; they were stunned by what they saw. Hitler was now truly the *Führer,* and the Nuremburg rally was a Nazi sermon extolling the power of Germany. The message was clear: Germany had reclaimed its pride, and everyone must respect Adolf Hitler, the man behind the vision, the man who had made it all possible. Recently voiced Nazi anti-Semitic views were absent from the film, but the images showed an Aryan ideal of what Germany should be. The Jews weren't mentioned, but their omission conveyed its own message: there was no room for people who did not fit the ideal. The film ended with the crowds lifting their arms in Nazi salutes and crying out, "*Sieg Heil!*" over and over again.

Sophie and Harry looked around to see many in the cinema doing the same thing. Then Sophie caught Harry's eye as they looked down from the screen to see Nancy and the cousins all joining in, giggling. Sophie stared at them in shock. Harry said nothing, but took Nancy's hand and forced it down. Not being allowed to join in with the others made Nancy very cross with her father. She started to protest but stopped when she was shushed by both parents.

The adults came away feeling drained. Sophie had a real sense of foreboding, but her mother came out all smiles as did the grandchildren, who had had enough of sitting still and wanted to race their grandmother back home. "Oh, I'm too old for that," Anke said with a chuckle, apparently unruffled by the two hours of propaganda she had just watched.

***

Karl looked up from the day's receipts when he heard a knock at Perle's door. It was Harry, come to pay his brother-in-law a visit. Karl smiled and walked over to the locked door to let him in.

"Good evening, Harry. How are you?"

"Fine, fine."

"And the cobbler's, how's business?"

"Never better, especially now that Rudi is back," Harry said with a hint of pride. "How are things here at Perle?"

You know, I never thought I'd say this, but Hitler has really turned things around, and I couldn't be happier that a good year has meant we could re-hire Rudi. I think the worst is finally behind us."

"I certainly hope so. After everything that's happened in the last decade and a half, I think Germany has earned a quiet spell."

"So, to what do I owe the honour of your visit?"

"Look, we both love our families; we're good fathers and husbands, but don't you sometimes feel a certain nostalgia for the old days, when we were young, free and single?"

"Oh, God, yes!"

"So I figured 'to hell with it all'. Let's just, for one night, forget about work, forget about children and families; let's go out with some friends and get royally drunk. Sadly Max isn't around, but you could get a couple of your friends to come along, and I've even managed to persuade Rudi to join us. It's a chance to be men together, to tell macho stories and talk crap. Let the beer flow; let's act like drunken idiots for one night … tonight. What do you say?"

"That, my good sir, is a brilliant idea!" Karl said, slapping Harry on the back.

Time was short, so Karl rounded up a couple of the neighbours and banged on the door of an old friend. Frederick had just become a father for the first time, and his wife was not best pleased with the idea, but Karl quickly explained that this would be a business meeting over dinner; surely she wouldn't want her husband to miss out on a lucrative opportunity, would she? His wife reluctantly agreed, but Frederick knew that by returning home, roaring drunk, with no business proposal, there would be an argument tomorrow. But, damn it, it was worth it for a night of fun!

Within the hour, six men sat in a *Bierkeller,* singing and drinking and sharing the rudest of jokes. After a couple of steins, completely unexpectedly, Rudi suddenly burst into life. It turned out he had been a soldier in the late nineteenth century in a colony called German New Guinea, a place to this day he still couldn't find on a map. All he knew was that it was somewhere in the Pacific. He had spent most of his time in the administrative capital of Herbertshöhe, where he busied himself either by carrying the dead-drunk colonial governor home from parties or trying to explain to the indigenous population how to pronounce Herbertshöhe.

As the evening wore on, the stories became more outlandish and incoherent. There were general declarations of undying friendship as the men were overcome with exuberant camaraderie. It was the perfect way to blow off some steam and celebrate the fact that, just by keeping their heads above water, they had all survived the past few years. There would be hell to pay from disapproving wives tomorrow, and the hangovers would be punishing, but right here, right now, they were having the time of their lives.

***

Sophie was worried. What she initially had thought was just a cold was now becoming more of a cause for concern. Nancy's temperature was rising rapidly, and her daughter was now lying in bed, sweaty, pallid and breathing with difficulty. Her normally talkative daughter was listless and quiet. Sophie had called the doctor, and within the hour, kindly Doctor Apfelbaum was at Nancy's bedside. He had attended both the Wald and Woods families on many occasions and was now regarded as a family friend; he had even been at Sophie and Harry's wedding.

The doctor checked the little girl's pulse and her temperature, then he took Sophie to one side. "She has flu, unusual for the time of the year, but it's common enough. She needs time, but she'll be fine," the doctor explained.

"But look at her, doctor," Sophie said, bristling with anxiety. "She is clearly not fine!"

"There, there Frau Woods, I see this all the time. While she will get weaker, the fever should break in a few days. When she gets worse, you must keep her temperature down with cold compresses - and make sure she keeps hydrated with lots of sweet drinks; try milky tea with three sugars. I promise you she will recover."

"But, Herr Doctor, 'flu 'is another word for 'influenza', is it not?" Sophie challenged.

"Well, yes, but ever since the Spanish flu, people get unnecessarily worried about influenza," the doctor replied calmly.

"That may have something to do with the fact that Spanish flu killed millions around the world, and right now, my daughter Nancy, who is named after a young girl who died of that very same illness, also has influenza."

"Are you suggesting the influenza virus is aware of this coincidence?" the doctor said flippantly, his patronising manner doing nothing to address Sophie's concerns.

"Of course not!" snapped Sophie.

"Good, because I see cases of influenza all the time. Your daughter is a healthy six-year-old girl; she appears to be very ill now, but I have no doubt she'll pull through and be fit and well by this time next week," he said, trying but failing to reassure the worried mother.

"And if she continues to worsen, what then?" Sophie asked, refusing to be fobbed off with the doctor's reassurance.

"Well, as good as modern medicine is, there's no cure for influenza. She just has to ride it out," the doctor replied flatly, and not wishing to continue the argument, he grabbed his hat and case and hurried out of the apartment, leaving Sophie alone with her gently wheezing daughter.

Sophie didn't know what to do, but it was time to alert Harry. She rushed down to the shop and waited impatiently for her husband to finish with his customer. When she was finally able to drag him aside and tell him of her fears, Harry was dumbfounded. Nancy had a cold, didn't she? It couldn't be influenza … not his daughter, not another Nancy! He looked imploringly at Sophie, begging her to tell him it wasn't true. Sick with worry, Sophie could do nothing but cling to her husband. A tear rolled down her cheek as she felt her husband's body crumple with the weight of dread.

Harry broke from her arms and, with tears in his eyes, instructed Sophie to go back to Nancy. He opened the cash register, took a small piece of paper from the back and grabbed a fistful of coins. Informing Rudi that he was now in charge, Harry took off his apron and rushed out.

***

Major General von Thoma was smoking a cigarette, lost in thought, when his telephone rang. He blinked himself back to his office, put his cigarette on the edge of the nearby ashtray and reached for the telephone. "Thoma," he said bluntly.

Harry had rushed to the nearest public telephone where he'd frantically shoved coins into the slot. He had managed to track down Thoma on his third call, but anxiety had made him hyperventilate. "Hello, Wilhelm von Thoma, this is Harry Woods," Harry managed to get out between gulps of air.

"Ah, Harry, how are you?" Thoma said, changing his tone instantly as he recognised Harry's accent.

"Not good, not good at all," Harry said truthfully.

"Whatever is the matter?" Thoma asked, changing his tone for a third time, now to one of concern.

"It's my daughter; it's Nancy," Harry said, fighting back tears.

"What's happened?" Thoma demanded, hearing the desperation in Harry's voice.

"She is deathly sick; she has influenza," Harry said simply.

Thoma had lost a cousin and an uncle to Spanish flu and felt the hairs on the back of his neck stand up. There were only two words he feared: 'cancer' and 'influenza'; both seemed to him like death sentences.

"How can I help?"

"The army has some of the best doctors and hospitals in the world. If I were to join up, could Nancy be seen immediately?"

"Yes, yes of course."

"What do I have to do?"

"Well, technically, you have to go to an enlistment centre, enrol and wait for your records to be checked."

"That will take too long," interrupted Harry.

"Yes, Harry, I'm getting to that. How old are you now?"

"Thirty-five."

"Good, you're still within recruitment age. I'm working on security for the upcoming Olympic Games in Berlin, and there's a role for a captain on my staff. Putting aside the unusual start to your military career, it's what happened after you joined the German Imperial Army that counts. Your war record, your Iron Cross and your service in the *Freikorp* practically guarantee your appointment. I will put you down for the minimum service time, which is five years. You'll be back in civilian clothes by the summer of 1941. I will get you to sign the paperwork when you arrive in Berlin. I assume you're still in Hannover …"

"Yes," Harry replied and gave his address at the cobbler's.

"I will see that your daughter gets to a military hospital by this afternoon. How does that sound?"

"It's more than I dared to hope for. I need to explain everything to my wife and make a few arrangements at home, but I will be in Berlin tomorrow."

"Excellent! Harry, I am very sorry to hear about your daughter, but I am happy that I could finally help, and I look forward to us working together … plus the Olympic Games in Berlin … that will be something to see."

"Thank you for everything, sir."

"Welcome to the *Wehrmacht*, Captain Woods."

"Thank you, sir. I'll see you tomorrow."

Harry hung up, and the major general immediately placed a new call. "Captain Woods' daughter is gravely ill with influenza. You are to despatch an ambulance to the following address …"

***

Harry raced home to Sophie. The implications were just dawning on him: he would have to live away from his wife and daughter, and the army life he had left behind was a reality once more. But there was no time for second thoughts, and he couldn't complain. The deal was a fair one, more than anything he could have expected, and a small price to pay to secure his daughter's health … her very life.

While Nancy slept fitfully in her bed, Harry sat down with Sophie in the kitchen. "Do you remember Major General Wilhelm von Thoma - from our wedding?" Harry began.

"Yes, of course."

"Well, I'm going to tell you something you never knew before: he was the one who arranged for me to join the German army. We met when I was a prisoner of war and still had a dressing on my head injuries. He had only my word that I wanted to fight for Germany, and yet he was willing to risk his reputation for me. The irony was that while I ended up being a good soldier, Thoma himself became a prisoner of war. We met up again during the uprising. It was then he said he'd do anything to get me back in the army. Thoma is a powerful man in the *Wehrmacht*, and the *Wehrmacht* has the very best doctors and hospitals. So I agreed to sign up for five years if Thoma could get Nancy into a military hospital *now*. The ambulance should be here this afternoon."

"You did what!" Sophie shouted. "You signed away five years of your life without even asking me?"

"Darling, I had to do something. I can't lose Nancy."

"How dare you! How dare you imply that our daughter somehow means more to you than she does to me!"

"That's not what I meant."

"If von Thoma is such a good friend, why couldn't he pull a few strings and get Nancy into a hospital without stealing my husband away for five years?"

"I don't know if there was another way to do this, but it was the only way I knew. Thoma has always wanted me back in the army, and if this is how it happens … well, he gets me, and we get Nancy the best possible medical care. It's true that I will have to live away, but it's not like there's a war on. It looks like my first posting will be working on security for the Olympic Games in Berlin, hardly a dangerous assignment. I'll only be a few hours away and, besides, five years isn't that long. It's a price worth paying to save our daughter's life, Sophie."

"But how could you make such a major decision, one that affects our entire family, without talking it over first with your wife!" Sophie shrieked, as angry as he'd ever seen her.

"Because I had just found out my daughter has influenza. Because my wife was crying in my arms. Because, for once, I didn't have to leave everything to fate; I could do something about it." He hesitated. "And because I panicked!" The room fell silent. Sophie and Harry stared at each other across the kitchen table. Harry knew he had made the right decision, but Sophie needed time to come to terms with it.

"I need to collect a few things and speak to Karl," he said getting up.

Harry hurriedly packed a suitcase and returned to the kitchen to say good-bye to his wife. Sophie sat where he had left her, arms crossed, refusing to make eye contact. He kissed her on the cheek and left for Nancy's bedroom. His eyes filled with tears as he said a little prayer and kissed her clammy forehead. If Nancy pulled through, this would be the best deal he had ever made.

***

Harry was in accelerated officer training. He had had to swear an oath of allegiance on re-enlisting: "I swear by God this sacred oath that to the Leader of the German empire and people, Adolf Hitler, Supreme Commander of the armed forces, I shall render unconditional obedience, and that as a brave soldier, I shall, at all times, be prepared to give my life for this oath."

It had not escaped Harry's notice that, in the past, as a soldier in both the British army and later, the old German Imperial Army, he had had to swear an oath of loyalty to the country, but the new *Wehrmacht* oath was different: it was an oath of allegiance to a man, not a state. This made him uneasy. Thoma had warned him that many officers were unhappy with the new circumstances, but in the end they had no choice but to comply.

Meanwhile, as Harry began to learn about the new technology and tactics of a modern army, Sophie was at the hospital with Nancy, where she was receiving the promised highest quality of care. Her fever broke and, within days, colour was returning to her cheeks; she had become more communicative, even asking her mother questions when Sophie was reading to her. Nancy was obviously over the worst and well along the road to recovery. Harry broke down when Sophie told him the good news, but he did his best to conceal it as they spoke on the telephone.

After ten days in the *Wehrmacht* hospital, Nancy was well enough to go home. While happy that the little girl had made a complete and speedy recovery, the staff members were all sorry to see Nancy go. They had clearly enjoyed the novelty of treating a child, and Nancy had charmed them all.

In her long days at the hospital Sophie couldn't help but notice how empty it was; there were the many medical staff, of course, but it seemed largely devoid of patients. There were a few men with injuries, sustained in military manoeuvres, but the hospital wasn't even at ten per cent capacity. Its size must mean that the authorities thought that, at some point, the beds would be filled, but when and why, Sophie couldn't say. The thought of a hospital just waiting for wounded soldiers gave her the chills.

Karl met Nancy and Sophie at the hospital in his brand new Opel Kadett. Business was booming in Hannover and, indeed, all over Germany; the good times were here again. Sophie's thoughts about the hospital were pushed to one side when she saw her daughter's face light up as she inspected the shiny maroon car with her uncle sitting proudly behind the wheel.

Sophie was worried that her brother's driving was not safe as he took corners fast enough to make the tires screech. She held on grimly, while Nancy cheered excitedly. Sophie accused Karl of showing off for Nancy's benefit and reminded him that her daughter was still frail, but her lecture was interrupted by a plea from Nancy, encouraging her uncle to drive faster. No one was paying her any attention, so Sophie sat back, hugged her seat and indulged her worst fears.

When they got home Sophie sat down to write to Harry. Not wanting to alarm her daughter so early in her recovery, she had explained Harry's absence by saying simply that 'Papa had to go away on business,' which Nancy, in her childish way, had accepted without questions. As Sophie came to the end of her news, she decided to leave room for her daughter to add something of her own. Nancy said she wanted to use her secret language to write to her father. Sophie knew this was English, but as she'd never learned the language, and as Nancy was only just learning her German letters, she could only wonder what her daughter was writing.

Using the German alphabet, Nancy attempted a few words in English and drew a picture of her father with an oddly round head and a substantial torso, surrounded by four sausage limbs. Her childish efforts were completed when she drew a red heart on the torso. Sophie assured her daughter that 'Papa will love it!' and put the letter in an envelope addressed to Berlin.

Harry and Nancy were close; his time in the army would be difficult for them both, but Sophie had decided to explain everything more fully at a later time – when the questions came.

***

The Olympic stadium stood before Harry like a giant monument to architectural perfection. Albert Speer was not only Hitler's architect, but the literal architect of Nazism. He had designed the Nuremburg Arena, where the major rallies took place, and now he had created this gigantic colosseum for sport.

As Harry inspected his company of men, assigned to police the perimeter of the stadium, it occurred to him how the Olympic ideal and the Nazi quest for Aryan perfection mirrored each other. Both were looking for links back to ancient times; both wanted the strongest and fittest to win. The Nazis had even combined the two with their original idea of lighting a torch on Mount Olympus in Greece and relaying it all the way to Berlin, where it was meant to burn permanently in its specially designed cauldron. It was an unmistakable message intended to show the link from ancient Greece to Nazi Germany. Yet there was a clear and significant difference: the modern Olympic ideal embraced men and women from all over the known world; all colours, races and religions were to be included and represented, whereas Hitler had distorted that ideal in an attempt to make Europe more 'European'. Germany chose to ignore multiculturalism, still on a high from Max Schmeling's victory over the African American Joe Louis, in a heavyweight boxing match in New York. This was said to be 'proof' of Aryan supremacy.

At the stadium Harry's biggest concern was discipline. The soldiers were too easily distracted by the pretty young girls who came to visit the venue, and pretty young girls like a man in a uniform. This was an unusual situation for everyone, and too often Harry had to reprimand the men for failing to pay attention to the task at hand. He observed that some were barely out of their teens and looked more like boys playing soldiers than the real thing. *Was I ever this young*, he wondered to himself as he saw off yet another flirtatious woman trying to catch a soldier's eye.

The Olympic Games and his assignment to the stadium were a welcome diversion from all the learning he had to work through. In the trenches he had begun to see the use of combined arms, linking tanks with infantry and air attacks, but in the nearly twenty years since he had been in battle, the technology in all of these areas had made enormous strides, and the concept of linking these three major services had been refined by *Wehrmacht* strategists. Now there were even *Fallschirmjäger*, entire companies of men dropping from aeroplanes in parachutes, ready to attack enemy lines from behind, an idea not even H.G. Wells had imagined. All of this was wrapped up in the unbreakable codes of the enigma machines, which transmitted radio messages, safe in the knowledge that anyone could listen in, but no one would be able to understand or decipher the messages.

It seemed to Harry that the era of protracted trench warfare was gone forever. Any future conflict would be about manoeuvre, and now that more and more soldiers were armed with the likes of the MG 34 machine gun, the damage that could be inflicted by a platoon of well-armed soldiers was ten times the magnitude of anything the same men could inflict when Harry last had a rifle in his hands. All of these images of war, mechanised divisions and aerial bombardments were a grim part of what he had signed on for, so the summer games in the capital were a pleasant way to drive this ominous new information and his darker thoughts out of his mind.

With rank came privileges. When Harry had free time, he was at liberty to do what he liked, and he liked to roam the Olympic grounds. On one occasion he happened on the Lightweight Freestyle Wrestling final. It was a tense match as the much-favoured German, Wolfgang Ehrl, was pitted against the Hungarian Jew, Károly Kárpáti. The crowd roared every time Ehrl made a move forwards, but Kárpáti silenced the crowd with a well-deserved victory. Harry couldn't help but smile; this encapsulated the difference between Hitler's twisted vision of perfection and the Olympic ideal. Hitler genuinely expected Aryans to excel; the Olympic ideal expected that the most talented would win, irrespective of ethnicity.

That evening Harry sat down with Thoma in a restaurant near the stadium. "I must say, Captain Woods, the uniform suits you," Thoma said, raising a glass of wine in a toast.

Harry looked down at his grey officer's uniform. It was smart and dirt free, a rare condition in any of his past lives as a soldier or in his most recent work as a cobbler. It seemed as if he had always been covered in mud, oil, dirt or polish. It was a little ironic that it was his return to a military career that gave him his greatest opportunity to be neat and tidy. "Thank you, sir," Harry said, returning the toast.

"Shall we stop with the titles and just talk as two men?"

"Agreed," Harry said, taking a sip of wine.

"Most importantly, how is your daughter?" Thoma asked.

"She's fine, thanks to you. Nancy always sends me something in my wife's letters, and she usually attempts some English, which can be more amusing than she intends because she only knows the German alphabet. My wife can't help her because she doesn't speak English, and Nancy won't share her thoughts, which must be frustrating for Sophie," Harry said with a wistful smile.

"Your wife can't speak English, but your daughter can?"

"I know what you're thinking, but Sophie's got a hectic life, and I'm busy …" Harry caught himself and corrected the tense, "I *was* busy with the shop. Besides, Sophie doesn't have much need to learn English, and it was easier for me to start with Nancy – a fresh young mind and a captive audience. We began with nursery rhymes. I haven't got a clue what Germans sing to their babies, but I remembered what I had heard as a child, and from there I just progressed to speaking to her almost exclusively in English. She calls it our 'secret language' because no one else she knows speaks it."

The waitress brought them their main courses. Thoma had ordered roast chicken with vegetables; Harry had opted for a sirloin steak, well done, because he had learned that whatever he ordered, it always came 'well done'. The waitress fussed over the two officers until Thoma shooed her away. "So, how does it feel to be back in uniform?" Thoma asked, cutting into his chicken.

"A little strange, but not bad at all. What I notice most is that the world of war has become far more technical than I could have ever imagined."

"I feel the same, and I've been able to watch it all develop: Panzer this, *Fallschirmjäger* that, Junkers the other. I tell you, Harry, the generation just coming through has so much more to remember than we old war horses."

"Who are you calling 'old'?" Harry asked in mock seriousness. "I'm ten years younger than you are, and I can still keep up with these twenty-year-olds."

"Of course, Harry, but you know what I mean."

They concentrated on their food for a few minutes before Harry chose a different topic of conversation. "The Olympic Games are a sight to behold, aren't they?"

"Yes, they are."

"I saw a Hungarian Jew win the lightweight wrestling today. Beat a German too. I wonder what the *Führer* made of that."

"Ah, yes, the Nazi obsession with the Jews and Aryan purity. There have been many great but unsung Jews who have contributed to Germany. I met one of them at your wedding. What was his name again?"

"Wilhelm."

"Yes?" Thoma replied, thinking Harry was addressing him.

"No, sorry. The Jew's name is also 'Wilhelm'."

"Ah, yes, I'd forgotten … I believe he had quite the reputation as a first-class sniper."

"Best shot I've ever seen."

"That's my point. Pretending that Wilhelm is inferior, despite all evidence to the contrary, is stupid. Hitler has rebuilt Germany and finally ended those lurches into economic catastrophe, but at what price? And will that price fall on the heads of all the so-called 'undesirables'? And I don't mean just the Jews, but Gypsies, Poles, the disabled … anyone who isn't 'Aryan enough' in the eyes of the law. 'Bread and circuses,' the Romans called it."

"Bread and circuses? What does that mean?"

"It's an old Roman saying. Rome was a republic, a democracy of sorts, but then came the time of the Caesars. The people of Rome lost their freedom, but in return, they were regularly fed by the emperor and regaled with magnificent shows. They were distracted from concerns about their loss of democracy by being bribed – bought off – with loaves of bread and entertainment in the Coliseum."

"And you're worried that Germany has become a modern-day Rome?"

"Well, yes, and if Hitler carries out all his policies, what role will the army play? That said, I'm glad we're providing the security for these Olympic Games; it's far more pleasant than anything else we might be asked to do."

"I'll drink to that," said Harry through a mouthful of steak, raising his glass for another toast.

Thoma raised his glass in acknowledgement.

***

Sophie sat down beside Nancy, who had finished her supper and was looking forward to a treat for eating all her vegetables. Sophie opened her hand to reveal a boiled sweet. "Thank you, Mama!" Nancy said, snatching the sweet and pushing it greedily into her mouth. Then, "When is Papa coming home?" Sophie had known this was coming and had been thinking how best to explain Harry's prolonged absence.

"Nancy …" Sophie began; "… you know we've been sending letters to Papa because he's been away in Berlin. He can't live with us just now, and that's because he's joined the army. He's doing very important work keeping all the sports men and women safe at the Olympic Games."

"Why does he need to keep them safe?" Nancy slurred her words through a mouth full of melting sugar.

The unexpected question caught Sophie off guard. "He needs to keep them safe from … bad people."

"Like Jews?"

Sophie was dismayed by the bigotry of Nancy's question. She and Harry had done their best to insulate their daughter from the obviously anti-Semitic news and public broadcasts, but they couldn't stop her from going to school. What were they being taught?

"No, Nancy, not Jews; Jews are not bad people. I'm talking about bad people like …" Sophie cast around frantically, trying to think of some genuinely 'bad' people. "… like gangsters and … um … pirates," Sophie said weakly.

"Oh, we know Papa is good at that," Nancy said confidently.

"Why do you think Papa is good at that?" asked a puzzled Sophie.

"Well, we never saw any gangsters or pirates in the shop, did we?" Nancy replied with watertight reason.

Sophie was lost for words. The conversation was not going as she had planned. "Anyway, my love, now that Papa is an army captain, he can't be here with us like he used to be, so we'll keep writing to him, and he'll keep writing to us, and we'll be together in a different way. Sometimes he'll be able to come home to visit us, so we won't always be apart. I know it seems a long time, but when you're eleven, Papa will be finished with his important work, and we can go back to being a family that lives together again. Do you think you can be patient?"

"Why can't Papa come home when the 'Lympics are over?"

"Well, because Papa is doing such a good job of keeping the athletes safe, they want him to do it in other places too."

"Yes," Nancy said, nodding sagely.

"I know you miss Papa."

"Yes, but can he come back for cuddles and bedtime stories?"

"Sometimes, not every night, but when he comes, you'll get to see him in his uniform."

"What's a 'uniform'?"

"Papa wears special army clothes to do his important work. He looks very handsome."

Satisfied with Sophie's explanations, Nancy had lost interest and wandered off to do some colouring. Sophie exhaled slowly. She knew Nancy could not fully understand what the long absences would mean, but her daughter seemed content for the moment. If there were problems, Sophie would deal with them as they arose.

***

It was early October 1936. The Olympic Games had been a huge success, and Harry had been able to visit his family once a month while he was in Berlin. After a fine summer, the weather was changing: every day seemed to be getting cooler, and the rain was becoming more frequent. After inspecting his troops in a light drizzle, Harry had left the parade ground and was heading towards his office, when a corporal came running up to him. He was struggling to catch his breath and salute. "Sir, Major General von Thoma wants to see you in his office immediately," he managed between great gulps of air.

"Thank you, corporal; that is all," Harry said, dismissing the man as he turned in the direction of Thoma's office. The guard in front of the administrative block snapped to attention, and Harry responded correctly but disinterestedly. As far as he was concerned, being a good soldier had nothing to do with the smartness of the salute; he was still getting used to his rank and the formality that came with it. As Harry walked into Thoma's office, he saw his superior packing a brown leather satchel.

"Sir," he said, saluting.

"Ah, Harry, you need to start packing," Thoma said, barely looking up.

"Where are we going?" Harry asked, caught by surprise.

Thoma stopped and looked at Harry, his face drawn and serious. "We've 'volunteered'," he said simply.

"We have? For what?"

"The Joint Chiefs of Staff are looking for a number of units to go to Spain to join the fledgling Condor Legion. Spain's involved in a civil war, and we're going in to do training and provide support for the nationalists. But I'm under no illusion; we're also going to fight for General Franco."

"I thought I was going to have a quiet few years in the army, and now you're telling me, just a few months in, that I'm going to a different country to fight in a civil war. It's not even our fight!"

"Oh, make no mistake; technically speaking, it is a civil war, but everyone is getting involved. The British have a blockade around the Spanish ports to try and stop the war, but it's actually making things worse. Stalin is sending in troops and heavy equipment to support the republicans, and Mussolini is backing the nationalists. I think our government reasons that it's better to have a pro-German Spain as our ally than a communist puppet state run by Stalin's cronies. I also think that this war is going to be a giant laboratory. All sides have new tanks and planes and tactics they want to try out. This war is going to see things no one has seen before."

"I didn't sign up for this," Harry said faintly.

"No, you signed up so that the *Wehrmacht* could save your daughter's life, which it did. Your service is the way to repay this debt. Meanwhile, I have selfishly promoted you, viciously treated you as my equal and unfairly bought you dinner on many occasions. I didn't start this war, and I couldn't have known when you called me that we would end up having this conversation, but here we are. Orders are orders. Don't whine, Captain Woods; it is most unbecoming."

Harry could feel himself blush. Everything Thoma said was true.

"My apologies, Herr Major General, sir, I will pack immediately and have my troops ready for transportation within the hour," Harry said with a razor sharp salute.

"That's more like the Harry I know," Thoma said, responding with his own salute.

True to his word, Harry's company was ready to mobilise forty-five minutes later. Troop trucks pulled up and took them to a nearby airport where they were due to fly out in JU 52s, with their distinctive engines: one under each wing and a third in the nose of the plane. Most of the soldiers had never flown before, but then, neither had Harry. He looked up at the sky. Was man ever meant to fly? He felt his stomach lurch at the thought of taking off but knew he had to set an example for his men.

As they boarded the aircraft, many were quiet, but many others chatted excitedly, pumped full of nervous adrenaline before their first flight. Harry was annoyed by their gabble and barked for quiet, giving the pilots the silence they needed for their pre-flight checks. As he waited for take-off, he absentmindedly patted his left breast pocket, where he felt a slight bulge. It was the book of poetry that Sophie had given to him all those years ago, still unread. He had become superstitious, thinking that if he opened and read it, the spell of protection would be broken, and the store of good luck would be released and lost. It was a silly idea he knew, but he found comfort in the notion of the book's protective powers. Having been pulled in and out of so many jacket pockets over the years, the cover was now a little scruffy, but it was his totem - and a reminder that wherever he might be, however awful the situation, there were people in the world who loved him.

His thoughts were shattered as the propellers began to turn and the engines roared into life. The noise inside the aircraft was enough to make their teeth chatter. As the plane taxied onto the runway and the pilot opened up the throttle, the sound of the engines grew to a cacophony, and the plane began to accelerate down the runway.

Harry looked down and saw that his knuckles were white as he gripped his seat to hide his nerves. The wheels bounced along the runway until the plane took off into the grey sky and headed for Spain.

***

Sophie sat with Frieda and Anke in their apartment, a selection of school text books open in front of them. "Here's an example," Sophie said, pointing to a line from one of Nancy's books. "'The Jewish nose is bent. It looks like a number 6'," she read and picked up another book. "This one comes from a maths book for older children," she said, indicating a marked page. "'To keep a mentally ill person costs approximately 4 Marks a day. There are 300,000 mentally ill people in care. How much do these people cost to keep in total? How many marriage loans of 1000 Marks could be granted with this money?'" I hardly know what to say I'm so appalled. Do your children have the same books?" Sophie asked Frieda.

"Yes, of course, this is all part of the national curriculum, and now that Sonia is ten, she has been automatically enrolled in the *Jungmadelbund*, the girl's version of the Hitler Youth. When Karl Junior is ten, he'll be in the Hitler Youth," Frieda explained in her detached way.

"This can't be right," Sophie said with an exasperated sigh.

"If the price of the rise of Germany is to make people aware of the treachery of the Jews, what's wrong with that?" Anke said, indignantly.

"What treachery?" challenged Sophie.

"We all know that it was Jewish politicians who stabbed our country in the back at the end of the Great War. The communist uprisings that nearly tore this country apart in 1919 were led by Jews, and of course, our financial crises were punishments inflicted on us by Jewish bankers," Anke replied, convinced of the rightness of her argument.

"I don't remember it that way at all. What I *do* remember is that once we gave Hitler power, he assassinated a number of his opponents and started blaming all of Germany's woes on the Jews. I also remember that he ordered all the books that disagreed with his world view to be burned. You should remember it too, Mother; we were all there when it happened right here in Hannover!" Sophie said this, overcome with emotion as she recollected the outrageous events of that night.

"Those are your facts, and here are mine: Who won the most gold medals at the Olympics last year?" Anke asked triumphantly.

"We did, with thirty-three." Frieda interjected.

"So?" Sophie responded tetchily.

"Doesn't this prove what we can do if inferior blood is eliminated?" Anke retorted.

"Jesse Owens," Sophie countered.

"Who?"

"The Negro sportsman who won four gold medals at the Olympics. Doesn't he show the flaw in your assumption of Aryan superiority?"

"The Negros are barely evolved from apes. Is it any wonder they are stronger than the more civilised Aryan stock?" Anke responded, seemingly unaware of the impact of her breath-taking pronouncements.

"Mother, you were just using the Olympic gold medal tally to prove a point of supremacy, but now you're saying it doesn't count. Which one is it?"

"Ladies, please," Frieda cut in, trying to diffuse the rising temperature. "Let's put aside sports, and let's forget about politics and history. Right now the Nazis have almost complete control over our children's lives. Hitler's agenda has influenced everything from science to history to physical education. Girls must grow up to be model mothers, and boys must grow up to be great scientists or brave soldiers. I may not agree with everything Hitler says, but you have to admit the Germany of today is doing a whole lot better than the Germany of ten years ago."

Sophie fell silent and nodded in agreement. Maybe putting up with propaganda was worth all the benefits she could see around her. Maybe.

***

It didn't take Harry long to discover that Spanish troops had nowhere near the levels of discipline and expertise that were taken for granted in the German army. So far he had spent most of his time in Spain training nationalist forces how to use, maintain and repair captured Russian tanks, and much of that effort felt like it was lost. He wasn't sure if it was a matter of poor translation or if the fact that the nationalists would take anybody meant a low level of literacy and an even lower level of interest in the war. Some of the men were farmers whose only motivation seemed to be money: they were financially better off fighting than they were harvesting lemons. Then there was the 'siesta', that interminable rest period when all Spaniards, regardless of their political affiliations, decided it wasn't worth fighting after lunch. Ridiculous. How could any country achieve an efficient economy with such regular and extended periods of indolence?

Where the Spanish recruits were concerned, Harry sometimes felt he was losing the will to live, but there was the relative solace of knowing his company carried out efficient patrols and ensured that security was robust around his Condor Legion airbase. The base itself might be rudimentary, but it contained the sleek, insect-like silhouettes of Dornier Do 17s and Heinkel He 111s, their glass canopies resembling the unblinking composite eyes of insects.

The bombers were like something out of *Metropolis*. For the first time in the short history of aeronautics they were made entirely of metal, with a single swept-back wing, a double tail and machine guns pointing out at various angles. They were able to reach the incredible speeds of 400 kph, while the fighter planes could go even faster. It was as if the future had arrived and was staring at him. Harry couldn't help but be impressed by the technical skill and vision it took to create such machines.

Life on the base was not hard. The greatest threat to his company was boredom; it degraded their vigilance and threatened their effectiveness. The tedium had been broken when they heard that Hitler had peacefully annexed Austria and then the Sudetenland in Czechoslovakia. However, those victories paled in comparison to the excitement around the 'Fight of the Century', the much lauded rematch between Max Schmeling and Joe Louis, who was now the Heavyweight Champion of the World. When they had met two years earlier, Schmeling had knocked out Louis in round twelve. Since then the concept of Aryan supremacy had only grown. Now far more was at stake than just the heavyweight title. This was not a fight between two men; it was a clash of ideals.

Harry saw the enthusiasm his troops had for Schmeling, assuming he would be the victor, and bets were being taken on which round Schmeling would knock out Louis. Harry wasn't so sure about the result. Why would an American boxer have a rematch in front of a home crowd in Yankee Stadium if he didn't think he could win - and win comfortably? Dozens of men huddled by the radio to listen to the fight in the early hours of that June morning in 1938. They were disgusted to hear that Schmeling was knocked to the ground three times in the first round and lost the fight due to a technical knockout before the bell had rung for the end of round two. It gave Harry a perverse satisfaction to see so many young men being so miserable. The Germans were good people, tough people, but they were no better than any other people, and Harry couldn't stand the constant rhetoric of Aryan superiority pouring out of the Nazi media.

That fight was now months ago, and the war ground on, but Harry never grew tired of watching the planes coming in to land. Some were just coming in from a mission called Operation Rügen, which they were conducting with the Italians. The target was not a republican base, but a town called Guernica, where republican forces were thought to be mustering amongst the civilian population.

Harry sat with some of the returning pilots and listened, at first, with admiration for the skills required to get into a bombing formation and the need to take into account wind speed, altitude and other factors necessary for a successful bombing run. His fascination slowly turned to unease as the *Luftwaffe* pilots talked so dispassionately about dropping bombs amongst houses, churches and apartment blocks. It was true that the republicans and the socialist soldiers would have had no refuge, no safe haven from the aerial bombardment, but what of the civilians? How many innocent families were crushed under falling debris or blown to pieces by high explosives? Not a minute was spared by the aircrews to consider the scale of the carnage they had inflicted on a small town full of civilians, guilty only of having enemy soldiers in their midst. How many had died in the aerial attack? Hundreds? Thousands?

Over the next few days Franco's troops easily captured the now shattered Guernica. The soldiers and the local population had been blasted into submission by wave after wave of German and Italian bombers. The news seeped out, and Harry was aware that the catastrophic damage inflicted on Guernica was being shouted from the front pages of almost every international newspaper, including *The Times* in London and the *New York Post*. There was talk at the airbase that this was one more example of Jewish-owned media cartels trying to influence public opinion and interfere with Condor Legion operations. The irony of German airmen muttering about an international conspiracy while standing next to their bombers in an airfield in northern Spain didn't seem to occur to them.

***

It was 23 December and, with Christmas almost here, Sophie had decorated the apartment in true festive tradition. She and Nancy had cut out paper snowflakes and hung them from the door frames and mantelpiece. A Christmas tree decorated with silver and gold ornaments stood prominently in their cosy sitting room. Nancy was anxious that it should be easy for Father Christmas to find so he could put a present under it for her.

Everywhere smelled of spice. Sophie was tireless in her baking, making her own *Lebkuchen*, gingerbread, *Stollen and Strudel*, not to mention her delicious spiced apple drink with cinnamon and cloves. The new radio filled the room with traditional holiday music. Sophie and Nancy were just sitting down, ready to tuck into an evening meal of sausages and sauerkraut with mashed potatoes, when they heard a key turn in the lock and the door to the apartment open. Sophie cocked her head to listen.

"Did you hear that, Mama?" Sophie ran to the hall. Nancy heard her mother cry with surprise before she saw her father's face at the kitchen door.

"Papa!" Nancy cried, jumping up and racing into her father's outstretched arms. She tried to put her arms all the way around his waist to squeeze him for all she was worth, but his heavy coat and uniform foiled her attempt. Harry whisked his daughter off her feet and up into his arms. "Did you miss me?" he asked in English, kissing her on the cheek. Without her father around, Nancy had forgotten much of the language, but she was able to reply, "Yes!"

"Oh, here we go again with the secret language. I had begun to enjoy conversations with our daughter and now this," Sophie said smilingly, only a little annoyed.

"Sorry, my love," Harry said, switching back to German for his wife's benefit.

"Why didn't you tell me you'd be coming home for Christmas?" Sophie asked.

"Because, to tell you the truth, I didn't know if I'd make it in time. I flew out first thing this morning and had to catch a train from Munich.

"How long you staying, my father?" Nancy tried in English.

"Ten whole days!"

"So you can see what Father Christmas brings me!" exclaimed Nancy, switching back to German in her excitement.

"The food smells delicious. Any left?"

"I'm sure I can find some for you."

"Good, I'm starving. Anything is better than those damned army rations."

Nancy giggled at the mild curse.

"Watch your mouth, please," scolded Sophie.

"Sorry … army life, you know; it's much coarser than civilian life."

"Isn't the food good in the army?"

"I've had worse, but no, it's not very good."

"But the *Wehrmacht* is the greatest army in the world!"

Harry looked quizzically at his daughter. Was it normal for an eight-year-old girl to have an opinion on the standing of her country's military force? He had no comparison, but he didn't think so. "That's as may be," said Harry, humouring his daughter, "but no army in the history of the world has ever been known for its good food." Sophie placed a loaded plate in front of Harry, who had already helped himself to bread. "Besides," said Harry, continuing his train of thought with a sidelong glance at his wife, "until the army gets Mama's recipes, they'll never be any good at cooking."

***

It had only been a month since *Kristallnacht*, when thousands of German businesses and hundreds of synagogues all over Germany had been destroyed by Hitler's SA paramilitaries. Shortly before this, Harry had lost contact with Goldmann. Whether his letters were being intercepted or whether Goldmann, for reasons unknown, couldn't write, Harry didn't know. Had he seen the destruction for himself, he might well have been worried, but he had been over a thousand kilometres away, preoccupied with a slightly surreal war, which his side was winning. The German army was advancing, gaining ground, getting stronger, all new experiences for him in war, and he recognised the dangers of allowing victory to intoxicate. That road led to hubris, and Harry wanted to avoid it at all costs.

Christmas provided a welcome relief from the ugliness on the streets of Germany and the fighting in Spain. Sophie, Harry and Nancy were expected at the Walds' apartment on Christmas Day. Nancy and Sophie dressed in new clothes, but they had both insisted that Harry wear his uniform: Sophie, because she recognised it was the smartest thing she'd ever seen her husband in and Nancy, because he was the embodiment of the Aryan dream. Under his captain's cap, Harry's blonde hair was now flecked with grey, but he wore his Iron Cross with genuine pride.

Anke smiled and gave her son-in-law a warm hug of approval. The uniform had been the right choice. Everyone admired his smart appearance and his good looks, while all the children wanted to touch the Iron Cross. The attention made Harry feel like a film star. Karl recalled his experiences of taking orders from Harry and gently teased him about becoming 'one of them'.

The ten days sped by but not so fast that Harry didn't savour the luxury of time with his wife and daughter. He was delighted to discover that Nancy wanted him to speak to her only in English, and she quickly recovered what had been temporarily lost, while also making significant progress. Together they decided that her lessons should continue in the letters they exchanged. Harry would set 'homework', and Nancy would send it back for him to correct. She was a smart little girl, her mind was clear and sharp – and she was eager to learn.

With Christmas and New Year's over, it was time for Harry to say his farewells. He didn't want Nancy and Sophie to see him off, so he had kissed them goodbye at the apartment. Karl drove him to the station and took the opportunity to ask about the situation in Spain. He knew the Nazi propaganda machine would never admit to any setbacks, but he had been in enough fights to know that what happened and what was reported were rarely the same. It took Harry most of the journey to convince Karl that things were going surprisingly well and that he wasn't just putting a brave face on it.

Harry collected his bags from the boot of the Opel, and clapped an arm around Karl, before him a quick hug. "Good luck," he said, "and if you take any stupid risks in Spain, I'll kill you myself!"

"I promise to stay out of trouble," Harry grinned. Then, seriously, "I have too many reasons to come home safely. Look after my girls for me."

"You know I will."

They shook hands and Harry strode into the station with a goodbye salute.

***

"We are in position," came the crackling voice in Harry's headset. The heavy accent meant that it was the Spanish Lieutenant Crespo.

"Engage, engage, engage!" Thoma ordered from his Panzer.

The engine of Harry's Panzer II went from a background growl to a deafening roar as his own tank lurched forwards. His head and shoulders were out of the turret. Rather than peering through the tiny slits of the periscope, trying to guess where he should look, he had a wide field of vision, while also avoiding the diesel fumes that clung to the interior and made him faintly nauseous. The chances of a republican marksman being able to hit a moving target that lurched from one side to another was highly unlikely, and if they took a direct hit from artillery, then it made no difference if the turret hatch was open or closed.

It was late January and the envelopment and capture of Barcelona was imminent. The Spanish Civil War was not a simple one between two sides; there were many vying interests. The Basques fought for independence; the communists were different from the anarchists, and Franco was separate from the Carlists. However, it was General Franco who had the momentum. He had the command and the loyalty of a unified fighting force, and his foreign support was better equipped and more in tune with his own goals than any other group fighting in the war. He had employed the strategy of 'divide and conquer' with brutal effect.

The *Wehrmacht*, *Kriegsmarine* and *Luftwaffe* had also achieved much since the start of German involvement. The war had been an opportunity for them to test their tactics and hone the skills of the officer corps. The power of combining and coordinating services, weaponry and strategies had been proven.

Thoma's armoured group was tasked with taking an old fort on a nearby hill, a strategic location both for spotting and for artillery. As they approached, they came under attack from a nest of machine guns firing pointlessly at Harry's Panzer, the bullets either missing or deflecting harmlessly off the tank's exterior. "Arnet, take out the machine gun on your one o clock," Harry ordered down the microphone.

The turret whined as it moved. The driver stopped (as training stipulated) to allow the gunner a chance to hit the target first time. Harry brought up his binoculars and saw the machine gun crew frantically trying to change the belt of ammunition. "What's the point? Their guns are useless against armour," Harry muttered to no one.

There was an ominous pause, the rumble of the engine the only sound as the gunner checked range and trajectory. The autocannon fired two rounds of high explosives into the machine gun nest, which fell instantly silent. "Good work, Sapp, but a little slow. Try to work faster; next time it could be an anti-tank position."

A Stuka arced in the sky above, looking for targets of opportunity. Its presence was a reminder of the formidable power that a modern, mechanised army could unleash. Airpower was available with just one radio call. The nationalists now had total air superiority, and the republicans had no answer to this new threat. The bravest men in the world, with hearts full of love for their country, couldn't stop an armoured spearhead, backed by airpower and radio communications.

The rest of the tanks were rolling forwards with little or no resistance. The armour group was a mixture of the latest German tanks, captured Russian armour and already obsolete Italian vehicles. Keeping them all running was a challenge, but enough preparation had been put into this push to ensure that every last armoured vehicle was in working order, and the crews were as well drilled as possible.

The republicans responded to the assault with a couple of pieces of artillery and some feeble mortar rounds. One Panzer Mark I was stopped by an anti-tank mine that blew out its transaxle. Meanwhile, Thoma kept the stream of orders and observations coming down the radio microphone to ensure co-ordination. The German crews obeyed with glacial calm, but as always, the Spaniards were ill-disciplined and lagged behind, fearing a non-existent ambush, or they rushed ahead, eager to reach the target and achieve glory.

Harry followed his superior's lead, ensuring that both he and the other Panzers under his direct command kept heading towards the goal, but he needed to check the situation with the immobilised tank. "Dreger, what's the situation with your Panzer? Over."

"We're out of action, but the crew is fine, if a little shaken up. Over."

"Good to hear. Sit tight. The infantry should be coming into the area in the next five minutes. Use their cover to come to me. I'll be in the courtyard at the fort. Over."

"Stay in formation," Thoma barked at some Spanish tanks, but he knew it was futile.

Harry's Panzer continued to grind towards the fort. A few riflemen on the battlements fired feebly at the oncoming amour. Harry looked up to hear the high-pitched whine of the siren on the Stuka as it dropped its bombs on the riflemen, then banked around and strafed the battlements for good measure. Harry waved his arm slowly from side-to-side in appreciation to the pilot, who wobbled his wings, his own response to Harry.

A T-26 tank smashed through the wooden gates of the fort, and Harry's Panzer was second in. There in the courtyard were eight men, gaunt and tired, with several days of beard growth. They looked beaten. Their rifles were on the ground, and their hands were raised in surrender. The T-26 manoeuvred itself to face the men. Crespo opened the hatch on his turret and smiled at the beaten republican troops. Harry watched him deliver a lecture, and then, without warning, the machine gunner in the tank opened fire and cut down the unarmed men.

Harry stared in disbelief at what he'd just seen. "What the hell do you think you're doing!" shouted Harry.

Crespo turned to him and smiled, "All's fair in love and war, my friend," he said casually.

"That's not war. At best, you've lost the chance to question some prisoners who might have had important information; at worst, it was cold-blooded murder."

"They didn't know anything; if they did, they would not have surrendered. And murder? Ha! They would have slit your throat in your sleep without thinking twice. All I did was secure the courtyard; I wasted some bullets but saved us some time. You're welcome," Crespo replied defiantly.

***

The long siege of Madrid was over. The city had fought off Franco for over two years, but the last bastion of republican idealism had finally been crushed by Franco and his foreign allies. The German contingent was itching to go home, but with the lull in fighting that came with peace, it was time to enjoy what remained of the sights in the Spanish capital.

Thoma had given all but a skeleton security force leave to celebrate their victory. He and Harry walked along the city's winding streets, relishing the spring sunshine and some leisure time. It was remarkable how quickly normal life tried to re-establish itself after war. People always longed to return to the status quo, and regardless of regime, people needed to work. Thoma pointed over to a tapas bar just opening its doors. The owner and his son were putting out tables and chairs, while the wife was placing white tablecloths, plates and cutlery on the tables.

"Lunch?" Thoma asked.

"I think we deserve it."

Food was scarce and there was no menu, so the two men said they would have whatever was available. Almost anything was guaranteed to be better than army rations.

"I must say, it's good to finally win a war," Thoma observed, sipping a glass of red wine.

"And we managed to do it in Spain too. Counting Germany's revolutionary uprising, this is my third war, and I have to say that the Spanish troops are the worst I've fought alongside."

"The Italians aren't much better," Thoma added.

"They are brave to the point of foolhardiness, there's no doubting that, but their organisation and discipline are all over the place. Give me the British stiff-upper-lip or good old German efficiency any day of the week," Harry concluded.

"That Crespo is a liability. More worried about exacting revenge than leading his troops. Nothing wrong with leading from the front, as long as you don't actually leave your men behind."

"You saw my report about the men he gunned down during the assault on the fort?"

"Yes, and that's not the first one I've seen, either. Some men see violence as the only option. Franco may owe a debt of gratitude to Germany and the *Führer*, but we may well have backed a savage."

"It seems to me that the one good thing about the Great War was that soldiers were fighting far away from civilian populations. The only ones getting killed were armed men. But now, with this era of rapid manoeuvres, too many innocents are in the way, like at Guernica. Even prisoners are seen as an inconvenience, something to slow down troop deployments. I'm afraid to think about where all of this is heading. At least Hitler made his territorial gains without a fight."

"And that's what *I* fear," Thoma replied ominously.

"How so?"

"Look at things from Hitler's perspective: Everything he wants, he gets. He wants absolute power in Germany, and he gets it; he wants the Rhineland to be returned, and he gets it; he wants Austria and the Sudetenland, and he gets them too. Did you know that the American *Time* magazine made him their 'Man of the Year' for 1938?"

"Germany is on the rise again, but this is all good, isn't it?"

"Yes and no. Hitler helped Franco win a war, with minimum casualties, because his army, and it *is* Hitler's army, had a clear technological advantage. Why shouldn't he try his luck again? If he waits too long, other nations will close that gap. Better to do things sooner rather than later as far as Herr Hitler is concerned. He's always talking about '*Lebensraum*', the territory he believes belongs to his vision of Germany - and not all of 'old Germany' is part of 'new Germany' – not yet. Mark my words: Hitler will try his luck with Poland. Normally the possibility of war would give anyone pause for thought, and the Poles won't give up without a fight, but Hitler has had an easy victory here in Spain. He must be thinking, why not go for the jackpot and reunify Germany?"

"You really think we're going to invade Poland?" Harry was wide-eyed.

"Both my gut and head say 'yes'. Everything is moving so fast, it may even be this year."

It was a grim thought, but Harry was determined not to let it ruin this victory celebration, this welcome end to a long fight.

And as if to punctuate the conversation, the food arrived.

***

Harry returned to a hero's welcome. Nearly everyone was waiting for him at the station. Nancy had been busy drawing countless pictures of her father driving a tank and shooting communists, all under a swastika banner. Sophie hugged her husband to her and kissed him warmly, hoping it wouldn't be too soon before he had to leave again. Anke and Karl and his family were also there, and Karl, always with one eye on business, insisted Harry come by the shops in his uniform. Outside were sandwich boards with 'Come and meet the hero of the Condor Legion' emblazoned on them. Harry frowned a little when he saw them but was cheered by the affection and enthusiasm of the people waiting for him. Everyone wanted to shake his hand, and children in their Hitler Youth uniforms came up to admire his Iron Cross and ask him what it was like to ride in a Panzer.

Rudi sat quietly in his usual place but gave Harry a nod and a wink of welcome. Harry didn't recognise 'little' Erik Zentz, the notorious toddler prone to tantrums, now a strapping eighteen-year-old, who told Harry that he had inspired him to join the army. Harry wasn't sure he wanted to be seen as a recruiting poster, an echo of the time when he had first joined the German army and was obliged to fulfil their propaganda requirements. He felt uncomfortable with all the attention but continued to greet people, trying to appreciate the sincerity of the many expressions of gratitude for his service and good wishes for the future. He could see that the day meant a lot to Karl and Nancy. They were proud of him: Karl, admittedly, had an ulterior business motive, while Nancy knew everyone would admire her brave and handsome father. Sophie had stayed in the background, just happy to have him home.

After a frantic day of congratulations and back slapping, Harry was able, finally, to spend a quiet evening with Sophie and Nancy. As they ate their meal of beef goulash with dumplings, Nancy looked at her father and asked in English, "Papa, were you scared?"

Harry hesitated, wondering which had priority: the truth about combat or his daughter's sensitivities.

"Well, were you scared when you swam across the river the first time?" Harry asked in English.

"Yes."

"But were you okay?"

"Yes."

"And didn't your fear make you extra careful and make you swim faster?"

"I guess so."

"Well, that's what it's like when I have to fight. A Panzer is made from thick steel; bullets bounce right off it. The soldiers I fight with are well-trained, and we all work hard to keep each other safe. But because we're all a little scared, we are careful, and that's why you can always count on Papa to come home." Nancy seemed satisfied with his answer.

After her bath, Harry took up his old routine for her bedtime story. Tonight it was 'Snow White', her favourite, but after the excitement of the day, Nancy fell asleep before the end. Harry bent over and gently kissed her forehead. He had missed these simple things. It was good to be home.

Sophie was listening to the radio while mending one of Nancy's dresses when Harry entered the sitting room. "You know, when you're speaking English with Nancy, you really shouldn't talk about fighting," she said, not looking up from her work.

Harry realised that the shine of the afternoon had worn off. Sophie was clearly unhappy, probably with him. "Tell me, if you can't speak English, how do you know I was talking about fighting? We could have been discussing which of the seven dwarves she likes best," Harry said defensively.

Sophie put the dress down and gave Harry a withering look. "Because, Harold Woods, 'Panzer' means 'Panzer' whether you say it in English or German, and I don't recall any Panzers in 'Snow White'." She had him.

"I'm sorry, my love," Harry said honestly, "but I think there's more to it than that."

"Oh, Harry," said Sophie, who began to tear up. "You don't understand what your being in the army is doing to us. Every time you walk out that door I'm convinced it's for the last time. Your letters come through sporadically, if at all. And I worry that you're dead in a ditch somewhere. In the meantime, we're losing our daughter, Harry."

"What do you mean 'losing' her?"

"She listens to you, but every day she pays less and less attention to me. Meanwhile, the school and the radio and just about everything around her are poisoning her mind. I never told you this, but she thought you were at the Olympics protecting everyone from Jews!"

"That's ridiculous."

"No, Harry, no, it wasn't ridiculous to her, and it's getting worse. After *Kristallnacht* I caught her with her friend singing a playground rhyme about sweeping the Jews out with the broken glass. Our daughter has been infected with Nazi propaganda, and I don't like what she's becoming. Then you arrive in your uniform, a symbol of this force I can't fight."

Harry took off his jacket and tossed it to the end of the sofa, then sat down beside his sobbing wife. She looked utterly distraught and helpless. He wrapped his arms around her, feeling her sobs as he held her close to his chest. His face was in her soft, sweet hair, his mouth against her ear. He whispered softly, "I made a bargain with the devil, but we got the better deal: we have our Nancy. And besides, between the two of us, there's nothing we can't fix. Two more years and this is all over; I'm more than half way done. You're a wonderful mother, and the best wife in the world. Together we can make it all better."

Sophie turned her head to rest over Harry's heart. The warmth of his embrace reassured and calmed her shaking body and her sobs receded. "But that's what I'm worried about; what if we can't do it together? This madman wants another war. I know you are going to have to fight *again*, that you'll be in danger *again* … that I'll have to lie awake worrying *again*. What if …" She cut the sentence short, believing that if she said the words, they would come true.

"Shhh," Harry whispered tenderly. He knew what she was going to say. It was his darkest fear too. "I may not look it, but I'm as a tough as tank treads, and it appears I am a hard man to kill."

Sophie didn't know whether it was the joy of having Harry back, the relief of telling him her fears or the intimacy of her husband's breath in her ear, but she suddenly felt the stirrings of arousal. She looked up and pulled Harry's face down, covering his lips with hers. Harry responded eagerly, their passionate kisses quickly becoming bolder and more pressing. Desire overwhelmed them as they became desperate with the need to be fulfilled. Soon they were tugging off their clothes before collapsing back onto the sofa where they explored each other's bodies as if discovering them for the first time. This had been more than lovemaking; this was a renewal of their unbreakable loving bond. They lay panting, their bodies still entwined. "I don't know where that came from," chuckled Sophie, her eyes bight in the afterglow.

"That's what every soldier hopes for when he gets home," Harry said with a big grin on his face, struggling to get upright.

Sophie pretended to be offended and playfully smacked her husband's still firm bottom. "Quick, put something on in case Nancy wakes up," Sophie ordered, grabbing her dress.

"But she's sound asleep, and you look a lot better naked than Corporal Sapp. We've had to bunk together, and I can honestly say you're much less hairy than he is."

"Charming," Sophie said, throwing a cushion at him. Harry reached over for one last caress of her breasts before they disappeared under the dress. Sophie playfully batted his hands away. "Show's over."

"Spoil sport."

Sophie looked over at Harry's discarded jacket and spotted something sticking out from the inside pocket. "Is that …?" Sophie said, reaching over. Harry realised what she had seen.

"No, don't," he begged, straining to get to the book before she did.

"Why, yes. You kept it!" Sophie said, fishing out the book of poetry.

"Put it back," Harry snapped, with more feeling than he had intended.

Sophie ignored him. "Why do you still have this?" she asked, bemused.

Harry could have explained that it had become a reminder of home or that he felt it was his lucky charm and that he had somehow decided that if he actually opened it, the magic would disappear. It all sounded so dumb in his head that he simply said,

"I really like poetry."

Sophie's smiling delight lit up the room. She carefully put the book back in the jacket pocket, stood up and reached out to run her fingers across Harry's cheek and chin, pulling him close for one more loving kiss.

Part 3: Götterdämmerung

Four of them sat underneath a great oak tree beside a country road. The sun dappled their shadows as it passed through the budding canopy; the green shoots of spring were pushing through the dirt in the fields nearby. The sun was not strong, but they welcomed its warmth on their skin. A breath of wind brought the scent of damp earth and new grass; birdsong seemed intent on waking the surrounding countryside from its winter slumber. It was a scene of bucolic tranquillity.

All of this beauty should have filled their hearts with joy, but it didn't. They were too exhausted and too hungry to care. All they could think about was food, food of any kind, but they had no idea what they could scavenge. Two nights ago they had tried to make a kind of soup. They had collected water from a stream and added whatever they could find, mainly old nuts and seeds, still on the ground from the autumn. In their desperation they had even added new grass, trying to bulk out their thin gruel. It had been inedible. The grass set their teeth on edge, and something had turned out to be mildly toxic. One of them had thrown up. Their ammunition was precious, and they dared not waste it hunting rabbits, fast moving and skittish as they were.

The biggest man of the four wore a grubby camouflage poncho, which they had tried to use as a cover during the long, cold nights. But large as it was, it was not designed for four, and it had taken half an hour after fitful sleep to stop shivering and prime their bodies back into something approaching usefulness. They could stretch and bend all they wanted, but it didn't stop their hunger pangs or their constantly rumbling stomachs.

The one with the poncho was also the leader. He excused himself from the others and walked over to a nearby thicket where he gulped down low sobs. How had he ended up here? How could he get out of this mess? And when would he have a proper meal again? He blinked away the tears in his eyes and looked down at his broken finger nails, black with dirt and grime. He ran his hand along his itchy chin, a reminder that he had nearly a week's worth of stubble on his face. He felt wet tears on his cheeks and angrily rubbed them off, unintentionally wiping away some of the mud flecks that spattered his face. Tears were for shame; tears were for the weak, and he was neither weak nor ashamed … but he was fearfully worried. He didn't recognise the world anymore, neither did his men. 'Men' – ha! His three subordinates were barely more than children. Their filthy, ill-fitting uniforms hung from their scrawny frames, but they were all armed and ready to fight. If only they could find someone to fight.

They had been sent to this roadside four days ago, with minimal ammunition, even less food and no support. Their objective was to defend the country road where they now sat… except there were no enemy units, and there hadn't been since they'd arrived. Day four was starting like all the others.

Were they to stay until relieved? Were the orders still valid? He didn't know and was getting to the point of not caring. But the others looked up to him; the others expected him to be decisive and have a plan of action. He sat there and sniffed. His weakened state meant he now seemed to be developing a cold, which meant a mild headache and sore throat were new additions to his repertoire of misery, more woe heaped upon uncertainty. He hefted the strap of his submachine gun which had begun to bite into his shoulder. He touched the cool metal casing for reassurance.

He sat there for several minutes, absorbed in his own introspection, trying to ignore the gnawing emptiness of his stomach, when his ears picked up a sound with a regular rhythm. It was man-made, the low whine of an engine - and it was getting closer. He carefully pushed aside some branches and peered out. In the distance were two enemy vehicles, both soft tops, no armour.

Good, he thought. A piece of luck at last. We'll take them out and head back to base, mission accomplished. Then we can finally eat again! He bolted out of the undergrowth, hunched down so as to keep a low profile, and raced back to his men, who were still lounging around under the oak tree. "Grab your gear! They're coming. We get this right, we can get out of here and finally get some food!"

And with that, the group quickly got into their ambush positions.

***

Summer 1939

Dear Harry

I know I have not written for a long time. I have received your letters and have read them but I still don't understand why you turned your back on us and stayed in Germany. I know you have made a good life for yourself but you could have done that here.

I am writing because we are about to go to war again and this is because of Hitler. Churchill got things wrong at Gallipoli in the Great War but he seems to have got things right this time. He said an appeaser is someone who feeds a crocodile and hopes it will eat him last. The problem is Hitlers appetite seems bigger than a crocodiles and the rest of Europe won't allow him to gobble up everywhere he wants. I hope you can see that.

Don't be on the wrong side in this war. I beg you to pack your bags and bring Sophie and Nancy to England before its too late. We have our differences but you have been in Germany for over twenty years and it's time for you to come home.

Your brother

Alfred

***

Harry leaned out of the hatch of his new Mark III Panzer. They were at the Polish border, part of a convoy of military vehicles stuck in a traffic jam that had come to a halt. It was the morning of 1 September 1939.

"What's the hold up?" asked Sapp from his driver's seat.

Harry took out his binoculars and watched the farce of a group of *Wehrmacht* soldiers dismantling the border crossing between Germany and Poland, while a film crew and photographer recorded the moment for posterity. "You're not going to believe this, but the invasion has been put on hold so a few commemorative photos can be taken." A general murmur of incredulity rose up from the hatch, but the photos took just a few minutes to stage before the armoured column roared forwards. The Panzers were the tip of the spear to be thrust into any resisting front. Right behind them were the troop transports to support the armour; buzzing overhead were the dive bombers and fighters of the *Luftwaffe*.

There were pockets of resistance, and the Germans were alert to the possibility of saboteurs as well as mined roads and booby-trapped bridges, but overall, opposition was light. Day-after-day, they pushed on, moving from town to village. The local populations were still largely present and were forced to come out and line the streets for their new masters.

The crowds in the footage of the *Anschluss* with Austria showed people clapping and cheering, some throwing flowers. The stark contrast with Poland showed the complete opposite: peoples' heads were bowed; some wiped away tears. A generation of Poles had fought for their independence; now it was in tatters again, with new German overlords. But the most pressing question on everyone's minds was where was the main Polish army?

By the evening of 8 September, a whole week had passed, and one Polish town had blurred into another. As the Germans approached Warsaw, they could hear the distant rumble of anti-aircraft guns and aerial bombardments. It came in waves but seemed to be relentless. On the horizon they could see plumes of dark smoke rising from the capital. If Guernica had caused an outcry, what response would there be to this pulverising of a capital city?

Thoma was in charge of the 2nd Panzer division, and it had kept advancing as ordered. They were now in a town called Płock. Harry's crew had parked up near an empty factory - the workers had fled long ago. Their Mark III had become known as 'Blitzen' after Dreger (now Harry's radio operator) had picked up the news about a 'Blitzkrieg'. Blitzen needed a crew of five: Arnet, a small, mousey man was the gunner from the Mark II, and Sapp, who was heavy and unusually hirsute, was still the driver. Dreger was handsome and lithe, the very definition of the Aryan ideal and a zealous Nazi; he had been moved over to Harry's command as had Fichter, just twenty, the youngest of the crew, their 'baby face' and another passionate Nazi. All had served in the Condor Legion in Spain and now, under Harry's command, had become a tight-knit fighting unit.

Harry, nearly twice their ages, was fond of his crew and sometimes felt obliged to have a fatherly word, although he did his best to avoid talk of politics, which Fichter and Dreger were bound to dominate. They sat in a circle by Blitzen, eating their evening rations.

"I thought the Poles were supposed to be fighters," Arnet pondered aloud.

"I know. It's like the damned communists in Spain all over again: all talk and no action," carped Fichter.

"We're too fast for them. Every time they try to regroup, we hit them again, and they just collapse backwards. This will all be over in a week," said Dreger between huge mouthfuls, waving his cutlery around to emphasise the point.

"No, they're falling back to a rallying point; then we'll see what they're made of. It's like a coiled spring: you push against it and it gives at first, but the energy builds up and pushes back harder. We're getting to that point; I can feel it," Harry said sagely.

"I don't buy that, sir. I think they know we have an insurmountable technological advantage, and they're running away, the cowards," Fichter said scathingly.

"Fichter, technology or no technology, people fight for their homes. Look at the American Red Indians: bows and arrows against guns, but they fought on," replied Harry.

"And with all due respect, sir, look what happened to them. Wiped out by the settlers," Fichter rebutted with a smirk.

Harry was about to say something more, when a corporal came by to inform him that Major General von Thoma wanted to see him. Harry made his way to the town hall, now the *Wehrmacht* HQ, where Thoma was just finishing a conversation with some other officers. Two radio operators sat side-by-side working an enigma machine in the corner of the room. "Ah, Harry, good to see you. Come, come." Thoma beckoned Harry over to the map spread out on a table. "You can see that we came into Poland from the northwest and have been steadily moving forward in a south easterly direction. We have pushed the Polish army into two main pockets: one in front of us, separating most of the German forces from Warsaw, and one on the other side of the river to the southwest, along our right flank. The concentration is such that I fear an imminent counter-attack," Thoma explained.

"Strangely enough, I was just having the same conversation with my crew. The Poles have been pushed back far enough to concentrate their forces for a real fight, and they have two directions to come at us," observed Harry.

"Exactly," Thoma replied, slapping Harry on the back.

"I'll have the men ready for a 05:30 start to ensure we're ready for any kind of dawn assault."

"Good. And there's something else," Thoma's sentence trailed off as he took Harry from the operations room to a smaller, private room. "With everything going on, I don't know if you're aware that our invasion of Poland has triggered declarations of war from France and Britain. I'm afraid you may end up fighting the British once we've finished with the Poles."

The news left Harry stunned and speechless. He began to feel hot and nauseous as his mind started to race.

"I thought you would want to know, to give yourself time ... but Harry ..." Harry was staring off into the distance. "Harry!" Thoma barked, bringing Harry back to the room. "I want you to remember you were seventeen when you switched sides; you're thirty-eight now. You've been German longer than you ever were English."

Still trying to get his head around the implications of Thoma's news, Harry nodded, saluted and went back to his crew. His mind was churning. Thoma was right, numerically at least, but wherever you were born and raised, those were your roots. Can that ever leave you? He owed Germany everything; it had given him a wife, a home and a daughter, but did that make him German? In the Great War his platoon had gone out of its way to remind him he was British by calling him 'Brit Bubi'. Wherever he went in Germany, his surname was mispronounced as 'Voods'. Germany had been good to Harry, but did he feel German? He honestly didn't know, but right now, he had more pressing matters that needed his attention.

***

Sophie desperately wanted to get away from all the talk of war but, even on the tram, she couldn't escape it; all around her were devouring the latest front page news. The army continued to advance. Hundreds of square kilometres of land were being absorbed into the Third Reich every day, and casualties, according to the reports, were light. Hitler had wanted to annexe Poland with the minimum of fuss, but now France and Britain were involved. Was it only Sophie who remembered what happened the last time these three countries slugged it out on the fields of Belgium and France? Somewhere in the middle of this carnage and Blitzkrieg was her husband. Was he safe? Was he hurt - or worse? The constant worry was giving her a permanent headache.

Nancy was at school, and Sophie was on her way to see her mother and Frieda. There was always something to do in the shop, but she didn't want to be in the cobbler's and listen to all the inane chatter about the war. Nor did she want to sit at home, alone with her thoughts. There was so much on her mind that by the time she reached the apartment she had tears in her eyes.

Frieda opened the door and, recognising Sophie's distress, hugged her and took her through to the drawing room where Anke sat listening to the radio. It was yet another account of the glorious *Wehrmacht* army pushing back the pathetic Poles. Anke's hearing was failing and the report was blaring out.

"Please, Mama, could you switch off the radio. I've had enough of the war today."

Anke turned the dial to off and went over to envelop her daughter in a warm embrace. She was nearly seventy and Sophie was in her mid-thirties, but Anke's powerful maternal instinct hadn't disappeared with age. She smoothed her daughter's hair and held her in her arms. "Oh, my Sophie, whatever is the matter?" Anke asked, already knowing the answer.

"It's Harry. There he is, off in Poland, God knows where, doing God knows what. I'm so worried for him. It was bad enough while he was in Spain, but this seems so much bigger, so much more dangerous."

"I know, I know," Anke said soothingly.

Sophie pulled away to rummage in her handbag for a handkerchief to blow her nose and wipe away her tears. "How do you know? I thought you believed everything Herr Hitler says!" Sophie said accusingly, angry, with nowhere to direct her feelings.

"My dear Sophie, we may disagree about the *Führer*, but we have never disagreed about your well-being, and right now, you are feeling low - with good reason. Harry hasn't gone away on a little business trip; he's off fighting a war. What loving wife wouldn't be sick with worry?"

Sophie smiled at her mother. It was the first uncontentious thing she'd said in a long time. Relieved at seeing peace return, Frieda went off to make coffee, while Sophie and her mother sat together on the sofa. A thought popped into Sophie's head. "Do you miss Papa?"

Anke hesitated, not because she didn't know the answer, but because she needed to articulate what had become second nature. "Yes, of course. He was at my side for nearly forty years, but the pain of losing him has passed; now there's just sorrow and loneliness. Sometimes it still feels like he's just stepped out of the room, but I feel his presence always. I know he's watching over me and preparing my place for when the time comes."

"Oh, Mother, don't say that! You still have decades left," Sophie exclaimed, taking her mother's hand.

"Well, I hope so, but saying that, my children are grown and married - and even the grandchildren are getting older. Sonia's twelve now. There comes a time when you feel you've done your bit, and it's time to move on and make room. I'm not there yet, but at my age, I have to be closer to the exit than the entrance."

Mother and daughter sat together in a comfortable silence. It was ironic that Sophie's anxieties had allowed her mother to mother her once again. After all the recent arguments, their relationship felt as if it had been renewed and refreshed.

***

On 9 September, the coiled spring of the Polish army pushed back in full force with a ferocious counter-attack. Hundreds of thousands of Polish soldiers, supported by hundreds of tanks and aircraft, clashed with the advancing Panzer divisions of the *Wehrmacht*. Harry and his crew were on the ridge of a hill firing at a mortar position to allow their troops to overwhelm it.

"Armour to our left!" Sapp cried out.

What looked like a metal pillbox on tracks rolled into view as it crested the ridge of the hill. The vehicle had no turret, just a heavy machine gun protruding from the front.

"It's a TKS," Arnet said, slightly disappointed.

The gun on the front of the tank snarled angrily at Blitzen but caused no damage.

"Arnet, use an AP round and put it out of its misery," Harry ordered.

Harry's Panzer paused its advance and fired. The armour-piercing shell punched straight through the front of the TKS and exploded inside, sending white-hot shrapnel around its interior, puncturing metal and flesh alike. The little tank immediately ground to a halt and fell silent as smoke began to pour from the damage. The men inside were dead.

"Enemy armour has been neutralised," Arnet announced unemotionally.

"What was the point of that? They stood no chance." Then, "Continue our advance to the farmstead at the bottom of the hill," Harry ordered into his microphone. As the vehicles moved across the field, they were supported by a Panzer IV and a halftrack full of troops. They heard the muted crump of an anti-tank mine before they saw the front of the halftrack burst into flames.

"Mine!" came the crackling call over the radio of the Panzer IV. Immediately the remaining Polish mortars, supported by a heavy machine gun, began firing again, eager to finish off the German troop carrier and the men inside.

"Sapp, get us side-on in front of the halftrack." Blitzen lurched into motion and powered over to the stricken vehicle to become a giant metal obstacle between the halftrack and the Polish guns. Harry leaned down into the tank and caught Dreger's attention. "Tell the Mark IV to keep firing at the Poles, and see if you can call in some air support." And with that, Harry leapt out of the turret of the tank.

"Where's he going?" asked an astonished Arnet. Dreger shrugged and got onto the radio.

Harry jumped down the far side of the tank and ran towards the burning halftrack. The driver was still in his seat, slumped over the wheel, dead from the mine's detonation. Sporadic mortar rounds exploded nearby as Harry made his way around the back to see the rear door open and a platoon of anxious faces staring out at him. "Who's in charge here?"

"I am. Sergeant Baumer," came the reply.

"Get your men out and form up along the nearside of our Panzer."

In a quick dash to the relative safety of Blitzen's cover, the men followed Harry, who clambered up the side of his tank and stuck his head and shoulders inside. "Sapp, arc around towards the farmstead, and make sure the right side of Blitzen is away from Polish fire. Arnet, you and the Mark IV keep pounding them with high explosives, and I want a smoke round down in front of the hedges to the right of the farmstead, just in case there are any Poles lying there, ready to ambush us. Fichter, you shoot anything that moves." Harry thrust his right arm into the cabin, hand outstretched. "Dreger, pass me my MP 40."

Dreger reached for the sleek metal submachine and passed it over to the waiting hand. Harry jumped down and explained to Baumer and his men how he planned to use the Panzer to get the infantry in close to the fortified farmstead. Blitzen began to travel forward at jogging speed, while Harry and the soldiers moved to keep pace, their heads down. Arnet created the smoke needed to cover their movements, then turned the turret and started pounding the Polish position.

"Got any spare grenades?" Harry asked one of the soldiers. Harry felt a tap on his shoulder. "Here's one," a soldier said, offering him a stick grenade. Before long they were close enough for the infantry to make a dash for the walls of the farm. Rifle fire rang out, and Harry heard the whizz of bullets passing his head.

A farmstead, exchanges of rifle fire … they echoed his very first taste of combat over twenty years ago. He might now be slower and greyer, but he was also a lot smarter and tactically aware of what was going on around him. The two Panzers stayed on the perimeter, ready to fire at anyone trying to break out, occasionally adding to the general uproar with their heavy machine guns. Meanwhile, the *Wehrmacht* soldiers fanned out across the scattering of low buildings.

There was a loud crack next to Harry and his face stung. A sniper had targeted him, but the bullet had struck the stone wall by his head. Shards of shattered stone had sprayed onto his face; the wounds were superficial but a sobering reminder of the high stakes involved in this game of cat and mouse. Harry flung himself to the ground then cautiously looked around. The building with the highest elevation was the barn, which had an upstairs opening. He raced to a nearby outhouse, keeping the structure between him and the barn, and continued to circle around.

The farmyard was now a cacophony of gunfire, explosions, shouts and screams. Harry couldn't tell who was winning; he was intent only on making sure the sniper was silenced. He came to the back of the wooden barn and crept inside. To his right he saw a ladder leading up to the second level. He climbed quietly and stopped just short of the top to peep across the floor, looking for any nasty surprises. There was nothing. He silently hoisted himself up and saw, diagonally to his left, a Polish soldier crouched on the floor, peering down the sight of his bolt action rifle, sizing up his next shot. As Harry brought up his MP 40, the movement in the Pole's peripheral vision made him look in Harry's direction. When he caught sight of the gun, he turned his rifle towards Harry, who squeezed his trigger and fired off five rounds. Two smashed into the wooden beams beside the soldier, sending splintered wood flying into the air; the other three hit their mark, ripping into the torso of the sniper, who fell to the ground, dead.

Harry moved forward and slowly peered out to see three Polish soldiers lying in wait as some of Baumer's men were approaching. Harry pulled out a grenade, primed it and tossed it at the Polish riflemen. The grenade smacked one of them on the thigh. The man instinctively looked up, and Harry opened up his submachine gun, spraying the troops with the rest of his clip. At the same time the grenade went off, eviscerating them all. After the flash and smoke had evaporated, what had, only an instant before, been three young men in their prime were now three bloody carcasses.

The *Wehrmacht* soldiers saw that Harry had saved them and waved their thanks. Harry acknowledged them with a nod. Suddenly the timber planks next to Harry came alive with angry insects punching holes in the wood. Splinters flew in the air, and Harry threw himself away from the opening and onto an empty hessian sack as more Polish soldiers fired at him. He scrambled along the floor and made his way back to the ladder, when he realised the shooting had stopped. Baumer's men must have caught up with the Poles. Within twenty minutes the entire skirmish had come to an end.

Harry walked out of the barn and made his way over to Baumer. "How are your men?"

"Three dead, including the driver, and four wounded. Would have been more if you hadn't come to our rescue, sir."

"We'll get on the radio to get the medics for your men," Harry said, ignoring the acknowledgement and turning back to his tank.

"Captain!" Baumer called out.

Harry turned back. "What is it, sergeant?"

"Sir, you were amazing, shielding the men, going into the attack yourself. Some of my men saw you take out a whole squad of troops on your own. All that and wounded too," Baumer said, pointing to Harry's blood-spattered face.

"These are just scratches; I get worse in my day job - and a 'whole squad' is an exaggeration, sergeant."

"You are some kind of *Übermensch*, a superman, sir. Thank you, sir."

Harry returned to his crew where he was greeted with whoops and cheers.

"Not bad for an old man!" Fichter said with a grin. Harry looked at him coldly. Killing people was never anything to celebrate, and the over-familiarity annoyed him. Fichter's smile melted away. "Er, I mean, good job, sir!"

***

Karl was in Perle fitting Frau Daigler's shoes. She was a regular, if awkward, customer. While she was not overweight, she was tall and physically imposing, with the longest, broadest feet he'd ever seen on a woman. And, of course, she always insisted on having the most fashionable, the most delicate styles available. Trying to cram her feet into unsuitable shoes sometimes felt like forcing sausage meat into its skin. "How's that, Frau Daigler?" asked Karl triumphantly. "You *shall* go to the ball," he added with a flourish.

Frau Daigler looked delighted and opened her handbag to pay. As she took out her purse, Karl heard the bell and looked up to see a beaming Sophie. She waited patiently for Frau Daigler to leave before she waved a piece of paper in front of him.

"It's a telegram from Harry," she said with a grin.

"Telegram?" Karl looked a little confused.

"I'll read it out; it explains everything:

POSTAL SYSTEM DOWN DUE TO INVASION+STOP+SENDING TELEGRAM TO SAY I AM FINE+STOP+RANK HAS ITS PRIVILEGES+STOP+NEVER BEEN IN AN ADVANCE THAT MOVED SO QUICKLY+STOP+CAN'T SEE THIS LASTING MORE THAN A FEW MORE WEEKS+STOP+LOVE TO YOU AND NANCY AND FAMILY+STOP+"

"The fact that it's a telegram means that this is only hours old, not days or weeks," Karl said.

"Yes! It's such a relief to know he's alive and well."

"Doing *very* well, by the sound of it. You always worry that we're being given a distorted version of the facts, but it seems we're genuinely pushing through the Polish forces."

"We?"

"Alright, *they* are pushing through the Polish forces."

"Is there a part of you that wishes you could be with them?"

"Oh, God, no! I'm in my mid-forties now, and soldiering is a young man's game. I have no idea how Harry does it. He must be the same age as some of the soldiers' fathers. Even if I was a decade younger and ..." he patted his stomach, "... a few kilos lighter, why would I want to put myself in danger again? Both Harry and I have already seen too much death, and I feel safe in saying neither of us wants to see any more."

"Harry didn't join up to see another war," Sophie replied tartly.

"I know. He did it to save Nancy; he did what any parent would do, and now he's paying the price in full." Karl paused then asked, "How is Nancy dealing with all of this?"

"That, my dear brother, is another worry. It's hard for her. She misses him, of course, but he's been gone for such a long time in her short life that I'm not sure she really remembers what it's like to have him at home. They have bonded over English. He sends her lessons and homework, and she sends it back for him to check. Of course it's not the same as speaking to each other, but they do their best with the circumstances they have. Saying all that, she can get despondent on her own, but mainly, she's busy with her friends. She is proud that her father is part of the brave German force expanding the Third Reich and giving the German people more *Lebensraum*. She's also happy that he is 'returning honour to the German forces and proving that they were stabbed in the back in the last war', to hear her quote the government's rhetoric. I can't bear to listen to the propaganda coming from the lips of a nine-year-old, but what can I do?"

"I'm sure it's worse for you with Harry away, but we get it at home too. Despite our concerns, it does seem Herr Hitler has found the formula for military success. It's not since the time of Bismarck that we have seen such sweeping German victories."

"Even business is good," observed Sophie. "Have we all made the same pact with the devil that Harry has ... lose a bit of your soul for a better tomorrow? Everything is great now, but what does the future hold?"

Karl didn't have the answer.

***

Harry and Thoma sat on the back seat of the *Kubelwagen*, the German military transport. The top was down, and they were enjoying a glorious late summer day as the driver sped them along a country lane through a recently captured area of central Poland.

"We're ready to push further east," Harry said over the roar of the motor.

"Actually, we are going to advance a little more carefully now as we are going to bump up against the communists."

"Soviet soldiers are backing the Poles?"

"No, no, quite the opposite in fact. About two weeks after we invaded from the west, Stalin pushed in from the east. It turns out there was a secret pact between us and the Soviets to do with carving up Poland. Ribbentrop's work."

"Ribbentrop got a treaty agreement between Hitler and Stalin? That makes no sense," Harry scoffed disbelievingly.

"I know. I always thought Ribbentrop was a self-promoting, pompous fool. It turns out he's a self-promoting pompous genius, who has managed to broker the most counter-intuitive deal in history."

"So what happens when the two sides meet?"

"We shake hands and put up a new border."

"You can't be serious."

"But I am and I mean that quite literally. We go up to the Ruskie, shake his hand, maybe get a photo or two and then out comes the barbed wire as Poland is carved up between its two bigger neighbours." Thoma stopped before continuing on another subject, "And before I forget, you've got your medal."

"Excuse me, sir?"

"Your action at the farmstead. You have been awarded a bar to add to your Iron Cross."

"Thank you, but I'm not in this for medals."

"None of us are, but it's the army's way of saying you're doing an outstanding job."

The *Kubelwagen* had entered the outskirts of another Polish town. Up on the left was a large municipal building with a line of SS vehicles parked in the front and clouds of smoke billowing out from the rear. Thoma frowned. Something felt wrong; Harry felt it too.

"Pull over by those vehicles," Thoma ordered his driver. A few seconds later they were crossing into the courtyard of what seemed to be some sort of medical facility. Three SS soldiers were sitting on upturned crates playing cards; a few more were milling around, smoking. Thoma approached the card players. "Who is in charge here?" Thoma asked, Harry right behind him.

The men looked up at the two officers and jumped to attention. "Sir! You need to speak to *Sturmbannführer* Dampf," came the crisp reply.

"And where is the *Sturmbannführer*?"

"He's out back, supervising, sir."

"Supervising what?" Harry asked suspiciously.

"You'll see, sir," came the ominous reply, while the rest of the SS men sniggered at the private joke.

Thoma and Harry walked briskly towards the back of the facility. As they drew closer, the acrid smoke grew stronger, hitting them hard, reminding them of a barbeque. The smell flooded Harry's mind with memories of S's final moments and his horribly burnt body lying on that cold Berlin street. This was the same; it was the smell of burning flesh, human flesh.

Harry raced ahead and rounded the corner. There, in front of him, was a bonfire of human corpses. A few jerry cans had been discarded around its edges, and a half-dozen SS troops were gazing intently at the blaze. An SS officer had his back to them. "*Sturmbannführer* Dampf? " Harry called out.

The man turned around, the skull on his officer's cap and the lightning bolt double S on his collar marking him out as *Waffen* SS. Framed by the flames behind him, he looked all at once, smart, proud and terrifying.

"What is going on here?" Harry demanded.

"Easy there, captain. I'm in charge here," said Dampf, making his position clear.

"That may be, but I outrank you, and I expect complete co-operation," Thoma interjected forcefully, catching up with Harry.

"Sir," Dampf said with a click of his heels and a Nazi salute.

Thoma gave a nodded acknowledgment and nothing more.

"What is this place?" queried Thoma.

"This is an insane asylum for mental cases. We have been sent here to make room for the new order."

"Make room?" pushed Thoma. "All I can see is a pile of human remains being burnt at the back of an empty hospital."

"The mentally ill are bad blood. They serve no purpose except to waste resources. The retards and loonies aren't going to get better, so it's best to get rid of them and turn the facility into something useful, like a hospital for good German stock, or perhaps a block of flats. I am not here to do the re-building; my orders are to wipe the slate clean."

"So you rounded up the inmates and set fire to them!" exclaimed Harry, feeling light-headed and nauseous.

"Certainly not! What kind of brutes do you take us for? There is no reason to create unnecessary suffering. Besides, it's not their fault they are like this. No, we rounded them up and shot them in batches. Then we put all the bodies in one place to burn. I assure you there was no unnecessary cruelty here."

"No cruelty?" Harry shouted, taking a step forward.

"Shhh, Herr Captain. The *Sturmbannführer* is only following orders. Thank you for educating us in the ways of SS support groups," Thoma said raising a hand to stop Harry in his tracks.

"To be precise, sir, we are part of an *Einsatzgruppen*," Dampf said with a proud smile.

"Thank you for your time," Thoma replied, gripping Harry by the elbow and turning them both away.

The two men quick-stepped past the SS soldiers and jumped into their waiting *Kubelwagen*.

"Drive!" Thoma barked.

"Where to, sir?"

"Anywhere, but get us out of here. Now!" Thoma ordered angrily. The vehicle pulled out and away. Once the hospital was a safe distance behind them, Thoma leaned forwards to touch the driver's shoulder. "I'm sorry I snapped."

"What the fuck was that!" Harry exploded at Thoma, who suddenly looked extremely world-weary. Thoma pinched the bridge of his nose with two fingers.

"I have heard the rumours, but I have never witnessed anything until just now. These *Einsatzgruppen* are apparently all over the place, busy making things fit their concepts of Nazi ideology and Aryan blood purity. But shooting and burning defenceless mental patients ..." His voice trailed away, then continued, "The SS are fanatics. That whole scene was like *Götterdämmerung*," he added, barely audible above the noise of the engine.

"*Götterdämmerung*?" Harry queried. It was a word he'd never heard before.

"Literally, 'the twilight of the gods', but to be more Biblical, 'the end of days'."

There was nothing more to be said. They sat silently, lost in the horror of what they had just witnessed.

***

Harry was alone in his compartment on a train taking him back to Germany. He was gazing out the window in deep introspection. The victory in Poland had taken just five weeks. The Poles had been completely overwhelmed by the technological superiority of the *Wehrmacht* and the size of the German force. Of course it also helped that Poland was forced to fight on two fronts when the Soviet Union poured in hundreds of thousands of troops from the east. It had been one of the quickest and most emphatic victories in military history, but at what price?

The image of the burning bodies continued to plague Harry's thoughts. Those asylum patients were not a military risk, nor did they pose any threat to the wider population, and yet they had been executed like dangerous criminals. It felt to Harry as if the only criminals in that courtyard were the SS, and - he hardly dared frame the thought – he and Thoma too. Was following orders or doing one's duty reason enough to turn a blind eye to actions that are morally wrong, no matter how they were justified? Even if that was the case, what could Harry do? Desert and risk retribution against his family? He couldn't even begin to go down that road. Best to continue being the good soldier, and besides, Thoma had his back - and he wasn't a Nazi.

Harry was jolted back to the present when the door of his compartment opened and two *Waffen* SS lieutenants entered. Great, that's all I need, he thought to himself.

"Heil Hitler!" they said in unison, raising their arms in the Nazi salute. Harry didn't want any trouble so felt it best to respond in similar fashion. "Do you mind if we sit with you?" one of the SS officers asked politely.

"Please," Harry said, indicating the empty seats.

"Were you part of the invasion?" the second officer enquired.

"Yes, 2nd Panzer Division."

"Then you must have been at the Battle of Kutno," the first officer responded excitedly.

"Yes, we were."

"That was the hardest fight of the whole campaign. Did you and your men get through okay?" The first officer asked, genuinely concerned.

"Yes, it was okay for us; we all got through," Harry replied, struck by the tone of sincerity from men he had assumed would be cold zealots.

"We were only on the edges of that, but we saw our fair share of combat," the first officer said. "But where are my manners? Apologies, I am Lieutenant Hortman and this is Lieutenant Kaltz."

"Captain Woods," Harry said with a nod.

"Voods? Sounds English," Kaltz observed.

"It is. I served with the German army in the Great War and stayed on."

"You're a veteran of the Great War!" exclaimed Hortman.

"I am," Harry replied neutrally.

"It's a shame that Germany and Britain are at war again. I admire the British Empire, its cultural achievements, its industry and its ability to rule so many diverse nations," Hortman commented.

"I agree, but it's frustrating for us that the British can't see we're trying to turn Germany into the same kind of European power that Britain is internationally. If we have to fight them, it will be like fighting our brothers," Kaltz said, supporting Hortman's sentiments. "I can't help but notice your Iron Cross. It is from the Great War, correct?"

"Yes," said Harry, uncomfortable with their enthusiasm for his war record.

"My God, you also have the *Spanienkreuz*!" Hortman said, pointing to a medal on Harry's left breast. "You were in the Condor Legion, yes?"

"Yes, I was."

Kaltz turned to Hortman. "We have a genuine war hero in our midst," he exclaimed. "Please, is there anything we can get you? We must mark this occasion. How about a drink when we're changing at Hannover?" Hortman asked.

"That's my hometown, so I'm anxious to get back to my family."

"Of course. Family comes first," Kaltz said, nodding in agreement. "I became a father just five months ago, and then I had to leave. I tell you, Hortman, it's easier without kids; you just follow orders. But once you have a child you just want to get through everything so you can get back and see them grow up."

Kaltz's comment struck a chord with Harry. Could it be that all fathers in war, no matter what side or what era in history, felt the same way? That to see the faces of their children again was all that any soldiers wanted?

"Well, I hope you get home to your family soon," Harry said, preparing to leave the train.

"No such luck. We've been assigned to duty at *Sachsenhausen* Concentration Camp," Hortman said with a sigh.

***

Harry and Nancy were sitting together on her bed, finishing her bedtime story.

"Papa?"

"Yes," said Harry, suspicious of any possible strategy to delay 'lights off'.

"You're my hero. I'm so proud of what you are doing for the Fatherland," she said, putting her arms around his neck and squeezing.

Harry hugged her back. He wasn't sure his work for the Fatherland was anything to be proud of, but the unconditional love of his daughter felt special. "Thank you, Nancy. Now it's bedtime."

"Will you be here tomorrow?"

"Yes, I will be here for another few days," Harry reassured her.

"And tomorrow, can we practice English?"

"I would like that very much," he replied, pleased and a little surprised that she was still interested. Nancy smiled as she put her head down on the pillow. Harry leaned over and kissed her cheek, then quietly left the room, flipping off the light switch as he went.

He walked into the sitting room and slumped on the sofa. Sophie was sitting at the other end, her legs curled up underneath her, listening to the radio. She looked over at her distracted husband and reached out to put a hand on his shoulder.

"Mmmm ..." he sighed, letting out a long, slow breath as he turned his head towards her.

"How bad was it?"

"Well, the fighting was some of the most efficient I've ever seen. It's almost ungentlemanly the advantages we have with our Panzers and air superiority and our radio communications. Make no mistake about it, the Poles fought bravely, but their equipment was decades out of date, and then they had to fight the Soviets as well. It was a brilliantly executed campaign."

"So what's the problem?" pushed Sophie as she leaned over to switch off the radio.

"It's what happened after we won."

"Go on."

Harry hesitated, his mind ablaze with the images from the hospital. "I can't. I've never told you much about what went on in my previous experiences in battle, let alone this."

"Well, share them with me, husband; my shoulders are broad," Sophie encouraged, thinking this might be the opportunity she had been seeking for years to get him to open up.

"Actually, your shoulders are slender and beautiful. The truth about war, the truth about combat is that it brings out the best and the worst in humans. I've seen nobility and self-sacrifice, and I've seen cowardice and brutality."

"So what are you in these situations?"

"A coward," Harry said, matter-of-factly.

"But what about your medals? Cowards don't get those."

"I wanted to live; it's as simple as that. And the medals ... the medals are reminders of how desperately I want to live. I didn't win them because I tried to be brave or do noble things. They were all born of the necessity to survive."

"Tell me about those times," Sophie pleaded.

"I can't; I just can't. I told you I'm a coward. I'm scared that once I start, I won't stop, and by the time I've finished, maybe I will have unburdened myself, but you would be drowning in all the horrors I have witnessed. Besides, I am home now. Home is a refuge from the real world."

Sophie nodded, trying to understand.

***

Six months passed and now Harry stood with other officers in front of Thoma, who had a large map of the Low Countries and France. The room was abuzz with rumours that they were finally going west, and the map seemed definitive proof. For a few of the old guard like Harry, there was the anxiety of history repeating itself ... of what would happen when the large and well-equipped army of France, backed by the limitless resources of the British, met the German Blitzkrieg. Would the Allies buckle, or would they all get bogged down in yet another war of attrition?

"Gentleman, welcome to Case Yellow or, as it will eventually be known, the 'Battle for France'. After the last war, the French built the Maginot Line to protect their border. This is a hugely complex fortification bristling with artillery, tank traps and pill boxes. An assault on this would be folly. However, the French, being the French, only built these defences as far as their border with Belgium. They assumed after that the Ardennes Forest would be too dense and too rough to allow an armoured spearhead to penetrate. Gentlemen, next week we will prove that the French were very wrong about this."

A sprinkling of laughter spread across the officers sitting in front of Harry. "Our methods will be identical to those in Poland: we will act quickly, decisively and with full force; we will strike like a hammer. We will drop *Fallschirmjäger*, paratroopers, into Holland while they're still having breakfast, and they will surrender before lunch. Then we will move into Belgium before the British and the French have time to respond. If all goes according to plan, we will separate the French from the British, push the English back into the sea and take Paris about a month after we start the campaign.

"Now at this point I have to inform you that this, for me, is personal. I served in the last war and we never got close to Paris; indeed, I ended up getting captured in that war. It will not happen this time. We are going to push and push and push until we can see the Eiffel Tower. Do I make myself clear?"

"Yes, sir!" came the booming response.

"Good. Look over the plans. Make sure your men and equipment are ready."

The meeting finished to the sound of scraping chairs as the room filled with excited chatter. Captain Schmidt, in his twenties, and another captain in the 2nd Division made their way over to Harry. "You served with the old man in the last war, didn't you?" Schmidt asked.

"Yes. Why?" Harry wasn't sure where this was going.

"Is what he said true? Was he captured?"

"Yes. Why would he lie about it?"

"No reason, I guess. It's just … well … it's strange for us who weren't around then to understand what it must have been like. It was so different, sitting in the trenches, exchanging artillery fire, going nowhere for four years."

"It wasn't quite like that, but if this plan works, France will fall faster to us than it did to the Prussians back in 1871. If it fails, we won't have the men left to start digging trenches," Harry said, honestly assessing the situation.

Schmidt laughed, not realising that Harry was deadly serious.

Harry made his excuses and joined the other officers to review their roles in the invasion plans.

By the morning of 10 May 1940, the Panzer divisions were lined up; the aircraft had taken off, and the great flood of troops was ready to pour inexorably across Western Europe. Within days Harry was passing towns that echoed with history, and once through the thick woodland of the Ardennes, they were in the Somme Valley, the very same Somme that, twenty-four years earlier, had been the site of unimaginable bloodshed between the British and the Germans. Today though, it was the scene of mechanised warfare: engines reverberated with power; planes streaked across the skies, and guns flashed fiery death.

Harry and his crew fought through a number of tank and infantry engagements. What Harry couldn't understand was why the French insisted on keeping their armour, infantry and air support separate. The Germans had clearly shown the advantages of mutual support and, while the German Panzers were at times outnumbered, the *Luftwaffe* or the infantry, with their anti-tank devices, compensated for the lack of numbers.

Harry's unit was making progress as it rolled across the countryside of eastern France, and he had assumed his usual position in the turret, his eyes scanning the horizon for threats. "My God!" Harry gasped down the microphone, not realising he was articulating his thoughts.

"What is it, Captain?" Dreger's voice came back at him.

"There's a squadron of French tanks on our ten o'clock."

"So, why the 'My God!'?" queried Arnet.

"Because the two small tanks next to the Char B1 … those are Renault FTs," Harry replied.

"So?" Fichter called out.

"I fought them last time around in the Great War; they're almost as old as I am," Harry commented, dismayed.

"That's pretty old, sir," Fichter smirked.

"I heard that, private, but on this occasion you're right. Sapp, ignore the FTs; they're pretty much harmless, but let's try to get around the B1 so they can't use their front-fixed heavy gun. Arnet, take out the tracks of the Char so it can't turn," Harry ordered.

"Affirmative, captain," Arnet responded. He immediately let loose a volley while the tank was still lurching from one side to the other. By now the crew had learned, through bitter experience, where to cut corners. The shot was a lucky one and took out the right track of the heavier and more modern French Char tank.

"Good work, Arnet. Keep going, Sapp," Harry said into the radio.

Blitzen continued to roll forward. The FTs fired at the Panzer but missed their mark, while the Char had yet to fire. The hit had either panicked or disorientated the crew, but the turret was turning to get a bearing on Blitzen. The Panzer shuddered as a shell fired from the FTs glanced off the side of the turret. "That was a little too close," muttered Sapp to himself as he guided the Panzer around the stranded French Char.

"Arnet, hit that Char in the flank," Harry ordered. Sapp dutifully stopped to give Arnet a clear shot. There was only the briefest of pauses as Arnet lined up and fired. The shell whizzed into the rear of the tank, where it blasted a hole, resulting in dozens of pieces of shrapnel shredding its crew into a bloody mess. The French tank was now a still and silent smouldering wreck, a steel mausoleum to the dead men inside. But nobody had time to think about the dead. The two lesser threats, the FTs tanks, were now trying to outflank Harry's Panzer, when all of a sudden, an FT exploded. Harry looked over his shoulder and spotted the low profile of a StuG tank destroyer, supported by infantry.

"Schmidt here. We got one of the toy tanks. Do you want the last one or shall we?" a voice crackled over the radio. As Schmidt was speaking, Sapp stopped Blitzen, and Arnet fired again. This time the turret of the last FT was ripped cleanly away, and almost immediately black smoke began to billow out of the burning wreck. With that final act, the fight was over.

The German divisions swept on. They charged past the furthest points the *Kaiserschlacht* had ever reached during the Great War – and they kept going. Their success in sweeping away all that lay before them was intoxicating. Harry's crew remained professional in their roles, but the banter increased as the feeling of supremacy grew.

In a dash to cut off the British Expeditionary Force from the French forces, the division turned northwards. The plan was to isolate the British and force a mass surrender or drive them into the sea. Harry saw regular waves of Heinkels, Stukas and Messerschmitts flying overhead, while in the distance there was the rumble of exploding bombs and yet more smoke drifting into the sky. With every passing kilometre, Harry felt uneasy. This attack wasn't against the Poles or the French; this was an attack against his own people. Thoma was right: he had been in Germany longer than he'd ever been in England, but he had English roots, an English family - and fighting the British felt fundamentally wrong.

Harry and his crew were sitting on Blitzen, chewing their way through some rations, when Sergeant Baumer appeared. "There's a temporary British field hospital up ahead. It's protected by a Humber armoured car and about a platoon of soldiers."

Harry put down his lunch and swallowed a mouthful of food. This would be his first contact with British troops since his time in the POW camp twenty-two years earlier. "Okay, Baumer, you and your men wait for my signal. While you advance from the south, we'll go a kilometre down the road and then double back to come from the north. But I want to make one thing clear: this is a field hospital; wounded soldiers don't deserve to be killed. If the British start shooting, you return fire, but let me see if we can handle this peacefully." Baumer nodded.

Harry and his crew scrambled back into the Panzer. "What I told Baumer goes for you as well: no itchy trigger fingers. Arnet, your main target is the Humber. Fichter, keep the machine gun on the nearest group of armed soldiers. But if any of you fire without my signal, I will take out my Luger and shoot you myself. No unnecessary killing. Got that?" Harry glared at his men. His withering look did its job and they all nodded in acquiescence.

The Panzer trundled into view from behind a small wooded copse and stopped, its main gun turned menacingly towards the British armoured car. "Wait here," Harry ordered. He hoisted himself out of the turret and walked towards the vigilant British troops. A British captain, solidly built, in his late twenties, walked towards Harry clutching a revolver aimed straight at him. Harry held up his hands and opened his palms to show that his own sidearm was still in its holster, although behind him was more than twenty tons of war machine ready to fire at a moment's notice.

"That's far enough, Fritz!" the officer warned.

"Alright, but just to let you know, your men are surrounded. There's a platoon of soldiers coming in from the south, and the Panzer to the north is well within range of you and your men," Harry said in English, which he realised had become accented.

"Your English is rather good for a Jerry," said the captain, lowering his pistol.

"I was born in London. The name is Harry Woods."

"Good heavens! You're a Brit?" the captain said in shocked disbelief.

"Captain, it's a long story. Suffice to say I have no wish for any bloodshed on this day."

"You wish us to surrender?"

"Yes. What is your name?"

"Wilson, Captain Tim Wilson."

"Alright, Captain Wilson, you are surrounded and outgunned. I didn't see anything you have that can stop my tank, and surely your first priority is looking after the wounded men under your care."

"But surrender …" Wilson said in a whisper of disgust. "There's that saying, 'death before dishonour' …"

"Yes, there is that option, but I prefer, 'He who runs away, lives to fight another day'." If you choose to fight, you will only incur unnecessary casualties. Surrender and I guarantee your wounded will receive the best medical attention. The rest of you will be safe as prisoners until this war is over."

The English captain changed his focus and stared over Harry's shoulder. Dreger had emerged from the turret hatch and was holding Harry's MP 40. It was aimed straight at Wilson. Harry turned around and saw Dreger aiming his submachine gun at the captain. Instinctively, he switched to German. "What are you doing, Dreger?"

"You're taking too long; you're giving them time to flank us or call for support."

"Stand down, Dreger. That's an order," Harry barked.

"What's the matter, sir? You can kill Poles and Frenchies, but you can't kill Englishmen like yourself?"

"That's enough, private! Nobody is going to shoot anyone. I have no interest in destroying a field hospital, whether it's English, German or fucking Chinese!" spat Harry. He turned to Captain Wilson and switched back to English. "With all due respect, captain, some of my men have less patience than others. Tell your men to surrender, or I will have difficulty stopping mine from attacking."

Wilson looked at Harry, then at Dreger, then back to Harry. With little in the way of choice, he tossed his revolver on the ground and raised his hands in the air. Harry scooped up the pistol, and the two captains walked together towards the main body of British troops.

"For heaven's sake, someone get a white sheet and wave it around before the madman in the tank starts massacring us all," the captain ordered his troops. There was a flurry of activity as rifles were stacked and a makeshift white flag was hastily raised.

Harry turned and shot a steely look at Dreger. "Stand down, private. You can see they're surrendering." Dreger was still pointing Harry's gun at the British soldiers. Then he slowly slunk back into Blitzen and out of view.

It had been a close run thing, but Harry had ensured that no blood was spilt that day.

***

Despite it being a cold winter's evening, Sophie had taken Nancy to the *Konditorei* for a celebratory ice cream. Her excited daughter, dressed in the uniform of the Hitler Youth for girls aged 10-14, had just passed the physical tests required to complete the *Jungmädelbund* challenge, and she was now proudly wearing the prized black neckerchief with the brown leather knot. Even though Sophie had ongoing concerns about the propaganda messages that Nancy seemed to absorb from the organisation, she had been genuinely impressed with her daughter's dedication to completing the tasks. Besides, attendance was compulsory.

"Nancy, I am so proud of you," Sophie enthused. "You are growing up to be strong and smart and responsible," she added, putting an arm around her daughter as they walked along.

"Thank you, Mama. I tried really hard," Nancy said between licks of cold ice cream.

"I know you did."

"I learned a new word today," Nancy continued.

"An English word?"

"No, not this time. It's German, 'to coventrate'," Nancy said proudly.

"Coventrate?" Sophie replied, not knowing the word herself.

"Yes, my leader said Hermann Göring was using it after the *Luftwaffe* destroyed the English city of Coventry. Coventrate is a new verb meaning to destroy a whole city in one attack. Imagine that, Mama. We have the power to destroy cities in one day."

Nancy wandered on ahead, unaware that Sophie had stopped dead in her tracks, unable to believe her ears. Why was anyone teaching her daughter to be proud of wanton destruction? Why would anyone think this was suitable information for children? Sophie caught up with her daughter, "Nancy, my dear, why did your leader teach you this word?"

"Because it's another example of our superiority to all others. We have been held back by the *Untermenschen*, people of other races and countries who are inferior to us. Now we have the power of the *Luftwaffe*, the Panzers and the SS to make certain Germany has its rightful place in the world. We are living in the 'Thousand Year Reich'!"

Suitable or not, the 'lesson' had found its mark. Sophie spun Nancy around and gripped both her shoulders. They were face-to-face, Sophie's long repressed rage boiling over. "Now, you listen to me, Nancy Woods: Everything you just said is wrong. *Wrong*! Do you understand? I know you hear this propaganda from everyone around you, and I'm the only one saying something different, but I know what I'm talking about. We are trying to raise you to have common sense and to understand that everything you hear is not fact. It's horribly biased nonsense to say that we are superior to other human beings. We are fundamentally all the same; there are no people who are 'inferior' human beings, and it's this kind of distorted thinking that is poisoning your generation. To hell with Nazi pseudoscience!

Sophie realised that as her grip was tightening, her ability to make sense to her ten-year-old daughter was a battle she had lost before she had even begun. Now Nancy was simply frightened by her mother's uncharacteristic behaviour and blatant rage. Shouting, "Let go of me!" Nancy struggled to break free and, in the process, dropped her ice cream. "Now see what you made me do!" yelled Nancy.

Shocked by her own outburst, as well as Nancy's, Sophie let go. Nancy looked down at her chocolate treat now splattered across the pavement. She was shaken by this unfair attack from her normally calm, loving mother. She couldn't understand it. Why was her mother angry with her? What had she said? Her face registered bewilderment, but through tears of indignation, she struck back, shouting, "Go away! I hate you!" and ran down the street. She wanted to escape, but her young mind knew only limited options, so she ran towards Perle, crying as she went.

Sophie followed at a safe distance. She watched from the street corner as her daughter burst through the shop door and into the arms of a confused Karl, who was just closing up for the day. Sophie smiled as she watched Karl sit down with Nancy, trying to calm her. She decided to wait awhile, to give Nancy a chance to let off some steam, but after ten minutes, she could feel the cold seeping into her feet and up her legs, so she walked hurriedly over to the shop.

Karl saw her coming and let her in. He'd guessed correctly that Sophie wouldn't be far behind. Nancy was still sniffling, but was able to talk about what had happened. Sophie apologised for her angry outburst but said that she would like to talk more about some of the things that had been said another time. Nancy said 'sorry' for yelling bad things at her mother, and a kind of peace was achieved before they headed for home.

All Nancy wanted to do was fit in and belong. All Sophie wanted was to save her daughter.

***

Harry and Sophie were cuddled up in bed. Sophie knew his moods and sensed that he was not yet, mentally, fully back with them. "What's the matter?" Sophie asked, running her hands though Harry's thick hair. Whatever was on his mind, her caresses proved immeasurably soothing.

"The Battle of Britain stopped us invading Britain. It was Hitler's first defeat, not a decisive one to be sure, but it was his first major strategic setback."

"Okay … so far I feel like one of your lieutenants in a particularly dull briefing," came Sophie's sarcastic reply.

"I'm glad. I'm relieved the *Luftwaffe* failed," Harry said, leaving his statement hanging in the air.

Sophie nodded her head. "Well, that makes sense," she said after a pause.

"What?" Harry exclaimed in genuine surprise.

"Harry, let's not kid ourselves; you're English, not German. Nobody can pronounce your surname properly, and you've spent years teaching our daughter English just so you could have someone else to talk to in your native tongue."

"But I swore an oath, and I'm a captain in the German army, living in Germany, with a German wife."

"But does any of that actually change who you are?" Harry sat thinking while Sophie continued to play with his hair. "When you signed up in '36, I was angry, as you no doubt remember. I knew you were doing it to save Nancy, but we were both losing you. When you fought in Spain and then Poland and the Germans won, I thought Hitler had achieved what he wanted and that you would be released, as Thoma had agreed, the next year in '41. But after France … well, it's clear that Hitler will keep going until his luck runs out … and for this family it means we may never get our Harry back."

Not wanting to dwell on the implications of all that Sophie had voiced, Harry retreated into the familiarity of military strategy. "Britain is unconquered, and Hitler lacks the ability to invade the mainland."

Sophie fell in with him. "And the British have begun bombing here. Berlin has been attacked a few times, and with the resources of an empire at their disposal, the raids by their bombers will only increase."

"Maybe that will bring Hitler to the peace table," Harry said wistfully.

"Maybe. Or else it will harden his resolve to conquer ever more territory, to build his own empire, to make most of Europe and Asia his *Lebensraum*," Sophie said scornfully.

"I'm not sure I could go to war against a British army," Harry said flatly.

"I understand. I hate Hitler, but I feel sorry for the Germans who eat up his lies. I am ashamed of what my country has become because I know how much better this country could be. I feel this way because I am German, just as you feel the way you do because you are English. Your roots are in that country, and you grew up there at a time of war."

Sophie's hand drifted down from his hair to his left hand and held it. "How many wars have you fought in?" Sophie asked, drawing in her breath, almost frightened of the answer.

"To be honest, it's hard to say. The simple answer is 'too many'," Harry said with a sigh.

"So what are you going to do?" she asked, breathing again.

"I don't know," came Harry's honest reply.

***

10 February 1941, was like any normal Monday in Hannover. There had been a brief rain shower in the morning, and the rest of the day was cool, with patchy cloud in the sky. Sophie's mother had come by to hear Nancy play the flute in a performance that only a grandmother could appreciate. The mostly melodious sounds floated down to the cobbler's as Sophie let Rudi out before locking up and counting the day's takings.

It had been an average Monday's business. Sophie noted the money in the ledger she kept under the cash register and went upstairs to serve *Eintopf*, their one-pot evening meal. They were just finishing when an ominous noise echoed around the dark streets. Is that ... Sophie said to herself.

"Is that the air raid siren?" exclaimed Anke.

"Yes, it is," Sophie said, leaping up from the table. "Quick, quick, everyone to the basement!"

"Turn off the lights!" Nancy shouted and Sophie complied.

Nancy ran ahead, leaping down the steps. Sophie helped her mother, who while mobile, was slow on the staircase. As they were still making their way to the subterranean refuge, the siren cut out. Was it Sophie's imagination or could she hear the distant droning of aircraft engines? She hurried her mother down the last few steps and sat beside Nancy on the floor, while Anke, loathe to make the effort it took to get down, sat on a little chair. Sophie didn't know why she thought they should all be as low as possible; it just seemed the right thing to do.

No sooner had they taken their places when they heard the first distant rumble of explosive detonations, followed by the barked retorts of the German anti-aircraft guns. The noise of propeller engines grew louder as the roar of explosions drew closer, each detonation now showering them with a light rainfall of dust and plaster. The three women sat gazing anxiously at the ceiling above them. A single naked lightbulb illuminated the gloom and swayed with the shock waves, sending wild shadows across the workroom.

Sophie held Nancy in her arms, using her own body to shield her daughter from the potential destruction of their refuge. She was terrified, fighting hard to control her rising panic. She glanced over at the battered table in the corner. She smiled, remembering that this was where she had seduced Harry for the first time. Her thoughts took her on to all that had followed, good thoughts, something positive to help her hang on to her sanity as the bombing continued.

Anke saw Sophie's wry smile as she looked over at the table. "What is it?" Anke asked. "Nothing," said Sophie as she buried her face in her daughter's hair.

Anke moved stiffly from the chair to the floor and wrapped her arms around Sophie; three generations hugged each other close as death poured down from above. If they could have looked out, they would have seen the night sky slashed by harsh search lights trying to aid the German anti-aircraft gunners in their attempts to beat back the never-ending wave of silhouettes.

Then, as suddenly as it started, it stopped. The man-made storm of metal and fire passed and they had survived. The air raid siren wailed the 'all-clear', and the three of them made their way back upstairs to the apartment. That night they all slept together in Sophie's double bed, reassured by the closeness of loved ones.

The next morning they woke early, ate a hurried breakfast and set off towards the Walds' apartment. The streets were busy with anxious onlookers, and fire engine bells rang loudly as emergency services and volunteers alike tried to cope with injured people and bombed-out properties. No one knew how many were trapped in the ruins. In an attempt to hamper German wartime operations, the British had sent at least two hundred bombers to attack Hannover's industrial district and train lines. While there had been serious damage to both, houses and shops had also been demolished. The destruction was widespread, and craters and rubble peppered the city.

There had been no news from Karl, and they were anxious as they walked towards the Perle apartment and the family business. Thankfully, the building had survived unscathed, as had most of the neighbourhood, but they had passed unrecognisable streets on the way. Karl was there to greet them, relieved that they were all in one piece. He'd been able to contact Max in Heidelberg and, like the Hannover Walds, they were shaken but fine.

Karl had gone earlier to check that the cobbler's was still standing and that the women were safe, but they had left by the time he'd arrived. Meanwhile, Rudi had also arrived to see for himself what had happened. He now had a little place near his brother on the outskirts of the city; their neighbourhood had been spared, but he had worried for the people he knew in a now scarred Hannover. It was only mid-morning and they had already seen enough destruction to last a lifetime.

That night Sophie tucked in Nancy with more than the usual amount of loving hugs and kisses. She wanted to reassure her daughter that everything was alright, that the threat from aerial bombardments had gone and that the British would find other targets, but Sophie was wrong. That Tuesday night the RAF returned in full force, just as she was getting ready for bed. She looked up in horror when she heard the chilling sound of the air raid siren for a second night.

Sophie ran into Nancy's room, scooped up the still groggy girl and pounded down the steps into the basement. The routine was distressingly the same: more furious detonations, more defiant anti-aircraft fire, more shadows from the swaying light bulb and yet more hugging her daughter's body close. When the all-clear finally sounded, they went up to Sophie's room, where they fell into bed and slept curled up together.

The next morning, even though they were rushing to leave the house, Sophie took the opportunity to make a point about the horrendous bombing. "Nancy, bombing cities is wrong. Destroying Hannover is a crime, but don't forget that we started this. You know what we Germans did to Coventry; now the British are responding to our country's attacks. You reap what you sow, and might is not right. It's not right to destroy cities just because you can. This is what I was trying to explain to you the other evening." This time Nancy appeared to take it all in and nodded seriously.

Mother and daughter set off for Perle, knowing they would see more destruction after another night of bombing. As they rounded the last corner, Sophie's heart stopped. The row of shops had taken a direct hit. The bakery two doors down from Perl was nothing but a smoking crater; the hardware shop adjacent to the blast was half standing and still smouldering. Perle's shop front had been blown out, and many of the roof tiles had been ripped off. Large cracks had appeared on the front of the upper stories. The street's occupants were listening for the sounds of anyone trapped; others were pulling people from the rubble. Sophie spotted Karl, the sleeves of a now filthy white shirt rolled up as he helped an elderly neighbour. Frieda and the children spotted Sophie and Nancy and ran to them. Everyone was crying with shock and relief as they held each other.

"Where's Mama?" Sophie asked, looking frantically around. Frieda pointed to a woman sitting on the edge of the pavement with a blanket wrapped around her. "She's in shock, but she's fine," Frieda said.

Sophie gazed around at another night's worth of devastation. The war had come to Hannover with a vengeance, but the bombers had done their job and would not return for a third night. What would happen when the factories had been rebuilt and the train lines were running again?

***

"Congratulations, Major Woods," Thoma said shaking Harry's hand. "You are now officially part of my 2nd Panzer Division staff - and not a minute too soon. Consider this the army's way of wishing you a happy fortieth birthday and apologising for extending your terms of service."

"I would have preferred a gold watch and a retirement dinner."

"Trust me, major, this is better than either of those."

The two of them were in a nondescript office in the small town of Rastenburg in Poland. Thoma took the chair behind the desk, and Harry sat down opposite him. "Tomorrow we launch Operation Barbarossa, when more than three-and-a-half million men will invade the Soviet Union. We are in the Army Group Centre. Our task is to roll the Reds right back to the gates of Moscow, and we certainly have the resources to do it. I was in a briefing with Hitler, and everyone could see how excited he is. The communists are the ideological nemesis of everything he stands for, and he said something like, 'We have only to kick in the door and the whole rotten structure will come crashing down'. I'm not sure it's that easy, but he has given us everything we need to win this campaign before the brutal Russian winter arrives.

"I tell you this much, Harry: the whole war will be won or lost here on the Eastern Front. If we take Moscow and Leningrad, Stalin will have to surrender, and after that, we will have the concentrated resources to take out Britain. All of that said, the area of operations is vast, and even three-and-a-half million men are like an army of ants marching into the endless Russian steppes. We should not underestimate the enormity of this campaign."

The numbers were colossal. The Germans would have to travel hundreds of kilometres to Moscow, and every meter was enemy territory, likely to be defended by fanatical Soviet resistance. Hitler had done his calculations and had amassed an army ten times the size of Napoleon's 'Grand Armee', which had nearly finished off Russia in 1812. But Napoleon didn't have nearly 3,000 aircraft, over 3,000 tanks and more than 7,000 artillery pieces at his disposal. And, unbelievably, despite this colossal build-up of troops and equipment, the Russians were oblivious to it. Operation Barbarossa could turn out to be the biggest large-scale surprise attack in military history.

The next morning, after an almighty artillery barrage, this gargantuan force smashed into the Soviet Union on three separate fronts. Harry was right behind the front line in a *Kubelwagen,* getting reports of success after success. They were averaging more than thirty kilometres a day. Not all the troops had mechanised transport and those on foot or on horse-drawn carts were having difficulty keeping up with the spearhead, such was the speed of the advance.

Reports had come in that the Soviet air force had been all but obliterated in the first week of fighting, having lost nearly 4,000 aircraft. Soviet troops were being rounded up with such alacrity that the prison camps were overwhelmed by the flood of Red Army soldiers. It was estimated that already more than a million men had been killed, wounded or captured.

Harry had difficulty absorbing the sheer scale of the successes. Maybe Hitler was right; maybe the whole communist edifice was teetering on collapse. No country had ever before suffered such a string of defeats of this magnitude and been able to keep going, but shockingly, the stubborn Reds just kept coming.

With every passing kilometre, the supply lines lengthened, but so far, nothing serious stood in their way. Harry spent most of his time chasing up requisitions for fuel. The Panzers were hungry beasts, always needing more petrol and diesel as they sped towards the Soviet capital. Harry met up with Blitzen and the crew at a rallying point where they were catching their breaths and checking equipment and supplies.

"I told you the Jewish-communist forces couldn't stand up to the supremacy of pure Aryan blood," Dreger boasted from the turret.

"Corporal Dreger," Harry said, exasperated by the zealous Nazi ideology spouting from him; it always ruined a good mood. "I think our victory has less to do with Aryan blood and more to do with German steel and good tactical planning."

"It's six of one and a half-dozen of the other," Dreger said dismissively.

"As you were, corporal. You always were a better Nazi spokesperson than you were a radio operator."

Dreger banged the inside of the Panzer, and Blitzen lurched off with the other armoured units.

It was two weeks into the advance when the division spotted Smolensk on the horizon. The arrival of Germans in the area had goaded the Soviets into a counter-attack. Two communist mechanised corps were thrown at the advancing Germans; they were swatted aside like an annoyance. Thousands of men were dead; hundreds of burning vehicles peppered the countryside - and for what? The Germans had been delayed by a day. Within a week the Germans were sweeping through the large and relatively modern city, where resistance was street-to-street and house-to-house. The Germans were seeing some heavy action as the Reds finally dug in their heels and fought for every building.

Just as it seemed Smolensk was clear, the Soviets carried out a new counter-attack near Yelnya Salient, southeast of the city. For the first time the Germans were being pushed back by the newly arrived 24th, 28th 29th and 30th Soviet Armies. Were the situation not becoming serious, Harry would have been amused to see pompous certainty turning into sweaty apprehension as staff began to wonder if the Panzers had over-extended their lines. This amidst a dawning realisation that despite a series of shattering defeats, the Soviet Union had virtually unlimited men, could afford to lose millions and would still have more to throw at the *Wehrmacht*.

Every time a panicky report came in, Major Woods' response was always the same: "So what are you going to do about it?" The officers had the answers, but their confidence had been rattled. After a few days the Germans had found a defendable location on the edges of the city, and the Soviets wasted the lives of thousands of men throwing them against impregnable positions. While the four Soviet armies were attacking in vain, Thoma had been organising an enveloping manoeuvre, rolling reserves up to the sides of the Red Armies to encircle and trap them.

By the start of August the German plan had succeeded, and the Soviets were trapped. As their supplies ran low, they were forced to capitulate. Nobody was quite sure of the numbers, but it was certain that more than a quarter-of-a-million Soviet soldiers surrendered. Smolensk was now part of the Third Reich. It was another epic success for Germany, but it had cost them weeks by the time all resistance was quashed. While they had travelled hundreds of kilometres into Soviet territory, spearheading one of the most rapid advances in history, the Germans were still more than 350 kilometres away from Moscow, and now it was getting on for September. Harry's temporary HQ in the Smolensk suburbs was packed up, and they were on the move once more, but time was against them.

The terrain ahead of them was little more than flooded swampland, the perfect place for ambush. It was early October and there was a chill in the air. Harry's *Kubelwagen* was stuck in the mud on a dirt road that was just above the water level of yet another primeval stretch of bog. Harry and a sergeant were pushing the wheels of the vehicle while the driver slowly revved the engine. A SS halftrack had come back to help drag the vehicle from the mire, when shots rang out. "Partisans!" came the cry. Harry reached into the *Kubelwagen*, grabbed his MP 40 and crouched behind the vehicle. More shots whizzed past. They were frequent but not rapid, meaning the ambushers had rifles, not submachine guns. The SS soldiers in the halftrack used their height advantage to pour on fire at the two groups of Soviet soldiers on their flanks.

A grenade landed near Harry. Clearly, as the senior officer, he was the prize target. He took one look at the smoking device and instinctively threw himself towards the murky water of the roadside swamp. Time seemed to slow down as Harry jumped and the grenade went off, tearing the rear right tyre from the *Kubelwagen*. Bullets flew angrily past him as he fell into the swamp and a filthy sludge embraced him. Harry got a mouthful of the vile bilge and came up gasping, then gagged from the wretched taste in his mouth. Meanwhile, the SS showed their fighting prowess and suppressed the ambush. Now they were moving to take the initiative.

Harry was thrashing around, trying to get his footing in the slippery mud, when he saw one of the last partisans raise his rifle and take aim. Harry whipped up his MP 40 and was about to squeeze the trigger when the soldier got off his shot first. The bullet ricocheted harmlessly off the MP 40's metal casing, sending a shuddering jolt up Harry's arms. While the partisan was forced to work the bolt of his obsolete rifle, Harry brought up his submachine gun and fired two well-aimed bullets. The partisan's arms snapped up as he crumpled backwards into the swamp's stagnant waters.

Harry was helped out of the swamp by one of the SS soldiers. He was spluttering and shivering from the cold and wet, but he thanked them for saving his life.

***

Karl and Rudi had been spending their days doing what they could to re-build Perle, trying to make it habitable again. They had only basic handyman skills, which would have to do under the circumstances. Anyone with construction expertise was either off fighting or working on buildings with higher priorities than a shoe shop. Meanwhile, Frieda and the children stayed with Sophie and Nancy. The small apartment was crowded and bustled with the sounds of life.

While the noise was a reassuring sign of normal life, Anke had decided that the calm of a nearby friend's home suited her better. She was still numb from the impact of the bombing. Her home of a lifetime was cracked and broken, the windows blasted out, the bedroom she had shared with her husband, uninhabitable. It felt like a desecration not just of her home and sanctuary, but of her very memories. What had she ever done to the British? Hadn't she taken in one of theirs and treated him like a son? And now her home and her city were being punished from on high by the RAF's heavy bombers.

Sophie had been taken aback by all the gifts and kind offers the family had received. The Walds had helped many others, and now the local community rallied to help them. But they were not unique: other families, who had lost their homes and livelihoods, also found support from their neighbours and friends. It was what the people of Hannover did in this time of war.

Bombing raids were spreading across the country: Dusseldorf, Hamburg, Berlin and more. Thousands of tons of bombs were being dropped by wave-after-wave of bombers. The city of Hannover could rebuild, but the sound of warning sirens was becoming ever more frequent. Sophie found it disturbing that Nancy and the other children had adjusted to the routine signalled by an air raid. They had become used to trooping quickly down the steps and sleeping in the cellar. Sophie had even bought some fold-up cots for everyone.

Eventually Karl felt able to take his family back to a just habitable apartment. The chaotic living arrangements with Sophie and Nancy were over and missed by both of them. It had been a comfort to have the family around, and the little apartment seemed empty – no more spontaneous grown-up discussions, no more cousins to chase down the hall. Now it was just Nancy and Sophie with a framed photograph of Harry in his major's uniform to keep them company. With Harry so far out east, letters were sporadic, and while it was clear this was due to massive *Wehrmacht* ambitions, the reported successes gave Sophie no solace.

Despite the air raids and the possibility that each night might be their last, people cannot live in constant panic, and a new kind of normal life evolved. Nancy attended school and *Jungmädelbund*; she was busy with her friends and did her homework while her mother made dinner. Sophie still worked on designs, but as there was not much demand for fashionable shoes, she continued to make herself useful in the cobbler's. She couldn't replace Harry, but she was learning to do basic repairs while she looked after the shop and served the customers. This allowed Rudi to spend all of his time mending shoes, an arrangement which suited them both.

At night, like wraiths in the wind, the sirens howled and the low drone of engines marked the return of another pack of hungry wolves, their teeth, high explosive bombs, looking to tear chunks from the helpless carcass of Hannover. Sophie never dreamed she could sleep through the devastation that was being wrought all around her, but sleep she did. On the nights of the air raids, she pushed her cot up beside Nancy's, her arm draped protectively over her sleeping daughter.

***

Harry lay in bed shivering, his eyes sunken, his skin pallid. He felt an ice cold snake writhing in his intestines. There was nothing left to vomit, but he still had diarrhoea and cramps and was sweating with a fever. He felt his life force slowly ebbing away. A *Wehrmacht* doctor sat by his side. "Have you come into contact with any stagnant water?" he asked.

If Harry could have laughed, he would have. Instead, he stammered, "… fell into swamp; swallowed dirty water last week," said through chattering teeth.

"That would be the very definition of what I mean," the doctor replied dryly.

"What is it?" Harry managed.

"Cholera, you have a serious bout of cholera. You are rapidly losing body fluids, and we are going to have to give you an intravenous drip just to stabilise you. I'm sending you back to one of the field hospitals where you will be able to rehydrate and recuperate."

A feeble 'thank you' was all Harry could manage.

Harry was put on a stretcher and placed in a military ambulance along with a number of other wounded soldiers, who were being taken to the relative safety of a medical facility. Harry's head was throbbing and having to be regularly cleaned as he involuntarily soiled himself added a level of humiliation to his wretchedness. The other soldiers, wrapped up in their own torments, looked disdainfully at the officer who kept leaking diarrhoea all over himself and the ambulance floor, leaving a foul smell.

Eventually, the truck stopped to refuel. Desperate for fresh air, the patients scrambled out, all except for the man unconscious from a head wound and Harry, who was attached to a drip and too weak to get up. He was quite certain he couldn't feel more miserable. As he shivered on his stretcher, he looked through the open ambulance doors and spied a column of several dozen bedraggled men, women and children, all in civilian clothes, walking as if under a cloud. Some were babies, cradled in the arms of their weary mothers. They were the most downtrodden and defeated looking group he had ever seen, and yet they were being guarded by the *Waffen* SS. Harry didn't understand what was going on and tried to attract the attention of one of the soldiers. "Excuse me! Soldier!" Harry called out weakly, struggling to sit up on his elbows.

One of the guards marched briskly over to the truck and instantly recoiled as he raised his right hand to protect his mouth and nose from the stench. "*Ja*, what is it?" the soldier asked with a look of revulsion.

"Who are those people? Why are you marching them into the middle of nowhere?"

"They are Jewish saboteurs," snapped the member of the *Einsatzgruppen* squad.

"Saboteurs? What? Even the children?"

"Don't concern yourself with this. You just get better," the soldier said in a patronising manner as he turned to head back to his squad.

Harry lay back on his stretcher, not knowing if he was shivering from his illness or because of what he had just witnessed. Everything about it felt wrong. He was lost in his thoughts and his wretchedness when the rest of the patients got back onto the truck, each one giving Harry a look of disgust.

Just then, to the right of the truck, there was the crackle of gunfire … then silence. Before their driver could secure the rear doors, Harry saw the *Einsatzgruppen* squad emerging from a stand of trees, their guns slung nonchalantly over their shoulders. There was no sign of the civilians.

***

Winter had arrived in Hannover, and a blanket of snow had settled on the streets and buildings, giving them both a crisp, clean look. Despite the air raids and the destruction, the Christmas market was in full swing, spreading festive merriment to a population in need of some good cheer. Sophie's holiday mood was enhanced when she received a message that Harry was in hospital, recovering from a fever. He was *alive* and, for the time being, out of danger.

Sophie was vacuuming when their front door burst open and an excited Nancy rushed in, her rosy cheeks framing a huge grin. Sophie turned off the vacuum cleaner and looked expectantly at her daughter, who was obviously bursting with news.

"Mama! Mama, I have something wonderful to tell you!"

"What is it, my love?"

"It was announced yesterday by Herr Goebbels that we can help with the war effort!"

Sophie had noticed that the usually optimistic-sounding Joseph Goebbels, the Minister of Propaganda, had changed his tone over recent weeks. Instead of talking about the imminent demise of the communists, he was now to saying things like, 'Let us not ask when victory will come, but instead, see that it does come'. This was a sure sign that the war in the East was neither going to plan nor going well.

"However can *we* help?" Sophie asked, wondering what the answer could possibly be.

"At school today our teacher said that the Reich Minister has decreed that, 'As long as a single object of winter clothing remains in the Fatherland, it must go to the front.' So Mama, we must go to our cupboards and get out our winter clothes to send to Russia for our brave troops fighting in the snow."

"My dear Nancy, how could a strapping *Wehrmacht* soldier ever fit into your winter jacket?" Sophie said, scoffing at the idea.

"But Mama, the Reich Minister said! We have to do everything to support the Fatherland. We will be helping Papa who could sew two of my jackets together. He's good at things like that." Nancy's imploring eyes were welling up with tears.

Sophie looked at her distraught daughter. How could she say 'no'? "Okay, you win, but Herr Goebbels would not want a little girl to be cold, so you're keeping the coat you're wearing." Nancy nodded enthusiastically. "And Mama gets to keep her best coat, but we can give the others, alright?"

"Yes, Mama!" Nancy said, jumping up and down with excitement.

Sophie and Nancy spent the next hour going through the closet. It was fun searching through forgotten clothing. Sophie found some of the more daring fashions from her time at university and wondered what she had been thinking, while Nancy, who was in awe of her mother, said she wanted to go to university too. They giggled at the idea of a soldier wearing a coat designed for a night out dancing. When they came to Harry's coats, Sophie wavered. Clearing out his things felt like she was giving up on him, as if he were dead … a bit like when they had cleared out her father's clothes after he had passed away.

"Would Papa mind if we donate his coats?" asked Nancy when she saw Sophie falter over the stack of men's clothing laid out on the double bed.

Sophie hesitated and then said, "I don't think he'd mind. He's in the army after all."

"Imagine if Papa got one of his own coats. That would confuse him," Nancy grinned, enjoying the notion.

Sophie laughed. It probably *would* confuse him.

***

Winter had arrived on the Russian front, and a blanket of snow had settled on the soldiers and the countryside, giving them both a crisp, clean look. While the army was no longer bogged down in the autumn mud, it was now snowed in by the winter weather. The soldiers loathed winter.

Thoma looked out across white scrubland with his binoculars. The army had advanced hundreds of kilometres; more than four million Soviet soldiers had been killed or captured; Leningrad was under siege, and Moscow was now within artillery range. It had been one of the fastest and most effective military advances in world history, but it hadn't been enough. Operation Barbarossa had come to a grinding halt. Even Hitler had admitted it with Directive No. 39, which had outlined a defensive strategy to retain what they had. Not allowing the army to fall back to defensible positions, which would enable their forces to regroup and concentrate, was a terrible decision, but Hitler was obsessed with holding onto every last meter they had already captured, even the utterly useless frozen bogs.

Stalin had pulled in reserves from Siberia and the Far East and, despite the Germans' sweeping successes, there were still a million fighting men between the German army and Moscow. The result of all this was that the soldiers of the Third Reich and its allies now sat in hastily dug trenches, where they were slowly freezing to death. The Soviet army's winter uniforms were far superior to anything the Germans had, and the corpses of the Red Army infantry were stripped of their warm clothing, the dead bodies left to freeze solid on the tundra. The fuel in the tanks of the vehicles, including the Panzers, had frozen. Some of the men had resorted to building fires under the fuel tanks in an attempt to de-ice them and get them running again. Sometimes it worked; sometimes it killed those foolhardy enough to try. At least they died warm, Thoma thought and cursed himself for being so callous.

Hitler had assumed another easy victory. He had counted on a Blitzkrieg that could continue its momentum for a thousand kilometres, and when that had failed, there was no backup plan. Now Thoma and the other generals had to hold their ground at the vulnerable end of a supply line that stretched across parts of Russia, Ukraine, Belorussia and Poland. Partisan attacks on vulnerable convoys were increasing. The Blitzkrieg-lightning war had turned into the *Schneekrieg,* the snow war.

Thoma stamped his feet on the wooden pallet that was the makeshift floor of his observation post. In the corner of the crudely built bunker was a Christmas tree decorated with real icicles and spent bullet casings. He genuinely didn't know if it was a pathetic attempt to cheer up the troops or a cynical statement of their situation's futility. He looked around at the bearded soldiers hunkered down in their trenches lined with fir tree branches. Everyone searched desperately for scraps of food and warmth, yet tried to conserve energy by moving as little as possible. Some men died from the cold while on sentry duty, and nobody noticed until it was too late.

For those who could remember, it all felt much like the Great War. Thoma sometimes wondered if he had ever left the trenches of those long-ago battles. Perhaps he'd daydreamed the last twenty-some years, and he was still sitting in a bunker on the Western Front in 1918, his mind distorted by some kind of trench fever. He shook these insane thoughts out of his head. What was the matter with him? Two crazy ideas in as many minutes, while he had an entire Panzer Division counting on him. Such distractions could lead to hundreds of deaths. He reached over for his cup of hot coffee, freshly made just minutes earlier. It was already tepid.

The German people must know that their armies had not yet reached Moscow, but what lies had they been told to disguise the unimaginable scale of human misery going on around the edges of that city? And what of the Reds? Perhaps they were inured to the cold; certainly they had the protection of the best heavy clothing. While Germany can get very cold in the dead of winter, nothing compared to the -40 Celsius frozen hell of the Eastern Front.

***

Harry sat in his tent looking at the orders of the day, his face covered in stubble that now had flecks of grey. His winter coat was unbuttoned, a sign of the current thaw. His uniform and coat were filthy. He'd lived in them for months, and they smelled strongly of his unwashed body. He didn't want to think about why he itched all over. His men had clung on throughout a vicious winter counter-offensive, when Stalin had thrown more than a million men at the remaining German army. Many of the Reds had fought on skis for surprise and mobility, a tactic no one had foreseen. It had been so cold the *Luftwaffe* had been unable to operate, and for the first time, the Soviets had had air superiority.

Having recuperated from his bout of cholera, Harry had returned to the front just in time face this onslaught. Some German forces had been pushed back a hundred kilometres, but overall, the front had held. Now both sides sat in their fortified positions, waiting for the next move, exhausted from the carnage already inflicted. The Axis army and the Reds were spent. The communist counter-offensive had been a well-planned winter campaign, but after losing so many men and with the thaw now underway, the Third Reich, once again, had technological supremacy and air superiority. Somewhere in the middle of this maelstrom, Japan and America had joined the war.

The last few months had felt like a recurring nightmare to Harry. Still frail from sickness, he had been cast into the frozen wasteland of White Russia in January. His body had barely survived the ordeal of cholera when it was forced to endure brutally cold temperatures. The result of all this was a persistent cold; his throat was sore and he sniffed incessantly. He never wanted see winter again for as long as he lived. But now spring was breathing life back into the wilderness. Nobody complained about the churned mud roads this time; now they were regarded as a sign of improving fortunes, and the Red Army didn't have a weapon that could skim across such obstacles.

Harry was shaken from these thoughts when a dispatch rider arrived at his outpost. The soldier saluted Harry, who casually saluted back. "Major Woods, General Thoma orders you to report to HQ."

"Very well, private. Do you have sidecar on your motorcycle?"

"Yes, sir."

"Good, then let's go."

The motorbike ground across the muddy tracks to what had once been a Soviet light industrial complex, now Thoma's headquarters. Harry was ushered into a room where Thoma was pouring over a schematic with an *SS Standartenführer*. As soon as Harry entered, Thoma wrapped up the conversation, and the other man hastily rolled up the plans. Then the SS officer was gone, and Harry was left alone with Thoma.

"My God, Harry, you look awful! No need to ask how you're doing."

"Believe it or not, sir, this is me at my peak," Harry said, raising his hands flamboyantly but ruining the gesture with a hacking cough.

Thoma could see that the man in front of him was just this side of desperate and his face dropped. "The *SS Standartenführer* was showing me the plans of a new heavy tank we will be getting in the summer. It's a real monster, code-named 'Tiger'. It should give us the edge we need in armoured warfare. Of course the SS, as Hitler's ideological fanatics, will be getting it first."

"The SS are some of the best fighters I've ever seen. They have the best equipment and training, but it's their indoctrination and zealous belief in the Nazi cause that scares me. I've seen things …" Harry trailed off.

"We both have. Remember the hospital in Poland?" Thoma asked soberly.

"I will never forget the hospital in Poland for as long as I live," Harry replied, recalling the horrific images of burning bodies and the smell that filled his nostrils.

"I wonder if war has always been like this. I've given up everything most men want – wife, home, family – because I've believed that the career of an officer is a noble one, one that demands and justifies total commitment. Now I feel like I've been kidding myself."

"I'm not sure about the nobility of war, but what we're in … this is not war; this is something different, something new, something very wrong." Harry's comment gave them both pause for thought.

Then Thoma changed the subject. "So, how are your men doing?"

"We're doing better than we were. Supplies are now regular enough; the Reds are sitting in their trenches and we're sitting in ours. I could, however, do with a two-day bath and a new uniform," Harry said with a sniff.

"Well, I can actually do something about that. I need to make a report to the *Führer* in the Wolf's Lair; then I'm scheduled to go on to Belin. I'm taking you as my adjutant. You won't be going with me on the first leg; instead, you are going to get that bath, a razor and a fresh uniform. Then you are going home to Hannover before we meet up again in Berlin."

He was going home! The sweet words washed over Harry like a warm shower. At last he was going home. It had been ten months since he'd seen his family.

***

After days of traveling westward, Harry was riding a tram through the streets of Hannover. He was shocked to find that they were unrecognisable with their ruined buildings, piles of rubble and blown-out craters of earth. Once his uniform had brought him the accolades of an all-conquering hero; now he was ignored as people walked past with their heads down, avoiding his eyes. The population of Hannover knew war, and they did not like it.

Harry's heart leapt with joy when he saw the intact shop front of the cobbler's. He rushed up the stairs and into the arms of the two women he loved most in the world. The little Woods family held itself tightly in a three-way embrace. Everyone was crying tears of joy and relief.

Sophie broke from the hug and stood back, looking her husband up and down. She was not fooled by the crisp major's uniform. He was thin, painfully thin; hardship showed in the new lines on his pale face, but underneath … underneath her Harry was still there, as handsome and as dashing as the day they had first met.

Harry looked at Sophie in her green silk dress; she was the most beautiful thing he'd seen since he'd last laid eyes on her. And Nancy! He was struck by how much she now resembled her mother, and it took his breath away. She was growing up and he had missed much of it.

"Papa," Nancy said, interrupting Harry's train of thought, "did you get the coat we sent you?"

Harry glanced inquiringly at Sophie who, with an imperceptible nod, implored him to go along with the question. Harry cupped Nancy's head in his rough, calloused hands. "Of course, my love, and it kept me warm throughout the cold Russian winter."

"Oh, good!" Nancy exclaimed delightedly and gave her father another hug.

But Nancy didn't want to speak English anymore. She said it was the language of the enemy, and Harry could see her point. She was living in Germany and being regularly bombed by the RAF, but it hurt him to think that she thought of his home country as the enemy.

Home pushed the horrors of recent months to the back of his mind, and Harry decided to wear civilian clothes to see the family at Perle, but when he opened his wardrobe, he saw that most of it missing. He gestured at the few summer shirts and trousers, looking to Sophie for an explanation.

"Herr Goebbels wanted everyone's warm clothes," Sophie replied as if that explained everything.

Harry shrugged in acceptance and remained in his uniform.

As they walked through the streets, Nancy was desperate to talk to her officer father. "Is it true that you were within artillery range of Moscow?" she asked with a hint of awe.

"Yes, my love, that's true."

"But then you were tricked by the Jews and got snowed in."

"What did you say?"

"The Jews, they stabbed us in the back in the last war, and they are scheming against us again. All they know is deception," Nancy said with conviction.

Harry was horrified by the casual anti-Semitism coming from the mouth of his own sweet daughter. He grabbed her arm and loomed into her face. "Listen, and listen well! Your mother has been telling me she fears that you and your generation are lost in a sea of Nazi propaganda. Heaven knows I've heard enough of it too. I will fight for this country, but I cannot endorse policies of racial hatred." Realising that his anger had alarmed her, he tried to keep his voice calm as he said, "Let me tell you about Jews. In the last war I had the pleasure of serving with two of them: One was a private called David, and he was a British prisoner of war, just like all the other British prisoners of war. And then there was Wilhelm, who was the best soldier I knew in the Great War and probably the best shot in the entire German army. Both of these men served with honour, and I would serve with them again in a heartbeat. Remember these men the next time anyone speaks badly of Jews."

Nancy looked bewildered and broke away from her father. She craved his attention, but she didn't like him when he was angry with her. Once again she felt unjustly accused of something she couldn't understand, something everyone but her parents seemed to believe. What was the matter with them? Nancy walked on ahead and sulked the rest of the way to Perle. Sophie took the opportunity to move closer to her husband and walked with him, arm-in-arm, grateful for the frank exchange between father and daughter. At last someone besides herself was trying to get through to Nancy.

When they arrived at Perle's street, Sophie was pleased to see that things wouldn't look too bad to Harry. The road had been patched up; most of the rubble was gone, and apart from the cracks in the front of the shop, Perle looked pretty much as it always had. It was probably just as well that Harry had not seen the worst; as it was, he was horrified by the cracks and the boarded up shops on either side.

The evening was spent with the family. Everyone wanted to celebrate Harry's safe return, and the happy atmosphere was only enhanced by the usual Wald spread of food. It was true that some items were harder to find these days, but Anke insisted it was her duty to fatten up her son-in-law. Harry did his best to comply, but his stomach had shrunk, and it would take time for him to recover his old appetite and capacity for a good meal.

There was no disguising the fact that Operation Barbarossa had taken a lot out of Harry, who was physically diminished since they had last seen him. He was now forty-one, no longer a young man who could count on his body to snap back into fitness as it had done even five years earlier. Towards the end of the evening Karl took Harry into the kitchen. "Harry, you know how happy we all are to see you, but I have to say that, in spite of the very smart uniform, you look like shit."

Harry chuckled, "Thanks."

"No, I'm serious. Look, we fought together as young men. We watched friends die, and we sat caked in mud taking enemy artillery fire, so you don't have to explain to me how bad conditions can be and hard it is to survive. But every time you've come back from previous campaigns, you have looked fit and healthy. Now … now you look like a spent force. So, how bad is it in Russia?"

Harry peered into the drawing room where everyone was busy chatting and then slowly closed the door so that he and Karl wouldn't be interrupted. Karl was his best friend, and he knew he could tell him anything, things he could never even begin to tell Sophie. Besides it would be good to unburden himself, to talk about his experiences with someone who could understand, someone with whom he could be brutally frank.

"It's been hell on earth," Harry said bluntly, giving Karl a haunted look. "Either we're getting bogged down in swamps and seas of mud, or we're stuck in frozen wastelands so cold equipment stops working and fuel freezes. Then there's the Red Army; it's like a colony of ants: we smash one army and another pops up. We surrounded and captured a quarter-of-a-million men, only to have double that number attack us afterwards. And on top of everything the battlefield has to offer, I fell into one of those swamps and contracted cholera. This campaign makes anything in the Great War look like a seaside holiday."

Karl just stared at Harry, aghast.

"And that not the worst part. The SS are killers, not soldiers ... killers and cold-blooded murderers. They may fight like lions in battle, but after the fighting, they round up the 'undesirables': the Soviet commissars, the Jews, the disabled, and lord knows who else - and they execute them. This isn't war; it's mass murder, and it's beyond insanity. They have even requisitioned units of the *Wehrmacht* to help them with their dirty work. It taints us all. We're all complicit in this, and I'm sick to death of it."

"All for the Fatherland, all because one man's fevered imagination has infected an entire population," Karl whispered.

"Yes, Hitler has turned civilised Germans into murderous barbarians. It's incomprehensible."

The children were calling out for Uncle Harry, so they both returned to the dining room, but their appetites had gone, neither able to eat another morsel.

***

Sophie loved having Harry back in their cosy home. It was good to have another adult around; it was good to be a family again. Eager to make another connection with normality, Harry even helped out in the cobbler's and won an approving nod from Rudi when he appeared one morning in his old apron. It almost felt as if the past six years had never happened.

When Nancy was at school and Harry wasn't playing shops, he and Sophie took long walks, a simple pleasure that brought them joy because it was something they no longer took for granted. It was inevitable that their walks often took them to the Herrenhausen Gardens, where they had spent so much time together in the early years of their relationship. Their visits always felt like stepping back in time, as if the gardens were welcoming them back.

They stopped when they reached the fountains, where more than fifteen years ago, Harry had proposed to a slightly peeved and very cold Sophie. She remembered, too, and leaned into his arms as he planted a tender kiss on her cheek. The gardens, the fountains, the memories created an intimacy in this tranquil sanctuary. They were greedy, trying to make as many new memories as their time together would permit, their unspoken fears for the future never far away.

As the afternoon was drawing to a close, they set off towards Nancy's school, chatting amiably while sauntering along. When they turned a corner, Harry noticed a middle-aged couple coming towards them; something about them caught his eye. They were smartly dressed, but both had crude yellow stars sewn onto their coats. Harry had heard that Jews now had to wear the Star of David as a badge of identification, but these were the first he'd seen.

The couple's appearance caught him by surprise and he stared, offended by the unmissable racist implications of the stars. The couple could have no way of knowing his thoughts, and their eyes widened as Harry tipped his hat when they passed. He didn't know if his token gesture had caused fear or dismay, but he realised that a *Wehrmacht* officer raising his hat to Jews was probably unwanted attention, and he quietly cursed himself. Sophie commented that no matter how often she saw those yellow stars, she never ceased to be outraged – and that hat tipping had become a widespread gesture of defiance towards a regime whose racism was more overt than ever.

***

It had become their custom to meet Nancy after *Jungmädelbund* and stop at a *Konditorei* for tea and cakes on their way home. Nancy wanted her father's undivided attention, and Harry went out of his way to spoil his daughter. It had been too long since he'd last seen her, and he didn't know when he'd see her again. It was Nancy who initiated something of a renewal in their English language bond, though she was still hesitant, and Harry didn't press her. Sophie ignored Harry's indulgences, which were worth it just to see Nancy so happy and carefree.

However much time they might have had, it would never have been enough, and Harry soon received word to meet General Thoma in Berlin. It was unfortunate that the Woods' last night together had to be spent in the cellar avoiding RAF bombers as they pounded away, while German anti-aircraft guns roared ineffectually around them.

Harry felt a strange sense of familiarity as the bombs echoed and rumbled, taking him back more than twenty years to his time in the trenches, an artillery barrage raining down. Then he had been nervous and frightened; tonight his primary reaction was anger. He was furious that his country was trying to bomb civilian populations into submission. It was hypocrisy, and that's the least of what it was. After international outcries over Guernica, the London blitz and Coventry, it seemed all that had been learned by Allied bomber command was how to do it more viciously than the *Luftwaffe*. If Guernica was wrong, wasn't this ten times worse? If revenge was the motivation, was this kind of retaliation morally justifiable? If Germany deserved punishment for its crimes, and as far as Harry was concerned it did, did the annihilation of civilian populations fit the crime? After all, it wasn't the

Luftwaffe that was being bombed, or Hitler, or his Nazi stooges; instead, it was the vulnerable civilians of Hannover, who were taking the brunt of the punishment their leaders deserved.

Harry looked over at his sleeping daughter and was filled with sorrow and rage: sorrow that his daughter should be in such danger and anger that the danger had become so routine she could sleep through it. He sat next to her, stroking her hair, looking up when a bomb detonated close enough to make the roof beams shudder. This was no way for his daughter to live. This was no way for anyone to live.

The next day was hard for them all. After many tearful hugs, Nancy said good-bye to her father at the school gates, and Harry walked with Sophie to the station, where he handed her something heavy wrapped in a cloth. Sophie looked at it uncertainly and folded back the material to reveal Harry's Luger. Sophie gasped and quickly covered it again.

"Why?"

"Because if you think things are bad now, I want you to understand that they're worse than you know - and they may well become even more difficult, in which case I would like to think that my family is able to defend itself in my absence. What you're holding is a Luger, one of the finest sidearm ever made. It's quite the collector's item. I hope you never have to use it, but it's better to have a gun and not need it than to need one and not have it."

"But don't you need it?"

"I'll say I lost it in Russia and get a new one. We're at war and I'm a soldier; I can always get another gun."

"I don't know what to say," Sophie said, hurriedly putting the bundle in her handbag.

"Just keep it, then kiss me and wish me luck," Harry said with a smile.

And that's exactly what Sophie did.

***

Harry sat on a chair in the reception area of the busy *Wehrmacht* HQ in Berlin, surrounded by the comings and goings of men in uniforms. The marble hall echoed with the sound of military boots as they clipped along the stone floor. Thoma spied Harry, smiled and walked over. Seeing Harry's bag on the floor beside him, he said, "I'm glad to see you've packed."

"Yes, sir."

"After the freezing temperatures of the Eastern Front, is it fair to assume you never want to see winter again?" Thoma enquired.

"Yes, sir."

"Good, because General Nehring has been wounded in an air attack in North Africa, and I am being despatched to lead the *Afrika Korps*. You're coming with me."

Within hours they were on a Junkers transport plane and off to Libya via a stopover in Tobruk. Harry stared down at the Mediterranean beneath him. While it was not his first time in an aeroplane, it was the first time he had flown across a sea. The beautiful blue water stretched beyond the horizon, deceptively peaceful in its appearance; however, closer observation of the reality below would have revealed the vicious campaign of aerial and naval bombardments taking place between Britain and the joint forces of Italy and Germany.

It occurred to Harry that this was the fifth year in a row he was being shipped off to a new country. Since re-joining the army he had been to Spain, Poland, Belgium, France, the Soviet Union and now North Africa. He was seeing the world but not in a way that any traveller would wish.

If Spain had brutally hot summers, they paled into insignificance compared with North Africa in June. It was only going to get hotter, and already it was so hot Harry felt he couldn't breathe. On arrival in Libya, he had been issued with an *Afrika Korps* uniform. He resisted the idea of wearing no clothes at all and swapped his wallet and Sophie's book from his old uniform to the new one before putting it on. At least the peaked cap would keep the sun off his face. Drenched in sweat, he was as ready as he would ever be for his new assignment, and he joined Thoma, who was waiting in the shade before getting in an oven-like car. Thoma had opted for full-length trousers; Harry had chosen the shorts. Thoma looked at Harry and chuckled. Harry couldn't remember the last time he'd seen his superior officer snigger like a school boy.

"Is something the matter, sir?" Harry asked warily.

"Oh, Harry, with your English blood and your time on the Eastern Front, your legs look like two white fence posts sticking out of those shorts," laughed Thoma.

Harry stared down at his legs and smiled. Thoma had a point.

"Let's go. We need to check the situation at the front. I guess you'll have to bring those white saplings with you," Thoma said, still chuckling at his own wit, clearly enjoying Harry's discomfort.

Harry shrugged in defeat and got in beside Thoma. "Your legs wouldn't look any better," muttered Harry to Thoma, so as not be heard by the driver and the guard in the front seats.

"I can't argue with that," replied Thoma, "but I am smart enough to cover up my legs with trousers."

"I guess that's why you're the general and I'm the major," Harry wryly observed.

***

Sophie was just taking payment from a customer, when the air raid siren sounded. They looked at each other with confused expressions. An air raid during the day? That hadn't happened before. "Quick, in the cellar," Sophie called out to the woman and Rudi. They both nodded and headed for the stairs. Sophie had just begun her descent when a horrible thought struck her: Nancy was at school. Would she be safe? They had always been together during air raids. Would she be frightened without her mother? Sophie looked down at Rudi, who was beckoning her to hurry. Sophie pursed her lips, a feeling of steely determination pumped through her veins. She turned and walked back up.

Rudi stared at her in wide-eyed astonishment. "Where are you going?" he called.

"You go on down. I'll be back soon," Sophie shouted over her shoulder.

The droning in the skies wasn't the same today. Maybe it was because they were using new planes, or maybe it was because she was outside; she wasn't sure. She didn't know anything about Allied aircraft, but the sound was undeniably different as was the tactic of daytime bombing. What she didn't know was that the arrival of the American 8th Air Force marked the change in strategy.

Sophie rushed through the streets. She hurried past an anti-aircraft gun surrounded by sandbags; a crew member was staring through the site and range finder. Sophie winced when they fired; the recoil of the shell rippled through her whole body. She picked up her pace and covered her ears with her hands. The bombers were dropping their deadly cargo; explosions erupted nearby. Sophie looked up to see tiny specks of metal surrounding the large formation of bombers. The *Luftwaffe* had come to hunt, and like lions attacking a herd of buffalo, they picked and probed at the larger targets, wary of their formidable defences.

Sophie stopped in her tracks and watched in horrid fascination as one of the giant bombers exploded and nosedived towards the ground. Thick black smoke belched out of the aircraft and flames lapped its fuselage. The *Luftwaffe* and anti-aircraft guns appeared to be having an easy time of it as they homed in on their targets. The bombers were being decimated by fierce German defences. Good, thought Sophie, gratified that finally the Allies were no longer unopposed during their killing sprees.

As she ran on towards the school, more bombs exploded. Enough bombers were still getting through to wreak havoc. She realised – too late – that she had been incredibly reckless to go out on the streets during a bombing raid. A blast ripped into the road behind her, and the shock wave made her stagger. Sophie ran into the doorway of a nearby house and cowered. She tucked herself into the foetal positon: knees bent, arms wrapped round them, her head on her knees. She was close to the school but not close enough to risk any further movement. She didn't want Nancy to lose the only parent she had at home. "Stupid," she said to herself. She had been so intent on trying to save her daughter that she had put herself in mortal danger. She had been rash and, as the bombs rained down, she realised there was a very real chance she might not survive; she might never see Nancy again.

The anti-aircraft guns blasted away and the bombers pounded the city. Most of the bombs were falling in the vicinity of the railway lines and the industrial district, but some were falling in the shopping and residential areas too. Sophie's stomach lurched every time there was an explosion nearby, and she ached with the anxiety of not knowing her daughter's fate. She curled up in her pitiful refuge, sick with fear.

The attacks lasted for another half-hour before the bombers either headed for home or were fought back. As the all-clear siren rang out, Sophie leapt from her hiding place and dashed to the school. It had avoided any hits, but Sophie rushed into the school office, demanding to see Nancy. A few minutes later her daughter appeared with her visibly shaken teacher. Nancy fell into Sophie's arms as tears streaked down both their faces. Sophie's impetuous decision had been wrong, and she made a silent vow never to be so foolish again.

***

Harry and Thoma sat under the camouflage netting of the forward observation post. The netting gave some protection from the two dangers in the sky: it made it harder for RAF fighters hunting for targets of opportunity to see their location, and it gave some shade from the oppressive sun constantly beating down on them. But wherever they went, no matter the location, there were flies - huge clouds of buzzing black flies. The flies got into everything that stood still and much else that didn't, like their faces. The men hated them more than they hated the enemy. They made an unbearable climate even worse.

Thoma led Harry away from the outpost, which was situated on a rocky bluff. To the south there was a breath-taking view of the sea of dunes, their undulating contours in golden contrast to the crystal-clear blue sky and the white-hot sun. The two men made their way down to the bottom of the rugged stone outcrop, where Thoma leaned down and picked up a handful of sand. "There's more than a quarter-of-a-million men standing around in this stuff, killing each other over worthless sand," Thoma said, allowing the grains to trickle through his fingers. "The plan had been to blitz our way across the North African coast, supported by our Italian allies; from there we would drive the British out of Egypt and continue on into the Middle East, where there is oil and a chance to open up a second front against the Soviets." Thoma allowed the last of the sand to fall onto the ground with a sigh.

"Some said the plan was bold and ambitious; others said that it echoed Napoleon's insanity when he attacked Egypt. Either way, within in a year, all the goals were impossible to achieve. Now all we're doing is seesawing back and forth across the sand, leaving dead men and burnt-out vehicles to pockmark the endless barren desert."

Harry stood silently by Thoma. He had heard him being wistful and cynical before, but this train of thought was different: it was almost as if something inside the general had broken. He had lost faith in the *Wehrmacht* not because they were incapable of fighting, but because they were fighting for the wrong reasons. The Nazis had stolen his army and corrupted it into something ugly and evil, made to do the bidding of a madman.

"When I was last in Germany, I was taken to a secret government facility. I can't tell you where it was, but I *must* tell you the two things that horrified me: I saw technology of unimaginable power, including unmanned rockets that could fly across a sea and deliver a payload of bombs, all done automatically. The major who was showing me around said, 'Wait until next year when the fun will begin.' Fun? It's not fun; it's automated death.

"It frightens me that we are creating weapons like those rockets and other monstrosities like the Tiger tank or the colossal railgun, *Schwerer Gustav*. It frightens me that this desert we are in right now might be showing us our future - what we could end up doing to Europe. We might yet win this war with our technological terrors, but the result could be that we rule a continent covered with ash as deep and as endless as the sand before us."

There was a long silence before Harry said, "What was the other thing you saw?"

"The workers, Harry. The workers at this giant underground factory were like living skeletons. They were malnourished, yes, but more than that: they were utterly destroyed as human beings. We have perverted science. There I was in the most sophisticated and advanced facility in the world, surrounded by trailblazing technology, and yet in the shadows there was a constant reminder of the price that had been paid to achieve this. The wretched state of those poor creatures with their dead eyes is indescribable. They will never leave me."

"So what now, Wilhelm?" Harry said, dropping all pretence of rank.

"I have been ordered to fight with Rommel against the British General Montgomery, who has chosen a good defensive location. Impassable terrain to his south makes it impossible to flank him, so it will be a head-to-head slugging match. I suspect the fact that the British have delayed things means that they have been carefully piecing together an army with more of everything: more men, more tanks, more aircraft and more artillery. Between our two forces there are miles-upon-miles of land mines. The battle is stupid and pointless, and after it's over, tens of thousands of young men in their prime will be dead - and the desert will be as worthless as it ever was."

Harry was worried for his old comrade-in-arm; he'd never seen Thoma like this before. He wanted to tell him that he had no desire to fight his fellow countrymen, but his uneasiness about confronting the British army paled in comparison to Thoma's existential crisis.

"When the battle comes, I'm going to be commanding a Panzer. I plan on being in the thick of it, and maybe I will be put out of my misery. It would be an appropriate way to go. The army is all I know," finished Thoma.

"I'll be with you in battle. I will be in the Panzer on your right-hand side," Harry said, putting a reassuring hand on Thoma's shoulder.

Thoma nodded in appreciation.

***

Sophie's hands shook as she opened the envelope from Harry at the kitchen table. Nancy sat fidgeting across from her, urging her mother to hurry, her face a picture of eagerness. Over the years of travelling the world in the service of the *Wehrmacht*, a pattern had evolved. Harry always sent two letters; the first was for Nancy and other family members. The second was for Sophie, and it was in these that Harry shared as much of the truth of his experiences as he dared. Mainly, however, these were the love letters of a far-away husband to his wife back home.

Harry's enthusiasm for letter writing had begun when he was shipped off to Spain. It was such an alien environment that he took great comfort in both the writing and receiving of these messages connected to home; they made everything more bearable. Later on, in Poland and France, he had been travelling too quickly to write more than brief notes. In Russia, his bout of cholera meant that he had found it difficult to concentrate, and his handwriting betrayed his condition. Unsurprisingly, Sophie had picked up on this and, realising all was not well, worried about the reason. It had comforted Harry and swelled his heart to know that his wife understood he was ill without his need to say as much. Because they were separated by time and distance, they worked hard to maintain their loving bond.

Sophie cherished the ritual of Harry's letters. When she and Nancy wrote to tell him their news, they often enclosed additional letters from Anke or Karl and, sometimes, messages from Sonia and Karl Junior. Nancy drew pictures before she could write, but even now she frequently added a drawing, or some little 'treasure', such as a pressed flower or an autumn leaf. Sophie took pleasure in gathering together the latest collection and sending it off to her husband in some far-flung place. This connection, the only one they had, was important to all of them.

On this occasion, when Sophie pulled the papers from their envelope, a spray of sand fell across the table. Mother and daughter looked at each other, bemused. Sophie shook the pages and handed over the first letter to Nancy, who always read it aloud. She had only just begun when she exclaimed, "The sand is from the Sahara Desert!" She stopped reading and they both ran their fingers through the gritty film, making patterns on the table. They had no way of knowing if this was like other kinds of sand, but it had travelled all the way from Africa and came from the most famous and mysterious desert in the world. Mother and daughter both stared in wonder. For Sophie, the fact that Harry had touched the sand she was now feeling was a powerful link to her husband. Of course Harry had touched every letter they received, but there was tactile sensuality in moving her fingers through the grains.

The moment passed and Nancy continued to read aloud until she had finished her father's letter. The room was quiet. As wonderful as they were, the much-loved, the greatly-anticipated letters brought into sharp focus just how much they missed him. Sophie left Nancy still seated at the table and went to her bedroom to read the letter meant just for her. Harry was in Libya. She didn't know whether it was nearer or further than the edges of Moscow. Either way, he was on a new continent, in yet another alien environment. Apparently this one was the opposite of the fearsome cold of Russia, but the heat was just as harsh in its own way.

Sophie absorbed the letter hungrily and, at the end, yearned for more. It was always the same. 'How can I bear the wait for the next one?' was the question she was left asking herself. The answer never came but, if the pattern continued, another envelope would arrive within a few weeks. It had to; the letters were her lifeline. They were all she had of her husband.

Sophie could not know that this was the last letter she would ever receive from Harry.

***

It was late at night on 23 October 1942. A full moon hung in the sky and the heavens were washed in glittering stars. Harry was answering a call of nature and crouched at the base of a sand dune, a spade stuck in the ground to his right. He gazed up at the sky on a beautiful clear night, unaware that the British were about initiate a simultaneous bombardment from their nearly 900 artillery pieces. A night of death was about to descend.

As the guns erupted, Harry fell flat on his face but managed to scrabble to his feet, pull up his shorts, grab the spade and run towards his Panzer Mark III. The detonations were relentless, and Harry was blown over a second time by a nearby explosion. On slightly wobbly legs, he made it back to his tank, leapt in and slammed the hatch behind him. The pounding lasted for twenty minutes before the general assault turned into more precision strikes. The British were aiming for communications points, fuel dumps and ammo stores. It was clear that their intelligence was excellent. Panic was palpable in the German radio communications.

Hour after hour, the British artillery rained down death and destruction. Eventually, after five hours and a half-million shells had been fired, the incessant pounding and high explosive death subsided. Halfway through the barrage, Harry's driver, a man called Gunther Hahn, had begun clutching his ears and screaming. Harry had seen it before in the trenches; the man was losing his mind. Harry ducked down beside him and began talking to him as if nothing was wrong. His soothing tones had a calming effect, and Gunther quieted, much to the relief of the rest of the crew.

Somewhere in the hurricane of fire and steel, Harry lost his uneasiness about fighting the British. They were intent on killing him; he had no option but to fight back. Quite simply, it was kill or be killed.

The artillery assault was clearly a cover to allow British forces to penetrate the minefield, and once the barrage was over, the fighting began in earnest. It was tank-against-tank, plane-against-plane and man-against-man, with every other combination imaginable. The British attack had disrupted and damaged the German positions, but they were not defeated. Rommel had just returned to the front and ordered an immediate counter-attack, but the sheer weight of numbers in the British offensive was telling. Still the Germans and their Italian allies fought on.

Darkness turned into light and hours turned into days. The British were advancing on all fronts, but the frequency of the Axis counter-attacks and their well-prepared defensive positions made the going slow for the advancing British 8th Army. Harry and his Panzer had roared into battle but had been forced into a hasty retreat to shore up their position. The changes of momentum and targets were constant. The grit and grime kicked up by the battleground into their skins; their sweat was black with dirt, and their already tanned bodies were further darkened by the filth of war.

Aeroplanes screamed overhead, and artillery rumbled in the distance. It was not the biggest battle Harry had ever been in; the scale of the Eastern Front dwarfed Egypt, but the British were better equipped, better organised and better led, so the ferocity and intensity of the fight was terrifying for all involved.

Great clouds of sand rose into the air, churned up by the advancing vehicles from all sides. The wind took the clouds and blew them around the battlefield, creating a man-made sandstorm. The pale yellow plumes mixed with the black oily smoke belching out from shattered vehicles, set ablaze by ruptured fuel tanks. Despite Rommel's expertise in desert warfare, despite the fact that the Italian allies fought bravely and to the last round of ammunition and despite the fact that the German Panzers were still superior to the British armour, the *Afrika Korps* was being broken down. Montgomery's armoured spearheads were driving big wedges in the Axis units.

Thoma ordered his Panzers once more into battle, this time to attack a New Zealand force of armoured units. As always, Harry was at his side. Thoma and Harry knew they were outnumbered. The New Zealanders would invariably have air support, and they could call on artillery, but enough was enough; it was time to see what fate had in store for them. Harry was in his usual position, his head and torso out of the turret, using this wider vantage point to assess the situation. His group of eight Panzers met an oncoming force of thirteen British Imperial tanks, mainly Crusaders and Matildas. Their armaments were weaker than the German guns, so they would have to get in close. Meanwhile, the Panzers had the advantage. Harry used his experienced eye to choose his targets. One British tank was taken out, then another; but the jubilation was short-lived when Harry spotted two dots in the sky; they were coming in fast. Harry ducked down inside the Panzer and slammed the hatch.

"Bombers!" he cried. The temperature inside the Panzer was sweltering; the men could feel rivulets of sweat pouring down their brows, backs and legs. The bombers and approaching New Zealand vehicles managed to take out three of the German tanks, but Thoma and Harry fought on.

The Axis and Allied armour danced a dangerous waltz around the sands of the Sahara as each vehicle tried to gain an advantage or better target. Cannons fired; dust clouds rose, and soon there was nothing but swirling sand and flashes of metal in the harsh sunlight. A loud thud came from the left flank of the Mark III and reverberated through the crew space inside Harry's Panzer. The tank stopped dead.

"I think we've lost a track!" Gunther shouted.

Harry opened the hatch and leaned out. He couldn't see the damage, so he hopped out and scrambled across the tank's body, cursing its hot metal as it came in contact with his bare skin. When he leaned over the side, he saw that the Panzer's left track was gone. At that very instant a Crusader drew close and fired an armour-piercing round into the lightly protected rear of the Mark III. The shell punched though the steel plate and exploded inside, eviscerating Harry's crew and instantly killing them all. Harry was knocked over by the concussive blast and decided it was best to stay on the ground as the remaining Panzers fought to the bitter end. He peered around from his prone position, hoping to catch a glimpse of Thoma's Mark IV, but he couldn't see anything for all the dust and smoke.

The battle raged for another five minutes before the four remaining Allied tanks rolled forward, leaving Harry in a sea of sand and burning metal hulks. An eerie calm descended as the British armour rumbled off behind a sand dune. Harry lay and waited, pungent black smoke rolling over him, hot sand burning his exposed skin, the scorching sun beating down on him. Despite his intense discomfort, he remained still and silent next to the blasted husk of his Panzer. He had to be sure the 8th Army had moved on to another target; it was better to get sunburn and stay alive than move and become a target. The only sound he heard was his own breath, punctuated by the distant thunder of artillery and tank fire. Fatigue had built up over the long days of intense fighting. Now that the moment of danger had passed, he began to drift off. The bright light faded and the gentle oblivion of sleep began to wash over Harry as he lay peacefully in the sand.

Harry's calm was broken when a shadow fell over his face. His eyes snapped open. He had been stupid to play possum in the open, and he struggled to focus. Harry shielded his eyes, trying to make out the figure hidden by the glare of the sun. An extended hand was offering to help him up. Harry obligingly took it and was hoisted to his feet by General Wilhelm Ritter von Thoma.

"Harry, thank goodness you are still in the land of the living!" Thoma exclaimed, slapping Harry exuberantly on the back. "I'm afraid when I saw your tank take a direct hit, I radioed back to HQ that you and your crew were dead."

"No," said Harry, looking over his shoulder at the remains of his Mark III. "No, I was lucky; I got out to survey the damage to the track when we got hit." He was still staring at what was left of his Panzer, thinking of his lost men.

"Ah, I see. I'm sorry I spoke of your demise prematurely. Unfortunately the radio is now destroyed, so I can't tell anyone about your triumph over death."

"That's okay. We might get picked up by the *Afrika Korps*, in which case we can tell them of the error; or we might get picked up by the British, in which case I'm as good as dead anyway." Harry stopped. The shock of losing his tank and his men – and the reality of their dangerous situation were sinking in. Harry decided to turn the tables on Thoma. "And you … you get into a fight that's meant to write your epitaph, but I see you're still alive too."

Thoma shrugged. "What can I say? Either God loves me and has saved my life as a reward for my loyal service these past thirty years, or He hates me and has cursed me to see our armies lose another world war."

"I'm a major, not a priest, so I'm not sure I can comment either way."

The two men stood silently together, taking in the ugly scene of death and destruction. Thick smoke continued to billow up into the sky, and the paleness of the sand seemed to accentuate the sense of menace emanating from the twisted wreckage.

Still numbed by their experiences, they turned to practical matters and began to scavenge the derelict vehicles for water, then found some shade near one of the blasted Crusader tanks. They were sharing a canteen and exchanging stories, trying to make each other laugh, when they heard the sound of an approaching vehicle. Thoma stood bolt upright and saw a truck. Was it German or British?

Harry stood up beside him. Both reached instinctively for their binoculars, but neither pair had made it through the battle. Thoma tuned to Harry. "The truck could be anybody's, but it's coming from the direction of the British lines. Quick, get your pistol out and point it at me."

"What?" Harry said, utterly confused.

"Look, if they're English, you can always say that you were the one who forced a general of the *Wehrmacht* to surrender. That should at least stop them from shooting you on the spot."

"You think so?"

"Harry, I got you into this mess, *twice*. I was the one who agreed to allow you to join the German army in the first place, and I was the one who, for reasons of self-interest, lured you back in. You have been a loyal soldier, a fierce fighter and a good friend. This is something I can do to repay all of that. Now get out your gun and let's hope it's enough."

The truck shuddered to a halt in the middle of the mass of burning tanks. Out jumped a squad of British soldiers with their familiar steel helmets and Lee Enfield rifles that Harry recognised as the first rifle he had ever fired. Thoma slowly stepped out with his hands up. Harry waved at the soldiers as he pointed his gun into Thoma's back in what he hoped looked like a convincing 'I got the guy' pose.

The soldiers spied the two men in German uniforms, brought their rifles up and aimed. "Put the gun down and put your hands up!" shouted the officer, pointing his pistol at Harry.

Harry thought for brief second about his choices and decided that caution was the better part of valour. He dropped his Walther into the sand and slowly raised his hands.

The English captain craned his neck to get a better view of Harry's discarded pistol and looked faintly disappointed. "Shame it's not a Luger," the captain muttered to himself. Then, "Do either of you speak English?"

"Yes, I do," Harry said, cursing the German accent he had picked up over the last twenty years.

"And who are you?" the officer asked, approaching Thoma and Harry.

"My name isn't important right now, but I have a gift for the 8th Army. This," Harry said, risking movement in his right arm to point, "is General Wilhelm von Thoma."

"Thank you for the 'gift', but I must insist on having your name."

Harry sighed, knowing full well his name would only raise questions. "I am Major Harold Woods. And your name is …?" Harry said, trying to deflect the attention.

"I am Captain Allen Singer, and I have to say, major, your name doesn't sound very German."

"That's because I'm not; I was born in London."

"Well, Major Woods, rest assured we can take it from here with the general, but my men will be giving you some special treatment."

Harry had not noticed one of the Tommies move around behind him, and as Captain Singer finished his sentence, the soldier brought the butt of his gun down onto the back of Harry's skull. With an audible crack, Harry fell into a sea of darkness.

***

Harry took in everything about the room. It seemed to be a hotel room, nothing special, quite drab in fact. The beige walls were bare apart from one framed picture, a poor quality print of some exotic scene involving merchants, camels and a desert oasis.

Light poured in through the half-open curtains and onto the bed to his right, a slash of early sunlight falling across the dark coverlet. He had spent the night not sleeping, just lying there staring at the invisible ceiling. His senses were heightened even though he was exhausted, and time seemed to pass in slow motion.

The linoleum floor looked tired, and the rug beside the bed was too threadbare to make out the pattern, something black against a faded red background. What had once been a fine example of weaving skills had long since been worn into a shabby memory of its glory days, much like the room and the man in it.

The room had certainly seen better days, but was it a hotel room or was he in barracks? It certainly wasn't a prison cell. Still, any roof over his head and a bed to sleep in were luxuries. He had long ago lost count of the nights he had spent under canvas or huddled in ditches.

He sat on a wooden chair that matched the same light wood of the desk beside him and thought about writing something down, some sort of explanation. But what could he say? He wasn't sure he could explain anything.

He thought he saw some lint on his filthy left sleeve and plucked at thin air. If he was going to die, it should be with dignity; he should try to look his best, but even without a mirror, he knew he looked far from his best. That blow to his head must have scrambled his brain if he was worried about his appearance. Why would it matter?

Memories streamed across his mind as he thought of other times and other places. He could be standing on a mountain ledge, drinking in the scenery: a lush forest valley below, a single bird of prey in silhouette against the sharp blue sky and distant snow-capped mountains bearing silent witness. That would be magnificent. But then again, he could be lying in a hospital, surrounded by scores of men hacking out their diseased lungs, or he could be cowering in a muddy ditch, having wet himself and, in a flash of high explosives, ceasing to exist, no longer there. He'd witnessed that too many times.

He'd seen and done many things, but right now this room was his whole world. While it was no epic mountain view, it wasn't degrading squalor either. In the grand scheme of things, this dingy room wasn't a bad place to die. His thoughts were broken as he heard the key in the lock and saw the doorknob turn.

"Well," he sighed, "it's time."

***

Harry wasn't sure what to expect when two burly British soldiers approached him in silence, grabbed him in a restraining hold and marched him down the corridor to a dimly lit room where he was forcibly pushed onto a chair in front of a small table. A desk lamp had been turned to glare into his face. As he reached out to adjust it, he heard a shadowy figure behind the table say, "I wouldn't do that or Corporals Scothern and Guynan, the rather large soldiers who escorted you here, will be most displeased, and I can assure you that you really don't want to displease them."

Harry sat still, fully expecting a shot to ring out, but nothing happened. The figure placed a closed manila file on the table between them. Harry looked down and saw it was labelled 'Pvt Woods, Harold'.

"Harry … may I call you Harry?"

"You can call me anything you want as long as I know who I'm speaking to," Harry retorted, refusing to adopt a victim mentality.

"Harry, you don't know me, but I know you. I have been following your career with great interest over the many years you have been busy in Germany."

"You still haven't told me your name," Harry said bluntly.

"One of my very first jobs," the man continued, ignoring Harry's request, "was to keep all the propaganda about you joining the German Imperial Army out of the British press. I was also the one who intercepted and censored all your letters from Germany. I know you better than Alfred and, probably, even better than your wife Sophie."

The mention of Sophie's name triggered something in Harry, and he lunged at the man behind the table, only to be beaten back by one of the guards, who landed a crushing left hook in Harry's ribs. He doubled over in pain and wheezed. "Now, now Harry, I warned you about misbehaving. That, by the way was Corporal Guynan, and if you think his left hook hurts, you really don't want to be on the receiving end of his right."

"Can I at least see the face of my enemy?" Harry managed through gritted teeth.

"Enemy? I'm not your enemy, Harry. In fact, right now, I'm your best friend in the whole wide world." The man adjusted the desk lamp so it shone on the file, then he walked over to a switch on the wall, and everyone blinked as the room flooded with light. "And I would very much like for you to be my friend too. My name is Richard Barley."

Years of sitting behind a desk meant that the last two decades had given Barley a paunch. It was fate, however, that had taken away most of his hair, leaving him with a grey fringe around his bald pate. He had given up on the thin moustache of his earlier years, but like his middle, his glasses, too, had thickened with time, and he was now prone to squinting.

Barley hated Cairo and did everything he could to avoid being there, but El Alamein meant that the military had wanted their best intelligence officers on location, and Richard Barley was one of the most respected names in the entire Secret Intelligence Service. Far beyond anything the job required, Barley had developed an obsession with Harry Woods. Finding him in Egypt was totally unexpected and made the sweltering heat, the incessant flies and the appalling food worth the trip.

Barley had not seen Harry since the photos and footage from 1918, and while he had expected an older Harry, he was taken aback by the middle-aged officer in front of him now. Harry's frame and the way he carried himself exuded confidence, strength and calm. The broken nose had obviously never been repaired and the scar on his face, partially obscured by grime, had faded to a white pucker, but Barley knew those eyes. Harry's life was there in the lines on his face and in the eyes that had seen too much. This was a man hardened by war, one who no longer feared his fate. Barley knew he could not break this seasoned veteran; he could only hope for his cooperation.

"Am I to be executed?" Harry asked, more curious than fearful.

"Oh, heavens, no!" Then, "Would you like some tea?" Barley asked as if he were hosting a guest in his home.

"Yes, thank you. But I have to ask, what's going to happen if I'm not to be executed?"

Barley looked over at Scothern and ordered two cups of tea. If this was an unusual order, Scothern gave no indication and left the room. Meanwhile Guynan watched Harry's every move like a hawk with prey in its sight.

"Let me be clear, Harry: if you had been caught back in 1918, you would have been charged with desertion and treason, both punishable by death."

"*Two* death sentences. That feels excessive," Harry said wryly.

"If you were a member of the Nazi party, again, we might be having a different conversation. But you joined the *Wehrmacht* before Britain was the enemy, and as a letter from a Captain Tim Wilson to his wife attests, you went out of your way to save British lives during the invasion of France. It seems you make a better German officer than a British private."

"That could be the most back-handed compliment I've ever had," replied Harry as the tea was brought in.

Harry brought the cup to his lips and tasted his first proper British tea in twenty-five years. He stopped to savour it: the taste of Britain, the taste of home - via Indian tea, enjoyed while sitting in Egypt.

"I have to be honest, Harry. I don't have a complete picture of your career. You famously received an Iron Cross and a promotion to sergeant, and I know that you were promoted to lieutenant on what was essentially the last day of the Great War. After that, we lost you for a while. Were you in the *Freikorp*?"

"Yes."

"So you fought in the German Revolution of 1918-19?"

Harry's mind flashed back to a bitterly cold Berlin and S lying burnt under a charred winter coat. "Yes, I did, but that was meant to be my last time in a uniform."

"Then you settled in Hannover, married - and you have a daughter Nancy." This extensive knowledge of his private life made Harry uneasy. Barley continued, "Then, after eighteen years of civilian life, you joined up again. Why?"

"It seemed like a good idea at the time," Harry said sarcastically.

"Now, now, less sarcasm, please. Let's get the complete story, and then we can decide what's next."

"I joined up because my daughter was ill, and I knew the military doctors would give special care and attention to the child of an officer."

"So you reacquainted yourself with General von Thoma?"

"Technically, we'd never lost touch, but yes."

"So you were expecting an easy life in a peacetime army, but within months you were in the Condor Legion in Spain."

"Yes, I led the crew of a Panzer Mark II."

"And once that was over, it was only months before you were invading Poland … where I see you had a bar added to your Iron Cross. How did you get that?"

"I saved a transport full of soldiers in danger from enemy fire." He paused before adding, "Your intelligence is excellent. Do you have this much on everyone in the *Wehrmacht*?"

Barley raised an eyebrow. "That is, of course, classified information." He continued, "Then France in 1940, the Soviet Union in '41. You disappeared for a while in Russia."

"That happened a lot. It's a big place, you know. But before you ask again, I contracted cholera but was back on the Moscow front in time for that wretched winter."

Scothern and Guynan glanced sideways at each other, begrudgingly impressed. Was there anywhere Woods hadn't fought?

"And that brings us up-to-date with your transfer to the *Afrika Korps* and your capture at El Alamein."

"I guess so."

"So, why? Why did you change sides back in the prison camp in 1918?"

Harry sat staring off into the distance. He hadn't thought about Katarina for such a long time. Now, looking back, it seemed so immature and impulsive to have changed the course of his life over a German nurse he barely knew, but her memory lingered. After a time, Harry replied with, "Sometimes you do the right thing for the wrong reason; other times you do the wrong thing for the right reason. If the question is, do I regret what I did? I would say that up until going to Spain, no, I did not."

"What changed?"

"I've seen enough of war to know that there is no nobility in it. In the end it's just about killing, and killing is neither noble nor heroic. But the Nazis have introduced new types of killing, deliberate and premeditated killings intended to cleanse their own population of 'undesirable' and 'impure' elements. This is not war. It's worse than war."

Barley leaned closer, "What have you seen?"

"I am sure you are aware of Guernica and the other atrocities that happened in Spain, and for the record, all sides were guilty; but we helped Franco perpetrate more of them. After Spain I saw a mental hospital in Poland emptied of patients who were executed in cold blood and set alight on a human bonfire by an SS *Einsatzgruppen*. Their crime? Not fitting Hitler's idea of Aryan perfection."

The room was deathly quiet.

"Then, in Russia, I saw more SS *Einsatzgruppen* units rounding up Jewish men, women and children and shooting them in a forest. How can anyone execute a mother cradling her child? There are no words to describe such madness.

"I have been on the receiving end of an RAF bombing raid on Hannover and have seen the destruction you have wreaked on civilian homes and populations, all justified by the noble Allied fight against the evils of Nazism. The Nazis *are* evil and must go, but bombing civilians is not the way to defeat Hitler. If you give me an opportunity, I will fight them; I will do anything you want, carry out any task, as long as I can see my wife and daughter when it's over."

"But you're part of Hitler's war machine. If Germany hadn't invaded Poland, would those mental patients be alive today? If your Panzer hadn't charged across the Soviet Union, would those Jewish families still be alive? You might not have pulled the trigger or burnt the bodies, but you are part of what happened, what is happening still."

"No, I have fought only soldiers. I have never attacked civilians!"

"*You* might not have, but your army and the SS certainly have. Like it or not, Harry, you are part of these crimes; you are complicit in these atrocities."

"I'm a soldier. I do what I'm told. I was following orders." As the words slipped from Harry's mouth, he knew they were a pathetic excuse and that Barley was merely articulating what had been going around in his own head for years.

"You are the puppet of an evil regime," countered Barley.

"So, let's go through my options," Harry said, trying to rally from the body blows Barley had just landed. "When I re-joined the German army, it was guilty of nothing more than the crimes perpetuated by all armies. As time went on, the Nazis introduced the concept of Aryan purity and implemented their plans for the calculated slaughter of those who tainted their artificial ideal. I gradually became aware of these inhuman crimes, but realistically, what could I do? Desert? What do you think the Gestapo would have done to my family? Should I have gunned down the SS officers at the mental hospital? I would have been killed before I left the premises, and I would have achieved nothing. Believe me when I tell you that the thought did cross my mind. The irony is that I would rather have died at El Alamein than be here now. What do you think will happen to my family when the Nazis find out where I am? No, it would be better for them if I had died in 'glorious battle, fighting for the Fatherland'. But my family's welfare is not your concern. And my question to you remains: what would you have done in my position?" Harry finished defiantly.

Barley ignored the question and changed tact. "Before we go any further, perhaps you could help us with this," Barley said, placing a tattered book on top of Harry's file. It was E.E. Fowler's *Anthology of Melancholy Poetry*. "Is this a code book?" Barley asked earnestly.

Harry grinned; the grin turned into a smirk and, finally, he burst out laughing. Barley, Scothern and Guynan looked at each other in disbelief. They had all seen men cry or shout and swear in interrogations but never laugh. Harry's laugh filled the room. Caught up in a joke he didn't understand, Barley's mouth turned upwards in a smile. Eventually Harry calmed down and wiped a tear from his eye. "What kind of German code would use a Victorian book of English poetry?" Harry asked.

"I had the same thought, but there's nothing about your character that would suggest you're a fan of verse. So why carry such an item around with you?"

"Because it's good luck. My wife cannot speak English and bought it many years ago, thinking I might like an English book. Ever since then I have carried it, believing it has kept me alive."

"You can't possibly believe it's a lucky charm …"

"Say it like that and it sounds ridiculous, but you've read my service record. Quite frankly, I should have died several times over – in the attempted break out at the prison camp or in the trenches of the Great War, from cholera or in the snows of the Russian winter or in a tank amongst the sand dunes. But here I am, relatively intact. Under the circumstances, would you easily discard such an object?"

Barley gave a shrug of defeat and smiled again. Harry had been everything he'd hoped for, a worthy foil to his own intellect.

***

Sophie got to the front of the queue at the grocers and handed over her food stamps, along with her money. On top of the groceries was *Kaffee-ersatz*. She desperately missed the real thing, but while food was not scarce, imports were thin on the ground, and she missed coffee more than anything.

After gathering up her shopping, she made her way back to the apartment on the tram. As they trundled along, she gazed out the window. Her once splendid Hannover still had pockets of beauty, but it was harder to find them now. There had been dozens of air raids on the city and, while most of the targets had been infrastructure, there were times when it seemed the enemy bombers were simply trying to wipe the city from the face of the earth. Too often Sophie would see a row of houses with a huge gap in the middle, more homes forever lost to war.

As she made her way towards the stairs to the apartment, Rudi appeared to help with her load. They dropped her bags on the kitchen counter, and Rudi returned to work. Sophie put away her shopping and was just about to hang up her coat on a peg near the front door, when a loud knock made her jump. She laughed at herself, smoothed her hair and opened the door to find Rudi again, this time with the post.

She thanked him and shut the door, quickly scanning the envelopes to see if there was anything from Harry. What she saw was a brown envelope from the Reichs Ministry of War, and her heart froze. She stared at it as if a poisonous snake was coiled and ready to strike. She tore open the envelope with trembling hands, tears already filling her eyes as she prayed it was not the news she feared most. She began making deals with God: "If he's just injured, I swear I will go to church every day. No, if he's just injured, I swear I will go to church every day *and* do more for the community food kitchen."

Unable to delay any further, the terrified Sophie pulled out the letter and began to read. When she got to the second line, her frozen heart shattered, and she slumped to the floor, curled up in a ball and sobbed uncontrollably. She wept until she could cry no more, then she lay staring at the bottom edge of the door, not seeing it, overwhelmed by pain and sorrow. Waves of grief cascaded over her, each one sending a sensation of nausea through her body. She lay there, not knowing what to do. Had she been there for minutes or hours? She didn't know.

Her head was filled with images of Harry. It was beyond her ability to understand that she would never see him again. It wasn't possible, not for her, not for them. She was still lying there, lost in her broken world, when she heard footsteps coming up the stairs. It was Nancy, returning from school. Nancy! Sophie squeezed her eyes shut. What should she do? What should she say? She quickly pulled herself up from the floor, tried to brush the creases out of her skirt, hastily wiped her face with a handkerchief from her pocket and took a few steps back.

Nancy had had a good day at school. She particularly enjoyed biology and had been fascinated by the lesson on the lungs and how they re-oxygenate the blood. Eager to share the day with her mother, she turned her key in the door and let herself in, but she stopped dead in her tracks when she saw her mother standing there, her eyes red and puffy from crying. The open letter in her left hand could mean only one thing.

Nancy ran towards her mother, screaming 'no', in a fruitless effort to deny what she already knew. She flung herself into her mother's arms and cried from the depths of her grief, her heart broken. Sophie embraced her daughter and held her sobbing into her chest as her own tears flowed once more. They sank to the floor holding each other, the door of their apartment still open.

***

Barley mopped his brow. The heat, as always, was at its most relentless in the afternoons. Harry sat, shaved and washed, in his now clean but worn *Afrika Korps* uniform.

"Am I the only one who has seen the atrocities?" asked Harry.

"Atrocities such as?" Barley replied, looking for clarification as usual.

"The murders at the hospital, the shootings in Russia - am I the first person to tell you about such things?"

"No, you aren't. We've heard various reports of different types of crimes, but they all add up to a picture of barbarism ..." Richard trailed off, finding it hard to frame his thoughts about what was beginning to dawn on British intelligence. "I think we're seeing a level of crimes so great that new words will have to be created to describe what the Nazis are doing. It must be the most evil regime in all of human history." Barley stopped. This was the first time he had articulated these thoughts to anyone.

"We are seeing crimes against whole populations, against humanity itself. It is not hyperbole to say that Hitler has turned the German people, some of the most civilised in the world, into a society that has been duped into believing the lies about their superiority. They are intoxicated by Hitler's aspirations and blind to the Nazi crimes that are taking place in their very midst. They are complicit in all that is happening, and when this is over, the German people will have a lot of soul searching to do."

"And as you have so rightly pointed out, I have been part of that evil regime. If I have blood on my hands, why not hang me for the criminal I am?"

"You're not a Nazi; you're a soldier, no more a criminal than any other soldier, but for our purposes, you are also a weapon and a potent one at that. Why wouldn't we use this weapon against an enemy that is malevolent and ambitious?"

"So, I go from killing for one master to doing the same for another. I carry out the same actions, but this time they're justified?"

"Eventually the Allies will be fighting again in France, but we will not be killing Frenchmen; we will be killing Germans to free the French, to return them to independence ..."

"I know a fair few German families who wouldn't want me to send their sons home in a box," interrupted Harry.

Richard ignored the interruption and continued. "... the same will go for Italy and Belgium and all the other nations forced to endure occupation. The actions may be the same, but the justification is very different."

"Isn't all killing wrong? How did Britain build the largest empire the world has ever seen without killing? And as for 'independence', we don't allow India to be ruled by the Indians."

"Alright, Major Woods, if you want to play that game, you can sit out the war in a prison cell and indulge your sense of self-loathing; you can sit around and wait to see who wins this war. Maybe at the end you'll be released by some Gestapo zealot who will pin a medal on you and release you into a world built on the bones of everyone who doesn't fit the Aryan ideal. Or maybe it will be me, and I will lead you to the hangman's noose, along with every other German officer who can't see that their war machine is a force for evil." Barley paused. "Of course the other option is to fight, knowing that this time you are fighting on the side of those who want to stop Hitler's murderous ambitions."

The two men glared at each other across the table. The silence was palpable.

***

Sophie sat at the dining table in the Perle apartment where her family was in shock. She had managed to tell them the news and hand over the letter before she broke down again. Anke wept silently as she tried to comfort her daughter; Karl looked close to tears as he placed his arm around Nancy's shoulders, and Frieda had taken her children to the kitchen in an attempt to distract them by making some supper. But the news of Harry's death meant nobody felt like eating. The fact that Harry had fought in so many battles, in so many countries had, in a way, meant that inevitably, his luck would run out. At the same time, he had been so lucky so many times (and they didn't know the half of it), they had allowed themselves to believe that his good fortune would hold. It was a terrible irony that it was not the Spanish, the French or even the Russians who had killed him, but the British.

Karl had seen many good men die in battle, young men cut down in their prime, their potential lost forever. As sad as that was, as often as he had borne witness, Harry's death shook Karl to his very core. He had taken to Harry the minute they met; they had become the best of friends, brothers in every way that mattered. Harry, who remained cool no matter what the situation, who earned the respect of everyone around him ... Harry was dead? How was this possible?

It was getting late when Frieda served hot bowls of *Spätzle*, noodles, which everyone stared at, but nobody ate. The table was quiet when the meal was suddenly interrupted by the scream of the air raid siren. Please, not now, not while everyone was still numb from the devastating news. But the siren was no respecter of feelings; the RAF was coming. The room was caught briefly in the glare of a search light scanning the sky for the dark shapes of British bombers.

They heard the boom and thud of bombs exploding all over the city as the family rushed downstairs. Perle's basement was home to the workshop for the store upstairs, but space had long ago been allocated to the needs of the ongoing raids. This basement had the advantage of a coal chute in the rear, another way to escape if the building collapsed. But tonight they were less preoccupied with the danger around them than they were with their thoughts of Harry and his death on the sands of the Sahara.

Suddenly, Nancy started screaming at the top of her voice, *"Englisch Schweinhunden!"* Looking up, she shook her fist defiantly as tears streamed down her face. Sophie took her daughter in her arms and tried to soothe her. "Shhh, my love, don't forget Papa is English. The English people are not all evil, just the ones bombing our city, and the ones who ... killed Papa."

Nancy gradually quietened, and they all returned to their thoughts. After long hours of far-reaching destruction, the all-clear sounded. Nobody moved. Exhausted by the emotions of the day, they had fallen asleep in the basement of Perle.

The next morning, Sophie and Nancy made their way back home to change clothes and freshen up. Sophie didn't think Nancy should go to school, but Nancy was insistent. Sophie guessed that she was coping with her father's death by pretending everything was normal. There was comfort in familiar routines; she didn't have to think.

Nancy was now nearly thirteen. She had hit puberty, and along with all the physical changes, she was showing signs of wanting more independence. But today she welcomed her mother's company and took her mother's hand as they walked the familiar route together. It was when they turned a corner near the school that they saw the *Aegidienkirche* had taken a direct hit overnight. The roof had caved in; the exquisite stained glass was smashed, and the interior had been destroyed by fire. Sophie's heart stopped. This was where her parents had married; this was where Karl had married, and of course this was where she and Harry had exchanged vows all those years ago. This place of treasured memories, of joy and celebration, was now nothing more than a burnt-out shell. Was there no end to the destruction? Had she not suffered and sacrificed enough? It felt like her life was being destroyed, one memory at a time.

Shattered anew, tears in their eyes, mother and daughter turned back for home.

***

Harry had been going in and out of interrogation sessions with Richard Barley for weeks. Against his own expectations, he hadn't been tortured or even badly treated, but he had been intensely grilled – for hours on end. He was constantly asked the same things, over and over again: why had he not sided with the Brits in the prison break; what had motivated him to go over to the Germans; why had he fought so bravely and twice earned the Iron Cross? The questions were relentless, his explanations never enough. Barley always wanted more.

Harry assumed they were cross-referencing his answers to see if he was telling the truth. He had no difficulty keeping his story straight, purely because he was as honest as he could be throughout the sessions. But as gruelling as it was, as shattered as he felt, he couldn't complain. This was better than anything he had imagined under the circumstances. It was strange, but after being surrounded by Germans for so long, after trying to fit into their culture for years, he felt instantly at home with the Brits, even under the watchful eyes of Scothern and Guynan. He couldn't get over the fact that a simple cup of tea gave him comfort.

Once again Harry was sitting opposite Barley. By now he felt he knew his opponent well enough to see the thoughts buzzing behind his eyes, processing whatever information came before him. Harry knew he was dealing with the smartest man he had probably ever met. There was little point in lying, but he was becoming frustrated by this purgatory.

"So, you believe that the British tanks, such as the Matilda, are virtually useless against German Mark III's or higher?"

"Yes, I have already told you that."

"And you are aware of a new tank, codenamed 'Tiger', which is, in every way, an improvement over the Mark IV?"

"Yes, but as I have said before, I have only heard this; I haven't seen one, and I don't know its specifications, except to say you'd better build vastly improved tanks or Lord knows how you're going to stop them."

"I see and …"

"Now wait a minute," Harry said, interrupting. "I keep answering your questions; now I need to ask you something." Barley nodded for Harry to continue. "Can you get a message to my wife to tell her I'm not dead? I know she must have been told I died at El Alamein."

"Of course, Harry. We'll just pop a letter in the post, and it'll be with your wife by the end of the week." Then, "Harry, think it through."

Harry glared at Barley, hating him for being right.

"Let's say we do get a message to your wife, in which case, she will have been compromised by Allied spies. If the Gestapo gets wind of it, your family would be in mortal danger. It's the same scenario as when you talked about the implications of desertion, or when you said you worried for their safety if the Nazis found out where you are now. As frustrating as it must be for you, and as terrible as it must be for your family, it's better for all concerned if they believe you are dead. Sophie is now a war widow rather than the wife of a British turncoat. As this war drags on the German authorities will only get more and more paranoid. Your family's belief in your death takes them out of the spotlight."

"But …" Harry said weakly.

"But what, Harry? What have I just said that's incorrect? Do you know what Winston Churchill said about the Battle of El Alamein?" Answering his own question, Barley continued, "He said, 'This is not the end. It is not even the beginning of the end. But it is, perhaps, the end of the beginning'. It's a typically amusing bit of word play from the PM, but it's true. Hitler has mostly had his own way up until now. It's true that he failed to invade Britain, and right now an entire German army has been surrounded at Stalingrad, but El Alamein is the first offensive victory the Allies have had. The Third Reich has peaked, and now it will start to roll backwards. As that happens, Hitler and his regime will become more and more desperate. This will mean even more suffering for the German people, so let's try and keep your family on the periphery of that storm, shall we?"

"I hate to say it, but you're right … in which case, what can I do to help?"

"Harry, we've been sitting here long enough for me to know that while you are a formidable warrior, you are no Nazi fanatic. In fact, unusually for a man who has fought in so many wars, you don't seem to have much sense of national identity, but you *do* have skills and knowledge that can be useful. You are, of course, a fluent

German speaker, but you also have an in-depth knowledge of *Wehrmacht* weapons, tactics and strategy. So it has been proposed that we put you in a special advisory unit in the British army. You even get to keep your rank."

"And I get to see my family again?"

"Harry I work for the SIS, not Madam Frufru, the palm reader. The honest answer is, I don't know, but I hope so."

"Can I speak to General von Thoma?"

"No, all senior prisoners are isolated from each other. I'm afraid if Thoma saw you, it would undo everything we're trying to achieve with him."

"So I sign the papers and I am absolved?" asked Harry.

"Only God can give you absolution, but I can offer you a second chance."

Harry stared at the papers in front of him: one more army, one more war before he could see his family again.

"You know, Harry, you could be the only soldier who has fought in both world wars, on both sides. That's …" Barley searched for the right words, "… that's quite remarkable." He stopped to let the significance of his words sink in before continuing, "Meanwhile, you'll be getting a new uniform, of course, and I would like you to meet your, ah, chaperone, Sergeant Hannigan."

A shiver went down Harry's spine as a nightmare from his past walked in.

***

Sophie sat gazing out of the window. She was numb, adrift in a sea of ghosts and mists. Grief had overwhelmed her, but now her emotions seemed to have shut down completely. Nancy understood that since the death of her father, her mother had mentally moved to another place and, without a word, Nancy was quietly preparing lunch for the two of them. While she also felt keenly the loss of her father, she feared for her mother. Sophie had not eaten for days, and Nancy worried that she might lose her mother too.

Nancy chopped the onions, carrots, potatoes and turnips and scraped them from the chopping board into the boiling water already swirling with some old lentils she had found at the back of the cupboard. As she kept one eye on the soup, she kept the other on her mother, who stared at the street below, apparently taking in nothing of what she saw.

Nancy added some salt to the soup and tasted it. Pretty good, even though I do say so myself, she thought. She joined her mother at the window while the vegetables simmered and the soup bubbled away on the cooker. Sophie seemed to be unaware of her surroundings, of Nancy's presence, and said nothing. The silence was punctured only by her occasional sighs.

When the soup was ready, Nancy ladled out two bowlsful. She stared at what remained in the pot and guessed that there was enough left for their supper. She carried a steaming bowl over to her mother and placed it with a spoon on the window sill. Nancy had hoped for some kind of recognition that she had made the soup all by herself, but there was only continued silence from her mother.

While Sophie barely acknowledging the soup in front of her, Nancy began to eat, partly to curb the relentless grumbling of her stomach now that rationing had begun and partly to remind her mother that she should also eat. Sophie might be mourning a dead husband, but she was not dead herself.

"Mama, please eat something," Nancy pleaded.

Sophie sighed and half-heartedly picked up her spoon. She used it to stir the contents of her bowl, but showed little enthusiasm for putting anything in her mouth.

"*Please*," implored Nancy, her eyes filling with tears.

Sophie made a herculean effort and raised the soup-laden spoon to her open mouth. She chewed and swallowed, feeling the warmth of the liquid trickle down her throat. It tasted good; her body seemed to welcome the nourishment. The slight sting of heat at the back of her mouth brought her to her senses. She had been lost in a reverie for several days, but now she was back. There was her daughter, tears in her eyes, eating the lunch she had prepared all by herself. In that instant Sophie realised how selfish her grief had made her. Harry was dead, but Nancy, more precious than life itself, was still alive and full of surprises. How Harry would have scolded her for ignoring their daughter while she wrapped herself up in mourning. Sophie sniffed away a tear and reached over to squeeze Nancy's hand. "Thank you," she said simply.

Nancy beamed at her mother as the tears rolled down her cheeks.

***

Sergeant Hannigan and Harry, now in the uniform of a British major, were sitting in an Egyptian street café. Harry kept staring at Hannigan, unable to believe his eyes: Hannigan looked the same; his build was the same; even his Scouse accent was the same. Harry felt deeply uneasy. Hannigan had died in that POW camp; even if he hadn't, he would now be in his late forties, not the same age he was in the last war. He should have been relieved to be out of the barracks, knowing he had a future, but this walking reminder of his darkest moments cast a cloud over everything.

The waiter came over, and Harry ordered a beer. It had been months since he'd last had one. Hannigan did the same. "So, what's the deal? I put a foot wrong and you put a bullet in my head?" Harry asked, staring hard at Hannigan.

"That's about right, but I hope I won't have to. Mr Barley told me about your background. You are one battle-hardened soldier. Anyone who can survive a winter in Russia and still be fighting in his forties gets my respect," Hannigan replied bluntly but with admiration.

"Look, I have to get this off my chest. You remind me of someone I knew."

"You don't say."

"I have to ask, did your father serve in the Great War?"

"Yeah, he did, but he was captured at the Somme and was a prisoner of war," Hannigan replied matter-of-factly.

"Did Mr Barley tell you I was also a prisoner of war at that time?"

"No."

"And now I have to ask you a difficult question, so I apologise in advance, but did your father die in a POW camp?"

Hannigan's eyebrows shot up. Harry didn't need to hear the answer because he knew he was staring into the face of the son of the only man he'd ever hated. His mind churned with the memories he had suppressed for decades. The sneering face, the swaggering manner and the bullying threats all came back to him and turned his stomach. Was this a genuine coincidence, or was this Barley's idea of a joke - or even - a reminder of what might happen if Harry stepped out of line?

"Yes, he died in an attempted prison escape. He was given a medal and a citation posthumously. He was quite the hero for a while."

"What's your first name?"

"Simon."

"Then, Simon Hannigan, I knew your father; in fact, I was in the camp where he tried the prison break." The beers arrived. Harry grasped the cold glass with both his hands, enjoying the feel of condensation moistening his fingers in the dry heat of Egypt. He thought long and hard about what to say next, but his emotions overwhelmed him, and he blurted out, "Your father was an utter bastard!"

There was a pause as Hannigan leaned back in his chair before replying, "My earliest memory is of my pa beating my mother while me, my brother and sister cried and tried to stay out of his way. He would come home from the docks, drunk and in a mean mood, and one of us would get a thrashing. We never knew who it would be, but I took my fair share. When everyone was telling me what a hero my pa was, leading the break-out from a Kraut prison, I knew I should be proud, but I was just happy he wasn't coming back." Hannigan took a swig of his beer. "So, you're wrong, major, my father wasn't an utter bastard; he was a *fucking* bastard!"

"You look just like him," Harry observed.

"Yeah, I know; but I don't act like him."

"You see the scar on my left cheek?" Harry asked, pointing to his face. "I got it courtesy of a German rifle butt; your father made it a lot worse."

"That sounds like him."

They seemed to have reached a silent agreement to leave the past in the past. There was nothing more to be said about a man they both hated.

"So what's next?" asked Harry.

"Well Montgomery is rolling up Rommel along the North African coast at the same time as the Yanks have landed in the northwest, so it looks like the *Afrika Korps* is finished. Our services are no longer needed on this continent. We're going home to Blighty."

***

Harry's memorial service took place on a beautiful spring day, which was at odds with the sombre mood. The chief mourners were Sophie and Nancy, Anke, Karl and his family, Max and his family, with Rudi also in attendance. Sergeant Baumer and Corporal Arnet, both on leave, had heard about Harry's death and had travelled to Hannover to pay their respects. Word had spread quickly, and people from the neighbourhood, friends of the Woods and the Walds, and old customers came along to say their farewells. Frau Zentz was there, a mass of mixed emotions: sad at the death of a soldier she had known and liked, thankful and happy it was not her Erik, worried but hopeful he would not end the war in a similar way.

The family could have been forgiven for thinking that, under the circumstances, people would not turn out for an English foreigner, so it was both sobering and gratifying to know that those attending were able to separate their feelings about the RAF from those about the Englishman who had laid down his life for them.

Reverend Fischer, who had married Sophie and Harry, was still reeling from the devastation to his cathedral, but he was able to make arrangements with a local church for the conduct of the service. Fischer seemed to find his own solace in taking charge of Harry's service; it was a familiar routine, which created the illusion that everything was normal, when it clearly wasn't.

Having died in a battle so far away meant that there was no coffin, a state of affairs that was far from unusual in this time of war. Families of men who had died at sea or in the *Luftwaffe* also had to find closure without a body. In place of a coffin, Sophie had displayed a copy of her photograph of Harry in his uniform. The original still had pride of place in their sitting room but now had a black ribbon around it to show he had died in war.

The service was short and emotional, and afterwards friends and family gathered at the Perle apartment, where Arnet and Baumer were treated like heroes. Baumer found tears welling up in his eyes as he described the time in Poland when Harry had saved him and his squad, while Arnet regaled the group with stories about Spain, Poland and France. Some were serious; others were exciting; several were funny. A lightened mood encouraged Karl to continue the thread, and he reminisced about the months he had served with Harry all those years ago, each anecdote showing a different aspect of Harry's character. Sophie thought she knew her husband best; she even prided herself that she knew him better than he knew himself, but hearing his old comrades speak so openly, so movingly about his courage and bravery, in ways he never would have done himself, renewed Sophie's sense of pride and made more poignant the sense of loss for everyone in the room.

It was a day full of tears and laughter, but eventually, people began to think about heading for home. Karl offered to drive Sophie and Nancy back to their apartment, but they both felt like walking. As they drifted through the neighbourhood, people stopped to offer condolences and, sometimes, to share a memory. It warmed their hearts to know that Harry had been so well-liked, so well regarded in their community. As far as the Germans were concerned, he had been one of them.

But the day had been long, the stories bittersweet, and they were both exhausted, anxious to get home and into their beds. That night Sophie helped her daughter brush her hair and kissed her good night, lingering just a little longer than usual for an extra hug. Nancy was asleep before Sophie turned out the light and went to her bedroom. The double bed looked so empty. As the wife of a soldier, she had gotten used to sleeping on her own, but now she realised that the right side of the bed would never again be filled with her Harry.

She slipped between the covers and lay quietly on her side of the bed. She moved her right arm across to the place where Harry would normally sleep. It was cold and empty.

***

Harry never did see the mysterious Mr Barley again, and he assumed he never would. After further debriefs in a country house, which Harry guessed was in Wiltshire, he was assigned to an officer training course, where he learned not how to be a soldier, but how to do things the British way. While he was impressed with the motivation and the solid nature of the tactics, he couldn't get over the desperately short food supplies and the out-dated, almost antiquated equipment. If the Germans knew how close Britain is to collapse, maybe they would try to invade again, thought Harry.

When he was issued with his equipment, Harry was handed a Brodie helmet, the same head gear he had worn as a young soldier all those years ago in the Great War. He felt its smooth cold steel, a dead weight in his hand, and placed it on his head. The balance, the heft, the rough strap around his chin, it all felt so familiar. Twenty-five years melted away. This was it; this was what he had been wearing when his life had changed forever. Everything that had happened to him had begun with him wearing a helmet just like this. A smile crept across his lips. So much had changed in his life and in the world, but the British army was still issuing the same damn helmet they had been using for over a quarter of a century.

Harry's biggest concern was the Sten Mark II; it felt like a toy in comparison to his MP 40. He stared at his weapons and kit and wondered how Britain had been able to hang on for so long. Virtually everything was inferior to his German equivalent; the most reliable elements, such as the steel-rimmed helmet and the Lee Enfield rifle had been around since the last time he had served in the British army.

Designed as they were to prepare fresh-faced, twenty-something lieutenants for combat, the war games were laughably easy to Harry. The young officers were faster and better at forced marching, but when it came to the tactics and strategies needed to win, Harry's group excelled every time. Throughout the training, Hannigan never left his side. They both knew he was there in case Harry wavered, but both came to the conclusion that this wasn't going to happen.

After several months of being on-site at barracks and training grounds, Harry was finally given leave and, with Hannigan in tow, he headed straight to London. As he travelled towards Acton, he saw the scars and devastation from the Blitz. Three years on and Britain still hadn't found the means to rebuild; it was too busy fighting a war against annihilation, and it was slowly starting to win.

It was a drizzly Sunday afternoon when Harry walked up the garden path to a familiar front door. His palms sweated with apprehension; his memory burned with the words that had called him all but traitor and cut him off from his family. It had been twenty years since he had next heard from his brother, and while that letter was an olive branch, it was one Harry hadn't acknowledged. He had been too busy fighting for the Third Reich. Now … would the man inside hug him or hit him? Harry didn't know, but the time had come to find out.

Harry rapped on the door and after a few moments it opened to reveal a wiry, middle-aged man, wearing dark trousers and a white shirt open at the neck. His glasses were half-way down his nose, and his once fair hair was turning grey. He looked like a healthier version of Harry's father. It was Alfred, the brother he hadn't seen since 1918. Alfred stared at Harry, "Have we met?"

It was the moment when Harry realised how much he must have changed. It wasn't only time that had aged him, but the years of war and hardship had etched lines into his face and hardened his jaw. Then there was his scar and his nose and no doubt his bearing was different too. Alfred had last seen him when he was a naïve seventeen-year-old boy. He had changed so much that, while he instantly recognised his brother, his brother hadn't recognised him. Harry hesitated, the words sticking in his mouth. "It's me. I'm your brother … Harry!"

Alfred's eyes widened in surprise. He gazed up and down at the British officer who stood before him, absorbing every detail. Harry held his breath, afraid to think what might happen next. He had missed his family and now he feared the worst. He was terrified of messing up this opportunity, of losing this chance to re-establish the last remaining relationship from his old life.

"Harry?" exploded Alfred as he reached for his brother to grab him in a hug. "How long have you been here? I begged you to come back to us when the war broke out, but that was nearly four years ago." Harry opened his mouth to reply, but nothing came out. "You some kind of Jerry spy? You lived there long enough."

"Wait a minute," blurted Harry, but Hannigan stepped in between the two brothers, towering over Alfred. "Mr Alfred Woods, I am Sergeant Hannigan of the Secret Intelligence Service and, on behalf of the service, I apologise for keeping your brother away from you for some time, but I can assure you his knowledge of Germany has helped His Majesty's Government in many ways. Your brother is a war hero."

It was difficult to know which brother was more astonished: Harry, because Hannigan's quick thinking and articulate explanation were completely unexpected, or Alfred, who simply had no idea what had hit him.

Alfred looked at Sergeant Hannigan and then back at his brother. "Well why couldn't he write?" asked Alfred, addressing Hannigan as if Harry wasn't there.

"It's classified," replied Hannigan.

"Not even one letter to let us know he was alright?"

"No," Hannigan said firmly, making clear that this line of questioning was at an end.

Alfred hesitated, stroking his chin. Then he broke into a smile, grabbed his brother in another hug and pulled him by the arm in the direction of the sitting room. "Mary! Mary, come here!" Alfred called to his wife.

A plump, middle-aged woman with short, greying hair appeared in the doorway, hastily wiping her hands on her apron. "What is it, Alf?"

"Come here and meet my brother Harry," Alfred said, grinning from ear-to-ear.

"Can it be?" Mary exclaimed, shocked by the revelation. She approached Harry, holding out her hand. Not certain how to greet this stranger, who was his sister-in-law, Harry shook her hand politely. "My, isn't he the gentleman," she said, clearly impressed by Harry's uniform and demeanour. "And who is this?" Mary asked, nodding towards Hannigan, who was now standing quietly a few steps away.

"Ah, this is Sergeant Hannigan, my … ah … assistant," Harry explained. Hannigan raised an eyebrow at being described as an 'assistant' but played along.

"How long can you stay?" Alfred asked.

"Just until this evening, I'm afraid. And here …" Harry said, opening his briefcase, "…two tins of corned beef and some Bovril." Harry's experience of rationing in Britain was far more stringent than anything in Germany. He couldn't turn up empty-handed with two extra mouths to feed so had 'liberated' some items from army stores. Hannigan understood what was happening and turned a blind eye. He would have done the same.

Harry wanted to know about everyone. Alfred started with their father, who had succumbed to his illnesses just as war was breaking out in 1939. Their mother had died a year later during the Blitz not because they were bombed out, but because of a stroke brought on by anxiety over the nightly air raids. While Mary and Hannigan looked on, Harry and his brother swapped memories and told stories. Harry poured eagerly over the family photos Alfred kept in an album.

Too young to fight in the first war, too old for the current one, Alfred was now a volunteer for his local unit of the Home Guard. He fitted these duties around his job as a van driver. His son Robbie was now eighteen and had just joined the RAF as ground crew; he was being deployed to India. Their daughter Winnifred had been evacuated to a farm in the countryside and seemed happy there. At least she was safe, Alfred commented wistfully.

The war had brought an end to the letters that had meant so much to both brothers, but Alfred wanted Harry to know that he was never far from his thoughts; they had worried about him and his family. "Those damned Krauts! Have you seen what they've done to London?" Alfred asked.

"Yes, yes, I have, but the RAF is doing the same thing in Germany."

"Good, serves them right, the Nazi bastards."

Harry couldn't help himself. "They're not all Nazis, you know. There are millions of people in Germany who neither like Hitler nor want war; it's just that there's no alternative. Hitler and his Nazi stooges make sure there is no political opposition. I hope you'll remember that every time you refer to all Germans as 'Nazis', you're lumping my family into something they have always bitterly opposed."

Alfred opened his mouth to respond, when he felt Mary squeeze his arm. Whatever it was, he thought better of it and closed his mouth. For the first time, Mary entered the conversation. "It must be awful, separated from your wife and daughter, not knowing if they're safe or not, and I guess they can't know what you're doing either."

Mary's words hit home. How *was* his family? By now they must have been told he was dead. The frustration of not being able to tell them the truth was unbearable. Every fibre of his body yearned to be at home in Germany, but he couldn't say that. "Yes, Mary, it *is* hard, but we all do what we can for king and country," Harry deflected.

Hannigan coughed and pointed to his wrist watch. Harry understood.

Mary was on her feet, "But you haven't had your tea." They had been too busy reminiscing.

Harry turned to Mary and said, "Next time," with a warm smile as he took her hand in farewell. Then to Alfred, "I know one afternoon can't begin to make up for years of absence, but I'll be back."

Alfred nodded; the brothers exchanged good-bye hugs and slaps on the back. Hannigan and Harry returned to their base.

***

As his father had done before him, Karl Wald sat at the dining room table, smoking and reading his newspaper. "I tell you, the Italians are shit soldiers!" Karl raged, addressing no one in particular. And, as Anke had done in her time, Frieda emerged from the kitchen to see what all the fuss was about. "Whatever's happened now? And mind your language! The children, Karl, the children," scolded Frieda.

"What was that, Mama?" came a voice down the hall.

Frieda glared at her husband. Honestly, they seemed to have their ears tuned, waiting for someone to use bad language. "Nothing, darling, go back to your homework," she called back in reply.

Karl rolled his eyes and apologised by mouthing, 'sorry'.

"You were saying?"

"Ah, yes. So the Allies invade Sicily in the summer, a setback for Mussolini, but Italy is much bigger than Sicily, isn't it? Then the Allies invade mainland Italy at the start of September, and Mussolini has to be saved by our *Fallschirmjäger*. The Allies are on the mainland for only a month before the Italians capitulate – and then switch sides. I ask you! Poland lasted longer than four weeks."

"So the Italians are now fighting against us?"

"Well, as always, it's not quite as simple as that. The north has broken away as the pro-German Republic of Salò, wherever that is exactly, but quite frankly, the Allies can have Italy. It did pretty much the same thing in the Great War. It's ridiculous."

"Well, if they're that bad, aren't we better off without them?" Frieda asked.

"You make a good point."

"Thank you," Frieda said, savouring the moment.

"But if you read between the lines of our government's propaganda, Germany is being pushed back everywhere. Sounds like there was a huge clash between us and the Reds at Kursk, and while hundreds of thousands of communists died, we were the ones who retreated. Rommel has abandoned North Africa; Sicily and Italy are gone. It's not looking good."

"Winter is nearly here; there's never as much fighting in the winter," Frieda offered hopefully.

"You're right, my love, but will '44 mark the end of this butchery? I hope so," Karl sighed. He was about to start a rant against the stupidity and arrogance of the Nazis, when he heard his mother call out. The arthritis in Anke's hip was getting worse, and she needed help to get in and out of bed. Karl went to her assistance and hoisted her up and out, asking if she needed Frieda's help to dress. Karl realised that living on a first floor wasn't the best arrangement for his mother, but what could he do? He wished Harry was here; he could always talk things over with Harry. He missed his brother-in-law, his best friend. The realisation that he was never coming home stabbed him again.

***

For a time Harry had enjoyed a life of training and briefings. Most of his previous six or seven years had been spent fighting, mobilising and travelling; it had ground him down. But now, after more than a year of relative ease, he had begun to feel stale and frustrated.

He saw Alfred and Mary as often as he could, the 'faithful' Hannigan always by his side. Alfred took him to visit the family graves in the grounds of St Mary's in Perivale. His parents had not been religious, but the little medieval church was a place the two boys knew from their youthful adventures. There, in a line of tombstones, were Harry's parents and sister. Despite the years that had passed, it was something of a shock to see Nancy's name etched in stone, forever young. His own Nancy was about the same age as his sister had been when she died of Spanish flu, and his reflections brought tears to his eyes.

Harry missed his mother and sister, but somewhat surprisingly, he missed his father too. Now that he had been through war, he knew what it could do to men, and he no longer blamed his father for his harsh ways. He'd seen plenty of others do worse, and it had nothing to do with either bravery or cowardice. Terence Woods had been a victim of the things he had seen, of the orders he had had to obey. Harry, too, had seen terrible things and, like his father, these things were made worse by the fact that his army was targeting civilians. Harry longed to be able to tell his father that he knew, that he understood, finally, what he had gone through. That this wasn't possible left Harry with a profound sense of loss. Now that he was able to help his father carry his burden, to share it with him, he was too late, three years too late.

His thoughts turned to home, to his much-missed family. Were they safe? He couldn't know. The papers reported ongoing air raids by the RAF and, now, the US Air Force. Maybe his hope to be reunited with his family was a futile one. He tried to shake such thoughts from his head. No, he mustn't think like that; whatever happened, he was going to make it home; he was going to see his family again. Everything he was doing was for that. It was all he wanted.

Meanwhile, back at the base, it was becoming clear that all the training was in preparation for something big; and in May they were briefed about Operation Overlord, the Allied invasion of France. It was a chance to open another front on continental Europe in the hope that the war would be over by Christmas. Five Normandy beaches were the designated targets for landing: the Americans had Omaha and Utah; the British and the Commonwealth had Gold, Juno and Sword. Harry and Hannigan were to go in with the second wave on Gold beach, attached to No. 47 Commando, Royal Marines.

Harry and Hannigan met the troops, who were in peak physical condition, tough from training and half Harry's age. One of the marines called out in a mocking tone to Hannigan, "So, where have you been while we've been fighting?"

Hannigan shot back, "In Egypt, two years fighting Rommel in the desert."

Unperturbed by Hannigan's response, Private Trew continued, aiming his comments at Harry. "And what about you, Grandad? There's nobody here to help you up the beach. I bet you became a major fighting paperwork in the Home Office."

Harry opened his mouth to pull rank, but Hannigan came to the rescue again. "You're out of line, private. The major's career is no business of yours, but I promise you that it is long and distinguished; it is also classified, but rest assured he was killing Germans before you were a gleam in the milkman's eye."

The rest of the marines laughed and Trew shut up. Harry drew himself up to his full height, folded his arms across his chest and shot a withering look at the private. After the initial sparring, the two men got to work embedding themselves with the unit, where it was quickly recognised that Harry was no spare wheel. He talked knowledgeably about potential German tactics and weapons; he could even speak the language.

Eventually the men embarked on the ships and waited … and waited some more. The weather had deteriorated and everything was on hold, but the rough sea and the constant movement of the troop transport made even the hardened marines feel queasy as the hours, and then, the days passed. Their target was Port-en-Bessin, a small harbour on the dividing line between the British forces on Gold Beach and the Americans on Omaha.

Hannigan hung over the side of the vessel, dry heaving. Harry patted him on the back. "Remind me again why we are still sitting here," Hannigan groaned.

"Because the tides have to be right for the ships, and the weather has to be right for the paratroopers and, as we all well know, the British summer rarely does what we want it to do."

Still they waited until finally, on 5 June, a letter from General Eisenhower was read aloud, and they received their orders to head out. "Well, if the general has put pen to paper, the invasion must be imminent," Hannigan muttered under his breath.

***

At dawn on 6 June 1944, Normandy awoke to an ear-splitting barrage from the Royal Navy as rockets and shells marked the start of Operation Overlord. It was D-Day. The guns of the ships were supported by aircraft blotting out the sky. The bombers drenched the shoreline in high explosives, causing huge damage to the towns along the coast, while the army of the *Wehrmacht* sat safely in their reinforced concrete bunkers. As the explosions ripped across the shore, more than a million men were crossing the English Channel towards Normandy.

The last time Harry had been in France was four years ago, in Blitzen. What had happened to the crew? What had happened to the tank? So much had changed since then. Now, for the first time in a long time, Harry felt he was going into battle to fight a just cause. He had seen what the Nazis were doing, and it was time they were stopped, once and for all.

As their transport was coming in, the landing craft next to Harry's erupted in a plume of seawater and noise as it struck a mine. The transport lurched, nose down, sending the rear of the vessel into the air. It sank in seconds. The heavily laden marines were either killed by the blast or drowned as their gear dragged them down, while the life-jacketed naval pilot was left adrift and in shock on the water's roiling surface. There was no fire from the ridges overlooking the beaches as Harry and his men were coming in behind the first wave, but they could see bodies on the beach and the Centaur tanks, which had either been destroyed or had bogged down in the sand. The men landed and created a defensive perimeter. Harry approached and saluted the leader of the marines, a Lieutenant-Colonel Phillips.

"Sir, I can't get my bearings. The beach does not correspond with the map."

"Yes, major, that's because the navy, in its infinite wisdom, has landed us in the wrong place. I guess the battle starts here and not where it was meant to. Let's move on to the nearby town. If my guess is correct, it should be La Rosière."

The troops moved up. Phillips' guess had been correct. The town was lightly defended, and the commandos moved through it with ease. At the first opportunity Harry discarded his Sten and picked up an MP 40 and some ammunition. Hannigan looked at him a little dismayed.

"What?" challenged Harry.

"Use the bloody equipment you were issued," lectured Hannigan.

"Oh, yes, the Sten. It's less accurate than the MP 40; its effective range is shorter than an MP 40, and it's more likely to jam. I am not going into battle with something second best if I have a better option." Harry pointed to Hannigan's Lee Enfield. "You want to swap that for the Sten?"

"No, I'm fine," Hannigan smiled.

"Exactly," Harry concluded, satisfied he had made his point.

By that evening they had come to the edge of Port-en-Bessin. When Harry met with Lieutenant-Colonel Phillips and Captain Cousins to discuss the strategy for the next day, both men looked quizzically at Harry's German weapon but said nothing. Harry indicated where he thought the machine gun nests and strong points were likely to be and said that the hill would probably be mined. The harbour had two *Vorpostenboots*, light German torpedo boats, which Harry also pointed out had enough anti-aircraft armaments to be a worry for the infantry.

The next morning the commandos launched assaults on both the harbour and the town, and the battle quickly deteriorated into house-to-house fighting. Harry and

Hannigan flung themselves to the ground when a fence next to them exploded into splinters as an MG 42 fired from the front window of a nearby house. The two forward marines were not so lucky: one was hit in the chest and face and died instantly; the other was hit side on from a high velocity bullet that entered his left shoulder and passed across the top of his body before exiting through his right armpit. Harry and Hannigan clung to the pavement, willing themselves to be as small as possible.

Harry looked at the second marine who had panic in his eyes as blood flowed from his mouth and sides. The bullet had ruptured a major artery; the man was drowning in his own blood. He stretched a quivering hand towards Harry, who, against his better judgment reached out until their fingertips touched. Their eyes met; Harry saw the pleading desperation, but there was nothing he could do as the marine choked and bled out. At least the soldier did not die alone.

Harry tapped Hannigan's leg and whispered, "You keep low and head right, then go round the back. I'll head left and get up in front of the terraces, so I can move in from their front. Then I'll try to confuse them. Got it?"

"Yes, I go right and head to the rear; you go left and come in from the front."

"Go!" ordered Harry, and the two men scrabbled away in opposite directions as the machine gun barked into life again. Harry moved along the fence and called out in perfect German, "Don't shoot, don't shoot! My name is Gerhard Schmidt of the 2nd Panzer division. Thank you for taking out those English soldiers, but I don't want you to hit me."

Harry's comments were enough to stop the gunfire. An eerie silence followed. Harry flattened himself against the front of the short terrace of houses and began to edge his way back towards the window where the machine gun was positioned. He heard the sound of breaking glass as Hannigan entered from the rear. Harry quickly swung around to face the front of the window through which he saw the backs of three German soldiers, who had turned to see what was happening behind them. Harry raised his gun and unloaded his entire clip into the Germans. After the blaze of gunfire, the soldiers lay dead in pools of their own blood.

"Harry?" Hannigan called out.

"You can come out."

Hannigan stepped into the room and looked first at the three dead bodies, then at Harry, framed in the window, a murderous look on his face. Hannigan was taken aback; he barely recognised the man he thought he had come to know so well. At that moment, Harry was the epitome of war, the veteran soldier who knew how to kill. It sent a chill down Hannigan's spine.

The tempo of the attack on the French town was with the marines. Air support and naval artillery were used to pound the German resistance and their boats in the harbour. Harry spied Captain Cousins leading a charge up the hill through a minefield. He was a brave man.

After a few more hours, the call went out to Harry. It sounded like the Germans wanted to surrender. Harry met a German sergeant by a wrecked Citroën, its windscreen and driver's door smashed and riddled with bullets. The German held a pathetic flapping white handkerchief on the end of a stick. "What are your terms, sergeant?" Harry asked in German. The sergeant looked confused.

"We wish to lay down our arms, provided our wounded receive medical attention."

"Do you speak for all the German forces in Port-en-Bessin?"

"Yes, I do."

"Good. Tell your men to lay down their arms where they are and meet unarmed at the town hall with the wounded. You have thirty minutes, understood?"

"Yes, I understand and, I must say, your German is excellent."

"Sergeant, you're wasting time. Go!"

After Port-en-Bessin, Harry and Hannigan moved wherever they were needed, from one British unit to another. Harry was sometimes forced to fight, but more often he was interrogating captured officers or negotiating the surrender of groups of Germans. But there was one German unit that always fought on and never surrendered. Wherever Harry went, he warned the British troops of the fanatical resistance they could expect from SS Divisions. They rarely believed him until they faced one.

The landings in Normandy had been a success, but it would take time to turn the beachhead into a breakout across France. There was more hard fighting ahead for the British and Americans.

***

Karl and Frieda were out for an early morning walk. It was the one time of day there was guaranteed to be no bombing raids, and the fresh air took their minds off their growling stomachs. As Hitler's dreams shrank, so did the size of their rations. All the systems of government were starting to break down and shrivel; everyone could see that the Third Reich was declining rapidly. The Warsaw uprising may have been a victory for the Nazis, but Warsaw was the first capital city to fall to Germany, and now, five years on, it clearly felt the shackles had been loosened enough to try and break free. Meanwhile, Stalin's armies were gaining ground in the East, and the British and Americans had retaken France; they had only been halted when they reached Holland.

As they walked along the familiar streets, they saw the same 'Volkssturm' poster everywhere: on walls, on kiosks, on bus stops. It was the striking image of an older man and a young soldier, standing shoulder-to-shoulder with their rifles, declaring 'To live at peace and in freedom'.

Karl and Frieda approached a young boy, who was pasting up some of the posters. "Excuse me. Can you tell us what this is all about?" asked Frieda.

"There's been a decree by Reich Minister Joseph Goebbels to say that the *Volkssturm* 'will overcome our enemies' military strength through force of will'."

"And who are the *Volkssturm*?"

"It's a new conscription of all men aged between thirteen and sixty. I'm only twelve, so I can't join up," he sighed with real regret.

Karl laughed, "Oh, you're not serious. The *Führer* couldn't possibly want *me* to sign up. I'm fifty-two and too old to be of any use."

The boy gasped, put down his posters and gave Karl the Nazi salute. "Why, you're perfect: a man of experience! How I wish I could join you as you make a triumphant stand against Jews, Yankees and communists."

"What are you talking about? How is an old guy like me going to stop the millions of Allied troops heading at us from three different directions?"

"Our superior blood will prevail."

"I wish you good luck with that, kid," Karl said sarcastically and turned to head for home.

But the boy was not to be so easily dismissed and called out, "Police! Police! Deserter! Deserter!"

Karl couldn't remember the last time he had run at full tilt, but husband and wife both recognised the potential danger, bolted round the corner and zig-zagged their way back home, arriving at Perle through a back alley. The sharp sprint left them out of breath, and they fell in relief on the steps to their apartment. "You're quite a fast runner for a man in his fifties. Maybe the kid was right, and you still have some energy to give to the Fatherland," Frieda said sarcastically, still panting.

They regained their composure, stood up and found themselves in front of a military policeman (universally known as 'chain dogs' due to the metal plate and chain that hung around their necks). "What were you two doing down there?" asked the slightly bemused policemen, nodding towards the alley. There was no mistaking the guilty looks on the faces of this middle-aged couple.

"Nothing, officer, just thought I'd dropped my keys," Karl said, his mind racing.

The policeman frowned, "Papers, please."

Karl fumbled in his coat and handed over his papers; Frieda did the same.

"You're fifty-two, is that right?"

"Yes."

"In that case, I'll be escorting you to the nearest conscription centre."

"No!" cried Frieda.

"Frau Wald, please, it's a new directive. Your husband gets to fight for the Fatherland at last."

"I've done it before. Surely it's someone else's turn," Karl commented dryly.

The policeman grabbed Karl firmly by the right arm and thrust Frieda's papers back at her.

"Go home, Frau Wald. Please don't force me to report a respectable woman like yourself. As for your husband, orders are orders."

Frieda watched in shock as the chain dog marched her husband down the street.

***

Sophie was running the cobbler's on her own now. A few weeks earlier, for the first time in memory, Rudi hadn't come to work. She became concerned by the time mid-day arrived, with still with no sign of a man who was as reliable as he was quiet. Sophie shut the shop and travelled to Rudi's suburb, where she found his brother, who tearfully showed her the pile of rubble that had been Rudi's little house. He died when it had taken a direct hit.

Rudi's death had shaken all the Walds. He was so much a part of the business, so much a part of them all that it never occurred to them that he wouldn't always be there. Under normal circumstances, Sophie would have grieved, but she had lost so much that Rudi's death was just one more person on an already substantial pile. She was numb to loss.

At present, what most occupied Sophie was her ongoing concern for her daughter, who had grown rapidly over the past year and was maturing into a pretty girl with a small spray of acne on her forehead. Sophie remembered the embarrassed delight on Nancy's face when they had bought her first brassiere, but her daughter's hormonal development was not what worried Sophie; more than anything it was the increasing demands made on her by the *Jungmadelbund*. Nancy was coming home late; she had even been called on to perform duties during an air raid. Sophie had protested to deaf ears and only breathed again when her daughter arrived back home, but she could see the weariness on Nancy's face and suspected that her daughter had fears she could not admit.

Enough was enough. The next time Nancy was assigned Hitler Youth duties, Sophie planned to find out what was so important that they took priority over her school work and her home life, not to mention her safety. Sophie closed the shop early and waited outside the school until she saw Nancy leave in her *Jungmadelbund* uniform, accompanied by two friends. Sophie stayed well out of sight and followed at a discreet distance. They hadn't gone far when the girls stopped at an anti-aircraft gun emplacement, the barrel of the powerful 88mm gun pointing towards the sky. Someone handed the girls helmets that were too large for them, and the others who had been on duty drifted off. Those she was apparently replacing were wearing the cadet uniforms of the *Luftwaffe* and were only a few years older than Nancy and her friends. Now there was a lone soldier with three teenage girls, one of whom was her daughter.

Sophie's jaw dropped as she stood watching in disbelief. She was aghast! The *Wehrmacht* was now using school children to man their guns. She had seen the posters for the *Volkssturm* but never imagined that it would affect her own daughter. A red mist descended on Sophie. What was the point of protracting a war that needed fourteen-old-girls to fight their losing cause? Surely they were already defeated if this point of desperation had been reached. She stormed over to the pile of sand bags that surrounded the 88.

"Who is in charge here?" Sophie asked, seething with unbridled rage.

"I am," said the soldier.

"Mother!" Nancy said, turning from a crate of ammunition.

"What is your name?" Sophie asked the soldier, ignoring her daughter's cry.

"Corporal Stephan Krauss," he responded, looking bewildered.

"Well, Corporal Krauss, I am Sophie Woods, wife of the deceased Major Harold Woods and mother to Nancy Woods, who I see is over there sorting through an ammunition crate."

"A pleasure to meet you," Krauss said, completely misreading the situation.

Sophie gave him a withering look, which he finally understood. "Corporal, what do you think you are doing with my daughter?"

"She is a member of the *Jungmadelbund* and therefore, by extension, the *Volkssturm*. She is helping us defend the Fatherland. If she keeps working like she has, she could make corporal by Christmas," Krauss said with a weak smile.

"Young man, my husband fought for Germany in the Great War, then he fought for the interests of Germany in Spain, and he was a major in the *Wehrmacht* right up until his tank exploded in North Africa two years ago. I think my family has given more than enough to the Fatherland." Sophie grabbed Nancy by the wrist, "We're going home."

"You can't just leave," squeaked Krauss, unsure of his ground.

"Watch us," challenged Sophie, shooting the corporal a defiant stare as she began to drag Nancy away.

"Please, Mama, let go!" complained Nancy, squirming against her mother's vice-like grip.

"We're defending the future of the Third Reich," Krauss explained half-heartedly.

"Corporal, look around you. Hannover is in ruins, much like every other German city, and now Herr Hitler wants school children and old men to fight for him. What kind of future is that? When all the young people are dead, what future is left?"

"But, Mama, please! You're embarrassing me!" begged Nancy, still trying to wrestle her way out of her mother's grip.

"Good!" said Sophie, her hair falling into her face as her daughter struggled against her hold. "If you're embarrassed, you're still alive." Sophie pulled Nancy towards home. She noticed, however, that once they were out of sight, Nancy's protestations and attempts to break free tapered off. Nancy had been worried about letting her friends down and frightened of saying 'no' to an organisation that had been as much a part of her life as her school, but she had no desire to fire guns and wage war. The night was a turning point for Nancy, who finally understood the callous disregard the Nazi regime had for her life, for all life.

Sophie had saved her daughter in more ways than one.

***

Hannigan and Harry had been enjoying a refit in Ypres where the winter snow had made the conditions right for a Christmas lull in fighting. They were attached to the British 11th Armoured Division, when from out of nowhere, thirteen German armoured divisions smashed through the Ardennes Forest and into the American front line.

There was palpable panic amongst the Allies. Low cloud cover and winter weather meant they were unable to rely on their air superiority, and the Germans were using all their armour reserves, including their King Tiger Panzers, tanks so advanced that the Allies had nothing on the battlefield to stop them. While General Eisenhower was deploying every American unit he could find to try and absorb the shock of the German offensive, the 11th Armoured Division was also moving up to plug the edge of the lines.

Harry and Hannigan sat shivering in the back of a truck as they were moved forwards. "The fucking Ardennes!" Harry spat out. "Isn't that the same plan Hitler had in 1940 against France? Why did anyone think they should try this again? Maybe the timing and location are different, but the idea of one final assault was the big idea in 1918 with the *Kaiserschlacht*."

"The what?"

"The *Kaiserschlacht*."

"What's that?"

"Oh never mind, you were just a child then, but you'd think that with all the intelligence, all the generals and all the technology, an attack consisting of thirteen entire armoured divisions might be discovered or, at least, anticipated."

"Nothing to do with me; I'm just the sergeant looking after the major," Hannigan retorted, blowing and rubbing his hands in a vain attempt to warm them.

The 11th Armoured Division dug in, and as they did, they could hear the rumble of war as the Germans and Americans slugged it out in the snow-covered forest. Harry and Hannigan were based in a makeshift forward HQ with some officers of the armoured division and a radio operator, when some of the German armour attacked their location. Harry had gone a little way ahead and now lay in the snow, peering over a hillock with his binoculars.

"How can you lie in the snow like that? It must be minus fifteen Celsius," marvelled Hannigan.

"Because I've been in minus forty in Russia."

Hannigan shook his head. Sometimes he didn't know if Harry was telling the truth, exaggerating or just making it up.

Harry spied the tell-tale insignia of two yellow circles. The British tanks fired furiously at the oncoming and outnumbered German armour and infantry support. He turned to Hannigan, "Those are Panzers from my old unit, the 2nd Panzer Division." Machine gun fire crackled past their heads.

"I don't think they're in the mood to talk about the good old days," shouted Hannigan over the gunfire.

The two of them crept below the brow of the hill and into cover. The exchange of fire lasted for an hour, during which two Panzers were taken out, and the Germans were forced to beat a hasty retreat. It had not been a big engagement by the standards of the fighting around towns like Bastogne, but it was important in containing the German advance and suppressing the contagion of panic among the Allies.

As in 1918, this final offensive by the Germans had started well with the element of surprise, but it failed to break the Allied lines. Although the Germans now had nothing left to throw at them, they were not a spent force. There were millions of *Wehrmacht*, SS and *Volkssturm* soldiers still in the field, still willing to resist the Allied invasion of Germany.

Somewhere in all the snow and bullets, it turned into January of 1945.

***

Karl was standing in a courtyard in his civilian clothes along with a thousand other men, many his age or older and others, who weren't men but teen-aged boys. They were lining up to receive their weapons. Some were given *Panzerfausts*, a single-use anti-tank weapon; some were given rifles, and a few were handed MG 42s, heavy machine guns. Karl was handed a Gewehr 98; he snorted in disgust. With all the Nazi talk of technological superiority, with all the propaganda about super tanks, jet aircraft and powerful modern machine guns, he was handed the same rifle he had been issued thirty years ago in the Great War. Its design was nearly as old as he was. A young soldier offered to show him how to use it.

"No, it's fine. I was firing one of these with your father before you were born," he growled at the soldier, who backed off immediately. To be fair, the gun was well-made and reliable, but against the submachine guns of the Allies, it was woefully slow to fire and reload.

A captain stood at the front of the courtyard and waited patiently for the weapons to be handed out. After everyone seemed to be armed, the new conscripts formed into lines as if they were soldiers on parade. The captain addressed them: "Men of the *Volkssturm*, I salute you. You are about to embark on a noble defence of the Fatherland. To complete your induction, you must swear an oath to the *Führer*. Repeat after me: I swear by God this holy oath that I want to offer unconditional obedience to the *Führer* of the German Reich and people, Adolf Hitler, the commander-in-chief of the *Wehrmacht*, and be prepared as a brave soldier to risk my life for this oath at any time."

The gathered mass dutifully recited the oath, some more enthusiastically than others. It struck Karl that most of the boys shouted the oath at the top of their lungs. They still believed that Hitler was going to lead them to victory rather than annihilation.

"Thank you. I can now confirm that you are all officially *Volkssturm*. Go and speak to your platoon leaders about transport to the front."

Karl found the corporal who had handed him his rifle. "So when are the trucks going to pick us up?" one older man asked.

"Alright, this is how it works: for those of you fit enough to do so, you are going to march, and for those like papa here, you will have bicycles. There's even a clip on the front for your *Panzerfaust*."

Karl turned to the man next to him, a man about his age. "Oh, great, the bicycle has a clip for a *Panzerfaust*. I guess that makes us the 5th Armoured *Volkssturm* Division." The man sniggered; he clearly had no wish to be there either, but what could they do? "The name is Karl Wald," Karl said, extending his hand.

"Kurt Fleischer," came the response as they shook hands.

"So, are you too old to march?" Karl enquired.

"My pride says 'no', but my knees want me to say 'yes'."

Karl laughed. It was his experience that marching was more bearable if you had good company. Kurt seemed to be just that. It was a shame they had to meet under such abysmal circumstances and, pleasant company or not, they both knew they were probably marching to their deaths.

***

Frieda was using every ounce of her strength to hoist her mother-in-law out of bed to relieve herself. Anke's arthritis had been made much worse by the lack of fuel to heat the apartment and, without Karl to do the heavy lifting, it was just within Frieda's capabilities to move her.

After her husband had been conscripted into the *Volkssturm*, Frieda realised the same fate could befall Karl Junior – not to mention Nancy's duties at an anti-aircraft gun emplacement, so Frieda decided to keep her children in the house. Out of sight meant out of mind – she hoped. When the school made enquiries, Frieda explained that they had both come down with scarlet fever and would need long periods of recuperation. She was not pressed on the matter. It seemed there was an epidemic of illness affecting school-age children, and of course all the doctors were at the front.

Sonia and Karl Junior missed their father terribly. Unlike Nancy, they were not used to his absence. All too aware of what had happened to Harry, they prayed every night for Karl's safe return. They would much rather have been in school than doing household chores, but their help meant Frieda had time to tend to Anke and go out to collect their increasingly meagre rations. She and Sophie had agreed to pool resources to get black market food. It was a risk, but a risk their empty stomachs willed them to take.

In the present uncertain circumstances, new shoes were the last thing on anyone's mind, and the women had also agreed that it was time to close the Perle stores. They still had the cobbler's and, even though they had reduced the hours of opening, thanks to Sophie's basic skills, old shoes could be repaired, and the business was ticking along.

Frieda was filled with anxiety. Her husband was in danger and her children might, at any minute, be called back to school and the Hitler Youth – or worse. Never a rule breaker, let alone a law breaker, she was also worried about buying food on the black market. She couldn't stop staring through a gap in the curtains, scanning the street below for signs of the Gestapo or the SS on their way to her apartment. She jumped every time there was a knock on the door. She'd heard the stories; everyone had.

Sonia and Karl Junior were desperate for stimulation from the outside world. They sat glued to the radio at every opportunity and even enjoyed the martial music. If the radio provided some diversion, visits from Sophie and Nancy were even better. While their mothers drank what passed for coffee, the three cousins went off by themselves, whispering conspiratorially.

Today Sophie and Frieda sat hunched over the dining room table. Sophie was worried about Frieda. She could see that her nerves were shredded and that dealing with her invalid mother-in-law was taking a physical toll. "How are things?" Sophie asked, reaching across the table for Frieda's hand.

Frieda's eyes well up. "Oh, Sophie, I have to admit that at the start of this war, I believed all the propaganda about the Thousand Year Reich and the superiority of our armies, but look at things now. My husband is gone; my children are hiding, and our city is destroyed. On top of all this, there is Mama to look after, and either she's getting heavier, or I'm getting weaker."

Sophie knew that Frieda had lost weight; they all had, but whether, in Frieda's case, it was due to worry or dwindling rations was hard to say. "Go have a rest; you've earned it. I will look after Mama tonight. I should come more often."

"Thank you," said Frieda through a muffled sob.

The evening's respite was a brief escape from the harsh realities around all of them.

***

The snows had melted and been replaced by rain. The heavens opened, drenching all beneath as if trying to wash away the countless sins perpetrated by the long years of war. Karl trudged along the road with the rest of the *Volkssturm*, rain dripping off his hat. He had been thankful for his warm winter coat, but now it grew heavy as water wormed its way inside. He was miserable.

It turned out that Kurt, like Karl and many of the older men, had served in the Great War; all had assumed their years of military service were over. Kurt had never fired his rifle. He'd been a stretcher bearer, so while he had not seen much in the way of combat, he'd seen his fair share of horror and, by the sound of it, he'd been brave enough to rescue the wounded under fire.

They had been slogging along an *autobahn* for days. The occasional armoured convoy roared past towards the front, but that was the only military traffic they saw, although they passed scores of bedraggled civilians going in the opposite direction, desperate to get away from the fighting. Some were lucky enough to have carts that were groaning under the weight of their families and possessions, while others had to make do with hastily bundled necessities.

Karl's group was splitting into factions. The young ones were, for the most part, happy to defend the Fatherland; they were full of zeal, their minds filled with the lies of Nazi propaganda. Then there were those who were there under duress, waiting only for an opportunity to desert but too scared to leave. These were mainly the older men, but there were exceptions to both groups. Keeping the peace in the middle and doing their best to follow the increasingly fraught orders were the handful of *Wehrmacht* soldiers and their fanatical Captain Ostermann. It was looking like today would be another day of endless walking, when one of the *Wehrmacht* soldiers called out, "Alarm!"

He had spotted a couple of RAF Typhoons, which were coming in fast and low. The Allies had virtual air superiority and could carry out low altitude raids with impunity, and they had spied the group of *Volkssturm* marching down the road. The men scattered and, despite the knot of fear in his stomach, Karl was impressed that he still had the energy to hurl himself into a nearby ditch. Many didn't; the older men on bicycles found it hard to dismount and reach safety.

The Typhoons roared towards the men and loosed a volley of rockets, followed by the rapid fire of their heavy machine guns. There was utter chaos. Pieces of tarmac flew into the air, ripped up by the impact of the bullets, while the rockets exploded into a cluster of men and bicycles, sending seared chunks of flesh and metal across the *autobahn*. There were screams and cries. Karl curled into a ball in the run-off ditch by the side of the road, praying he was out of the line of fire. Puddles of muddy water drenched him and seeped into his clothes.

One of the *Panzerfausts* was struck by a bullet, ignited and flew off across the road. It fizzed past Karl, landed in a neighbouring field and, after puffing smoke for a few seconds, exploded. Karl peered over his waterlogged ditch. His heart sank. The Typhoons were turning and coming back for a second run. He spied Kurt, lying stunned in the road, a minor wound to his head. Karl swore under his breath and scrambled out from his makeshift cover. He grabbed Kurt, hoisted him to his feet and half-dragged, half-marched the still dazed man towards the side of the road. Karl heard the screech of incoming rockets and flung Kurt and himself into the ditch. The concussive blast shuddered through him as the two men landed in a heap in the cold, murky water.

There were two more explosions, and the chatter of machine gun fire sizzled around them before they heard the whine of the aircraft speeding off to find more targets. Karl helped Kurt to his feet and looked at his bleeding temple where he'd caught a chunk of tarmac. The wound wasn't serious, but it was an indication of how close they had come. "Thank you," Kurt said, grabbing Karl's hand and shaking it. Karl patted him on the back and surveyed the destruction around him. There were a half-dozen mangled bicycles and more than a dozen men lying on the ground, presumably dead.

This group of *Volkssturm* had just had its first contact with the enemy. It had been completely outclassed and had achieved nothing. After doing what they could to tend to the wounded, they placed their dozen casualties by the side of the road and moved off in the rain towards the enemy.

***

"Tecklenburg," began Harry to a group of soldiers huddled around a map on a requisitioned table in the tent, "is a picturesque town with a ruined medieval castle and a charming town square. I have been there a few times. It's a great escape from the hustle and bustle of Hannover, less than a hundred miles away. This beautiful medieval town has been in existence for the best part of a millennium, and at 06.00 hours tomorrow, we are going to raze it to the ground if we have to."

Now that he had everyone's attention, he continued. "We are targeting Tecklenburg because it has become the epicentre of activity for a group of SS units and fanatical Nazis who refuse to surrender. They are nearly surrounded; they have no support, and they are outnumbered, with only a minimum of armoured units in an unknown state of repair. They give us no choice but to destroy them. I will remind you that we are dealing with zealots who will fight to the last round of ammunition. No heroics, men. Use flame-throwers and grenades or armour support if they are dug into a building. Captain Lewis, deploy your men and tanks around from the north. Captain Lucas, you are going in from the south. I will take the rest from the west. Watch out for mines and trip wires. I would like to keep this town intact, but if it's a choice, I would much rather keep the men intact. Good luck. Dismissed."

As soon as the captains had exited, Harry's demeanour changed from that of a strong, decisive officer to that of an exhausted middle-aged man.

"May I have your attention, sir?" Hannigan asked.

"Yes, what is it?" sighed Harry as he ran his fingers through his hair.

Hannigan produced a chocolate bar and handed it to Harry.

"Thank you, but why?"

"Because it's your birthday, sir. Happy forty-fourth!"

"Is it?"

"Yes, of course."

"Thank you, Hannigan. This is much appreciated. It's just …"

"… it's just we're so near, yet so far from Hannover, right?" finished Hannigan.

"Correct. That's all I'm really thinking about. It seemed to me that the German army was ready to collapse in December, but here we are now in the spring of 1945, and they still haven't capitulated. Will I ever make it back to Hannover, I wonder."

"I hope so, sir." Hannigan looked at the unstoppable force that was Major Woods. Then, speaking as if he could not help himself, he said, "If you don't mind me saying so, sir, I have never seen you falter in a fight."

Harry glanced questioningly at the sergeant. "Is there a point to that statement?"

"I just don't understand how a man like my father could ever lay a finger on you without you killing him."

This bold statement, coming seemingly from nowhere, caught Harry by surprise. The ogre that was Hannigan senior still lurked in the back of his mind, his nemesis, the epitome of brute force. Harry still cowered mentally at the thought of those vicious fists. Had he changed so much? Was he the embodiment of violence? Was he the ogre now? He realised he hadn't responded and shrugged. "That was a long time ago," he said simply. "But speaking of killing, Hannigan, tell me what possessed you to get a birthday present for a man *you* might have to kill?"

Hannigan cracked a smile. "That assignment finished months ago, pretty much after we landed in Normandy. It's been clear for a long time that you're not going through the motions, just itching to re-join Jerry … so I requested a formal transfer under your command and Barley approved it."

"I guess that means, officially, I'm not a traitor anymore."

"I guess it does, sir."

Harry hesitated. "You're a good friend, Hannigan," he said. This time it was his turn to speak as if he could not help himself, but he meant every word of it.

The next day the 11th Armoured Division assaulted Tecklenburg. Just as Harry had predicted, the combat was fierce as every Nazi went down with a fight. Fortunately the British had superior numbers and tanks and were able to wipe them out with only light casualties to their own. Harry was only too aware of the difference between 'light' and 'no' casualties and watched sombrely as the stretchers with wounded or dying men were loaded onto the backs of military ambulances.

How many more would have to die before Germany surrendered?

***

The *Volkssturm* were dug into a forested ridge. It would have been the perfect defensive position had the men been well-equipped soldiers and not woefully under-equipped old men and boys. At least the weather was changing for the better; the days were getting longer, the temperature was rising, and for a while there had been no rain.

Karl's unit had not exactly showered itself in glory. There had been desertions and, apart from the Typhoon attack, they'd had only one other contact with the enemy, a lost American halftrack. The men had got into a haphazard position and fired a *Panzerfaust*, which tore off a track. Now alerted to the presence of enemy combatants, the Americans prepared to retaliate, but not before the Germans fired a second *Panzerfaust*. This one streaked past the halftrack and detonated on contact with a nearby grazing cow, sending a spray of bloody beef into the air.

Everyone revelled in the gallows' humour that followed the abrupt and spectacular demise of the cow, but their enjoyment was short-lived when their commanding officer, the diehard Nazi Captain Ostermann, failed to see the funny side. A third and final *Panzerfaust* smashed into the front cabin of the halftrack, which exploded and caught fire. Nobody could say how many Americans were inside, but the fact that an entire unit of more than 800 men had barely managed to overwhelm a single Allied vehicle was not an encouraging sign.

That had been a week ago, and now Ostermann had ordered everyone onto the ridge to 'repel the American *Schweinhunds*'. For the Great War veterans the present futile resistance felt like the end of the last war, but Ostermann prowled the trenches, pistol in hand, to ensure that nobody else dared to leave.

At dawn the next morning, Karl awoke to the sound of ordnance being fired. He hunched down into the foxhole and covered his head as the first shells and mortar rounds exploded on their positions.

"Oh my God! Oh my God!" the fourteen-year-old beside Karl kept screaming, over and over again. His face was as white as a sheet, and Karl noticed the boy had wet himself. Karl looked over to his left at Kurt, and they swapped grim looks. The

Americans not only knew where they were, but were ready to tackle them. What chance did the rabble of the *Volkssturm* have against this?

After ten minutes of pounding, the metal storm subsided and was replaced by the clanking and grinding of tanks moving forward. Karl peeped over the trench and saw a wall of armoured vehicles chugging towards them. American soldiers, weapons ready, were marching between the vehicles. Suddenly they heard the eruptions of the Sherman tanks' cannons firing, accompanied by bursts of machine gun fire.

Karl risked another look. They were getting close when a boy from the trench to his left fired a *Panzerfaust* at one of the oncoming tanks. Although the shot found its mark, the tank's armour was too thick for their weapons; the *Panzerfaust* exploded but did little damage. This was going to be a massacre. "Fuck this. I'm going," Karl said to Kurt.

"But wait!" begged the boy, reaching out to grab Karl's arm. "We can't leave; we can't let the Fatherland down."

"Kid, the Fatherland let us down the minute it thought old men and young boys could do the job of an army. I don't want to die here. Do you?"

With tears in his eyes, the boy shook his head. He was squatting above a puddle of his own urine, clearly terrified.

"OK then. We'll climb out and crawl backwards. When we're far enough away from the front, get up, keep running - and don't look back!"

Kurt and the boy nodded their heads in agreement. "Wait, what about Ostermann?" exclaimed the worried boy.

"He's a fanatic. He'll be so desperate to kill himself an American or a Jew, he won't be worried about us. Come on, let's go!"

As bullets buzzed around them, they climbed out and over the back edge of the trench and began crawling backwards. Machine gun and rifle fire were punctuated by the sound of exploding mortar rounds and the snarl of tank fire. The burning smell of cordite and gun cotton filled the air, making Karl cough and splutter. Some explosions were close enough to make his body shudder. All he could hear was the noise of war. After moving along some two hundred meters of rough forest floor, when the cacophony was finally dying down, Karl stopped, cautiously raised himself to his knees and looked around him. Twenty metres behind him, Kurt was on the ground, a bullet hole in his back; he had been shot through the heart. The boy was seventy metres further behind. A mortar round had sent shrapnel through his abdomen; he was bleeding out.

Karl was stunned and nauseous. These two people had trusted him enough to follow him, and he had got them killed. But would their fate in the foxhole have been any different? Besides, he hadn't asked them to come. He recognised how cold and unfeeling this blunt assessment was, and it pained him. This was war; this is what it did to men. His goal was survival, and right now he was alive. A branch next to him cracked as a stray bullet tore it from the tree. Karl snapped out of his reverie. He turned and ran as fast as he could through the forest. His only thought was of home.

***

Exhausted, dirty, his feet bleeding from blisters, Karl finally made it back to Hannover. He had walked for countless kilometres; he had hitched a cart ride with a farmer; he had jumped onto a supply train and stolen a bicycle, all to get back home. He leaned the bicycle against the wall and eased his weary bones up the stairs. He stood in front of the familiar door to his apartment and smiled. He had accomplished his mission.

Karl knocked on the door and heard footsteps approaching.

"Who is it?" a hesitant Frieda called out in what she hoped was a stern voice.

"It's me; it's Karl," he replied, breaking down.

Frieda flung open the door and gasped. She had never before seen her husband in such a state, with several weeks' worth of grey whiskers on his dirt-caked face. His clothes were torn and filthy … and was that blood on his sleeve? He looked – and smelled - more like a vagrant than a successful businessman. In spite of everything, she threw herself at him and held him tight; then she led him into the apartment as tears streamed down both their faces. "Children, come here! Papa is back!"

Sonia and Karl Junior sprinted down the hallway and piled into him, almost knocking the exhausted Karl over. The Walds couldn't stop hugging each other, laughing and crying as they did so, not knowing how to express their joy.

Eventually Frieda closed the front door and insisted her husband remove the filthy coat he had been wearing since their fateful morning stroll. While Sonia prepared some food, and Karl Junior ran a bath, Karl went to see his mother. She hadn't understood the commotion in the hallway and squealed with delight when she saw her son. Despite his protestations that he smelled like a pig sty and needed a bath, Anke demanded he come over to the bed. Tears streamed down her cheeks as she held her son close. No matter the age, he was still his mother's child.

Karl stripped off his clothes and left them outside the bathroom to be thrown away. He never wanted to see those rags again. He stood in front of the mirror and scraped away the grey whiskers to find his face had changed; his familiar features were lined and gaunt. Then he lowered himself into the steaming bath with a huge, satisfied sigh and scrubbed away all the grime. He ducked his head under the surface, enjoying the novel sensation of hot, soapy water. Surely this was paradise.

After putting on fresh clothes, Karl sat down in the dining room and devoured the bean soup and gritty bread Sonia had laid out for him. The family watched Karl wolf down the food like a beggar who had been given his first hot meal in weeks.

"Tell us, Papa, what happened?" Karl Junior asked, waiting until his father had finished a second bowl of soup.

Where to begin? What could he say? How could he tell his children that his actions had led to the death of a child about their age? "I've done things ..." whispered Karl, "... I've had to do things to get back home that I will never speak of," he said, gritting his teeth as tears welled up in his eyes. "I always knew I would do anything to be with my family, and now I have. Please excuse me. I must sleep," he said, his body shuddering as he started to weep. Karl got up and walked to the bedroom where he allowed the sheets to envelop him. He slept for sixteen hours.

***

When Karl woke up, he wandered into the sitting room to be hugged all over again by his family – and now by Sophie and Nancy too. Not without reason, they had all feared that he and the rest of the *Volkssturm* would be annihilated in the Allied offensive. And now there were growing rumours that the Americans were close to Hannover. After a happy reunion with her brother, Sophie returned home with her daughter to await the looming attack in their own little apartment.

As it turned out, Karl had arrived less than forty-eight hours ahead of the Allied troops pushing into Hannover. After a sleepless night, punctuated by the sound of approaching guns, Sophie drifted off, only to snap awake on hearing distant shouts and the chatter of gunfire. Wrapped in her bathrobe, she went to the sitting room where Nancy was peeping through the curtains at the street below. Sophie lunged and pulled her to the floor. "Don't do that! If a stray shot comes through the window, I'll lose my daughter too!" The two of them retreated further into the apartment as rifle fire and the occasional explosion continued to move in their direction.

Sophie decided to keep things as normal as possible, trying to block out the reality of what was taking place on the streets around them. They washed and dressed. Sophie made some *Kaffee-ersatz* and scrounged together a breakfast of stale bread and cheese, which they ate, as usual, in the little kitchen. It would all have been so ordinary but for the noise of urban warfare crashing into the apartment. Neither of them now had any desire to peek out from the sitting room window.

Sophie wondered where all her neighbours were. There had been a steady exodus over the previous week as the news from the front meant that Hannover would inevitably become a target for Allied troops. But this was their home and, in any case, where would they go?

Not everyone had gone. Sophie had recently met Mrs Zentz, who lived at the end of the street; she'd been a neighbour and customer for years. Her husband had been a switch operator at the railway and had died there in the first air raid. Mrs Zentz would never leave her house; she was waiting for her son Erik to return, but she was worried because she hadn't heard from him in eight months. Was he dead? Was he too busy fighting to write? She was sick with the uncertainty. But Mrs Zentz was not the only story of defiant stubbornness; more than a handful of families on the street would not or could not leave.

They could clearly hear shouts in English now. "What's going on? What are they saying?" Sophie demanded, desperate to know as they huddled under the table. "Nothing of consequence, Mama. It's just things like 'Come on, Georgie, keep up'; 'Go, go, go'; 'Watch your flanks'. It's all soldier talk. But it sounds like we've brought our 88 in to try and stop the Allied tanks." After ten more minutes of furious gunfire exchanges, there was relative silence.

"I guess they'll start to move on now," Sophie sighed. Mother and daughter got out from under the table and sat down, lost in their thoughts, when they heard the heavy footsteps of soldiers coming up the stairs to the apartment. Sophie and Nancy stared at each other in alarm. "Quick, take off your shoes so you won't make a sound. Get into my wardrobe and hide behind the clothes," Sophie whispered. Nancy nodded and quietly dashed for her parents' bedroom.

Someone hammered at the door. "*Öffne die Tür!*" came a heavily accented voice. Sophie walked briskly to the front door, where she paused to inhale deeply before slowly opening the door with trembling hands. There in the hallway were four American soldiers, carrying a fifth. They were all wearing the same drab olive-green uniforms and steel helmets, except for one who had a white circle with a red cross on the front of his helmet.

They pushed Sophie aside as they made their way to the sitting room, where they placed their bleeding comrade on the floor. The medic leaned over to tend to the bullet wound in the man's left thigh. Blood was starting to seep into Sophie's best carpet, and she chided herself for worrying about something so trivial when a man's life was at stake. The soldiers were panicky and shouted to each other in English. She could only make a guess at what they were saying.

The medic barked at one of the soldiers, who got up to leave the room. Sophie had no idea what he was going to do, but she did not want any of them to find her fifteen-year-old daughter. She moved swiftly to stand in the doorway, her arms folded across her chest as she stared defiantly at the American. He glowered at Sophie and roughly pushed her to one side so that she banged her shoulder against the door frame and staggered. Sophie turned to watch him open her bedroom door and stifled a cry of fear, terrified that he would find Nancy. But the soldier walked over to the bed, flung the covers aside and yanked off the sheet.

Sophie quickly realised that he needed a sheet to make bandages. This time she stepped aside to allow him to re-enter the sitting room where the injured man lay bleeding and whimpering. After a tense fifteen minutes, it appeared the medic had managed to stabilise the wound, and the Americans breathed a collective sigh of relief. But now the G.I. who had been searching for sheets spoke to his sergeant and pointed to Sophie. She didn't know what it meant, but she knew it wasn't good. Another soldier approached her and kept repeating in bad German, "Who here? Who here?"

Sophie played dumb and looked confused. The man realised he was not going to get anything out of her and shrugged. The four soldiers drew their weapons, and three of them moved to investigate the apartment. Shaking with dread, Sophie began to follow them when the remaining medic called out. She turned to see him using his gun to motion her into a far corner of the room. Terrified and now furious, Sophie complied, but inside she was screaming. What right did these men have to come into her home? What right had they to threaten her with a gun? Her worst fears were realised when she heard a husky shout of jubilation and a shriek from her daughter.

Nancy had been listening in the cupboard when she heard the men discussing the fact that her mother was hiding someone. They had assumed it must be the officer in the picture, not realising that her father was dead. The order was to search and find whoever else was in the apartment. It was at that point that Nancy realised the cupboard was likely to be one of the first places they would look. She thought about leaving but realised she didn't know where else she could hide, so she decided to stay where she was and pray they didn't find her.

She heard the sound of boots coming into the bedroom and held her breath. The American walked around the room, apparently checking behind the door and under the bed. Then the right hand door of the wardrobe was flung open, and a soldier stood there pointing his rifle at her. "Come out, slowly," he ordered in English.

Nancy nodded that she understood but didn't want the man to know she spoke English. The soldier called out to his buddies as he motioned her into the sitting room. "I think I found what the Kraut was hiding," he announced, staring hungrily at the terrified Nancy.

"I can see why the mother was keen to hide this bit of skirt," the sergeant said, looking Nancy up and down.

"What do we do now, sarge?" one of the soldiers asked.

"To the victors belong the spoils. I get first go with the daughter, and then we can have fun with Ma Kraut. Brown, keep your weapon on ma. She might try something stupid."

The sergeant turned to Sophie and said slowly and loudly in English, "YOU STAY HERE!", then he took Nancy's arm and tugged her towards the door.

"*Nein!*" Sophie cried and took a step towards her daughter. The other G.I.s raised their rifles towards Sophie, who stopped in her tracks, quivering with rage. "How could you!" she spat at them.

Nancy was dragged, struggling, into her parents' bedroom, where the sergeant threw her roughly onto the bed. He used his pistol to lift Nancy's skirt and reveal her thighs and underwear. She was too frightened to move.

Sophie stood in the corner of the sitting room, her mind racing. All she wanted was to tear these men to pieces and save her daughter, but she was unarmed and faced four battle-hardened soldiers, armed to the teeth. To attack them would be suicide. Time stopped as Sophie's mind filled with the most repugnant images of the fate befalling her innocent daughter, something inside her dying with every passing second.

Suddenly, the sergeant called out. Not knowing what this meant, the three men raised their rifles and motioned Sophie towards the bedroom. Was this some kind of trick? But the looks on the soldiers' faces indicated they were now as bewildered and anxious as she was.

Sophie edged past the men, carefully stepping around the wounded G.I. and made her way down the hall to the bedroom. There in the room by the bed, his trousers around his ankles, stood the sergeant, with his hands up. Nancy was kneeling on the bed, aiming Harry's Luger straight at the temple of the American. Tears were streaming down her face. Intent on his ruthless conquest, the sergeant had failed to see Nancy reach into the bedside table to find her salvation.

"*Du Hurensohn*!" Nancy cursed through tears and clenched teeth. Her father hadn't taught her English swearing, so German would have to do as she continued, "Order your men to drop their weapons, or I'll shoot you in the head. NOW!"

The sergeant did as instructed, and the American guns clattered to the floor. "I … I'm sorry," the sergeant stammered, not knowing what else to say.

"You're sorry you tried to rape a fifteen-year-old girl?" Nancy shouted angrily in English, never taking her eyes off her captive as she inched her way off the bed to stand upright.

The sergeant's face conveyed his surprise. "You can speak English?"

"Yes, I can speak English, because my father is English!"

"I'm sorry," the sergeant offered again, weakly, as he stared down the barrel of the gun.

"You wanted to rape me! Why shouldn't I shoot you, you *Miststück*?"

"I, I … hey, is that a Luger?"

It was Nancy's turn to look surprised. The man began looking curiously, rather than fearfully, at the loaded pistol.

"Yes, it is my dead father's Luger," Nancy said, feeling an overwhelming urge to pull the trigger just as she caught sight of her mother's grim expression. Despite the soldier's brutal intentions, she couldn't shoot him in the face, not now, not with her mother as a witness.

"So you want me *not* to put a gun in your face?"

"Yes, but I'm interested in the gun itself."

"I'll bet you are!" Nancy said, her tears now replaced with angry confidence.

"No, you misunderstand. Everyone wants to take a Luger home. It's a kind of souvenir, proof that we fought the Germans, ya know?"

"So you want the gun rather than sex?"

"Look, I really am very sorry. I honestly don't know what came over me. I'm just an ordinary guy from Indiana. Me and my men have been fighting our way across Europe since D-Day. We've seen a lot, a lot of bad things … I know that's no excuse for what I was going to do to you."

Sophie watched intently, astounded that her daughter had fought off a veteran soldier, amazed at her composure and proud of her bravery as Nancy conversed in English, the pistol still pointing at the American's temple. Her *Jungmadelbund* weapons' training was now paying off in this totally unexpected way. But the danger was far from over, and Sophie was still afraid for them both.

"So, if I give you this gun, you'll leave?"

"Yes, and before you say it, why should you trust me … after what we were going to do …"

"Not just to me; you were planning to rape my mother as well!" Nancy said, bringing the Luger even closer to the sergeant's head.

"I have a solution. How about you take my Thompson machine gun in exchange. You fire that at us, it'll kill us all, guaranteed. That way I get my souvenir; you still have a gun to protect yourselves, and we go on our way."

Still concentrating on her would-be rapist, Nancy spoke to her mother, "Mama, this man says they will leave us alone if I give him the Luger. What do you think?"

"Has this man touched you?"

"No, I didn't give him the chance."

"Good. I'm picking up his machine gun. Tell him his men can take out their wounded friend first, and then, when everyone but the sergeant has gone, we'll give him his precious Luger."

Nancy explained all this to the G.I., who, with no other choice, nodded in agreement. He hastily pulled up his trousers and headed for the hall where Sophie stood, aiming the Thompson at the open door as the G.I.s filed out. Nancy handed over the Luger to the eager American and slammed the door in his face.

Sophie leaned the gun against the wall, and the two women collapsed on the floor, hugging each other and crying in relief. They had been a hair's breadth away from tragedy.

***

Harry was fast asleep, dreaming that his name was being called over and over again. His eyes snapped opened when someone pulled back the tent flap and morning light flooded in. Hannigan's panting face filled the opening.

"Oh, what is it this time?" Harry groaned.

"The Americans have just liberated Hannover!" Hannigan said excitedly.

Harry grinned and tore his way out of his sleeping bag. He grabbed his helmet and ran towards the nearest jeep. Hannigan was one step behind him. As they sprinted past Colonel Ferguson, Harry saluted and shouted, "Sir, I have an urgent mission in Hannover. I will return once the situation is under control."

The astonished colonel saluted back and watched as the two men jumped into a jeep, and Harry tore down the road towards his home.

"Sir, just because you want to see your family doesn't mean the roads won't be mined or there aren't *Volkssturm* or SS units ready to ambush us."

"Yes, Sergeant Hannigan, I am aware of that. In fact I am probably more aware of that now than I have been for the last six months. I'm travelling fast because that makes us a harder target to hit, and I am depending on your young eyes to look ahead for any damage to the road surface where there might be mines."

"Yes, but sir, if we're travelling at this speed, you may not get out of the way in time."

"Hannigan, I'm older than you, but I'm not *that* old."

They roared along the roads, and within half an hour, they could see Hannover in the distance or, rather, what was left of it. Harry was horrified. How many air raids had attacked the city to cause such widespread destruction? Hannover looked more like the site of medieval ruins, surrounded by craters from the moon, than the city he remembered. He had been worried before; now his anxieties deepened. What would he find? Would the cobbler's still be there? Would Sophie and Nancy still be there?

As they travelled towards the city centre, they saw groups of American soldiers fixing vehicles, restocking equipment, smoking cigarettes and standing around talking. Harry and Hannigan came to a road block where an American private held up his hand to stop. Harry pulled over and the private approached. "Sir, you should be aware that there is still some resistance up ahead. Nothing serious, but the city is not yet entirely secure."

"Understood, private." Harry saluted, gunned the engine and roared off down the road again.

Nancy was the first to hear the noise of a jeep pulling to a stop in front of the cobbler's. She spied two British soldiers in their distinctive steel helmets jumping out of the vehicle and heading straight for their apartment.

"Mama!" called Nancy. "More soldiers!"

Signalling for Nancy to follow her, Sophie hurried over to the door and picked up the Thompson. It was cold and smooth and heavy in her hands, but it gave her a sense of power. Big or small, soldier or civilian, this gun would stop anyone who tried to harm her or her daughter. She positioned herself behind the door, her finger hovering over the trigger, ready to fire at the slightest provocation.

Nancy waited until there was a curt knock. Slowly and cautiously she opened the door a sliver and looked at the two men. One was a well-built Tommy, a powerful, muscular man; the other was wearing a British officer's uniform. She hesitated, then realised it was her father. "Papa!" Nancy screamed and lunged at Harry. He grabbed her and swung her around, surprised by how much she had grown. In the years they had been separated, she had changed from a lanky girl to a young woman. He was overjoyed to see her, and she continued to squeal and cry in happy disbelief. Harry made her stand back so he could get a good look. She had made it; he was proud of her.

Sophie couldn't understand what was happening on the other side of the door, but Nancy sounded happy, so she put the gun on the floor and peered around. It was her Harry.

"Hello, my darling!" smiled Harry.

Sophie gave him a stony look then slapped Harry as hard as she could.

"Ow!" cried Harry, rubbing his reddening check. The woman could pack a punch. What did you do that for?"

"Because you have to be a ghost."

"No, I am alive and well and standing in front of you."

Sophie slapped him again.

"And what was that one for?" complained Harry, still rubbing his cheek. This was not the welcome he had expected.

"Because for three years, I have been in mourning. I thought you were dead!" shouted Sophie as she burst into tears and fell into his arms. They held each other in a wordless embrace, Harry's face buried in her sweet smelling hair. He relaxed his hold as she brought her face up to his, and they kissed with the longing of absence and the bliss of reunion, her soft lips against his rough ones. She wrapped herself around him as if she would never let him go, as if to reassure herself that this was not a dream. *This* was the homecoming he had hoped for.

They caught their breaths and drew apart but had eyes only for each other. Not wanting to lose physical contact, they held hands as Sophie closed the door, and Harry introduced Hannigan. The sergeant had known that when Harry heard the news about Hannover, he would leave immediately, so he'd had the foresight to pack a knapsack with food and put it in the jeep. With perfect timing, he produced a tin of real coffee, a jar of jam and a tin of corned beef, which he and Nancy gathered up and took to the kitchen to make lunch. It was then that Harry noticed the Thompson machine gun by the side of the door. "Uh, Sophie dear, how did you get that?"

"Nancy did a trade," Sophie said nonchalantly, and Nancy shrugged when Harry looked at her.

As they entered the sitting room, Harry spied his picture in the old *Wehrmacht* uniform, now with the black ribbon around it. He told them how sorry he was for keeping them in the dark and explained the reasons for it. Hannigan stared at the

249

picture, which clearly displayed Harry's medals. The photo confirmed that Harry hadn't been exaggerating; he really was the warrior who had seen and done it all.

They chatted until late in the evening. After Harry had explained all that had happened, it was his turn to catch up with their news. He was shocked to hear about Rudi; he couldn't imagine the cobbler's without him. And he was devastated to hear that Karl had been conscripted but relieved to know that he was now at home, and the family was safe. The same could be said of Max and his family, who had escaped the worst of the Heidelberg bombings. The news about Anke was not good, but except for Rudi, they had all survived. They had made it. They were the lucky ones.

Harry told Hannigan they would stay the night and head back to HQ the following morning. Hannigan had guessed as much. After being thought dead for three years, the least the man deserved was a night with his wife. Hannigan slept on the sofa, the first time in a long time he had been somewhere warm, comfortable and safe.

Harry and Sophie had almost no sleep as they eagerly rekindled their passion and made love. Exhausted but ecstatic, they fell into blissful sleep, wrapped in each other's arms.

***

The next morning, after an emotional parting, Harry and Hannigan headed back to HQ. It was mid-April, and the Nazi regime was in its death throws. Surely it was only a matter of weeks before Harry would be home again.

They returned to the 11th Armoured Division to find it a hub of activity. Scouts from the Special Air Service had reported a major facility up ahead, and there was huge speculation as to what it could be. Heinrich Himmler himself had agreed to turn the area around this base into a demilitarised zone; such a designation from the SS *Reichsführer* meant it was important. Was it a secret weapons' base? Rocket facility? SS training camp? Nobody knew what to expect.

As an officer and a fluent German speaker, Harry, accompanied as always by Hannigan, was in the first convoy of British and Canadian vehicles to arrive at the scene. Four uncomfortable looking Hungarian soldiers were there to meet them. It was clear they were not looking forward to showing the Allies what had been tucked away in the countryside just over an hour's drive from Hannover. As they drove through the gates, the feeling of uneasiness increased. There was a smell in the air. What exactly had the SS been doing at Bergen-Belsen? The vehicles stopped and everyone got out, trying to understand what they were looking at.

Gradually they began to see but not believe. There were piles of human bodies everywhere. The stench was unbearable, and everyone fished for pocket handkerchiefs to cover their noses. Hannigan walked over to a corpse, its paper-thin skin stretched over the ribcage, the body naked except for a few disgusting rags. Hannigan retched. The body shuddered and he jumped backwards in shock. It was just beginning to dawn on everyone that the situation was so bad they couldn't tell the living from the dead. Bergen-Belsen was the rotting charnel house behind the lie of Aryan superiority, the physical embodiment of Nazi ideology. This was Hell on Earth.

A Canadian captain had wandered behind the huts and called out. The stunned group rushed over and stopped in their tracks. There before them was a trench, about as long as four train carriages and twice as wide. It was heaped with the skeletal remains of thousands of people. What they saw was horrific, made worse by the human wraiths around them. This place was the personification of evil, and its prisoners were humanity's most tortured souls.

Everyone present had been hardened by years of war; everyone present had experienced violence and brutality, but this … this was something beyond war, beyond savagery, beyond any inhumanity they had ever witnessed. There were no dry eyes in the Allied group on that fine spring morning in Bergen-Belsen.

Lieutenant John Randall turned to one of his sergeants and simply said, "For God's sake, get help!"

The sergeant looked around him, dumbfounded, surrounded as he was by an overwhelming sea of human misery. "Who should I get?"

"Everybody!" said the lieutenant. "Go, hurry, bring everything you can for these people."

Harry looked around. There were huts, scores and scores of huts; they couldn't all hold people, could they? That would mean thousands – no, tens of thousands. They couldn't all be political prisoners, could they? Harry stormed over to one of the Hungarians, "Who are all these prisoners?"

"They come from many places," the man replied in heavily accented German.

"What is their crime?"

"Some are Russian prisoners of war; some are Czech dissidents; others are homosexuals, but mainly they are Jews. We were getting rid of the Jews."

"How many people are here?"

"Maybe 60,000."

"60,000!"

"Maybe. So many come. Some are used for labour; others are too weak to work, so we let them die."

A group had gathered around, and Harry translated for them. The first reactions of shock and disbelief were giving way to anger. They were looking for an explanation, trying to understand the incomprehensible.

Hannigan tried to offer some water to one of the living dead lying on the ground. "No, stay away from them! We have a typhus epidemic," the Hungarian called out.

Harry translated for Hannigan, who moved away but became angry with himself. Why should he obey the order of a mass murderer? An inferno raging in his eyes, Hannigan grabbed the Hungarian by the throat, "You murdering mother-fucker, you utter cunt! You are so fucking despicable, I can't find the words to describe you, you revolting piece of shit!" Hannigan roared into the man's face while reaching for his pistol.

Harry put his hand firmly over Hannigan's holster. "Sergeant, this is neither the time nor the place."

"With all due respect, sir, this is the perfect fucking time, place and target!"

"Let's not turn this into a shooting gallery. There are still *Wehrmacht* and SS soldiers on site."

"But he deserves to die," argued Hannigan.

"You're right. He does, and there will be a special place in Hell for these Nazi bastards, but let's not start a battle in the middle of a camp full of civilians who have already suffered more than any other human beings in history."

Hannigan let go of the terrified guard, who hurriedly led the Allied group towards the main administration block. Two smartly uniformed officers, SS *Hauptsturmführer* Josef Kramer and SS *Obersturmführer* Franz Hössler were waiting for them. Harry stared long and hard at the second man. It couldn't be *his* Hössler, could it? Could this really be the same annoying private who had joined the German army at the same time he had? He was older and greyer, but it looked like him. Meanwhile, the SS officer was staring right back at Harry, focusing on the old white scar on his cheek.

"Brit Bubi?" exclaimed Hössler with genuine warmth.

Harry's mouth fell open.

"It *is* you! Oh, Brit Bubi, it's so good to see you! I must say, it was with heavy hearts that we planned to hand over our concentration camp, but now I see you're here, I know we're in good hands." Hössler's speech still had its familiar staccato delivery.

Harry was utterly dumbstruck, awash in memories. The last time he had seen him, Hössler was still a teen-aged boy, full of foolish ideas and nervous energy. Twenty-five years later, he was standing in front of Harry as a key perpetrator of unspeakable crimes against humanity. Hössler, however, seemed unfazed. He spoke to Harry as if the intervening years had been only days.

One of the British officers turned to Harry. "Major, do you know this man?"

The question brought Harry back to the present. "Regrettably, sir, I do."

"How, may I ask?"

"We knew each other from the previous war. I haven't seen *Obersturmführer* Hössler since 1919, when he was a private in the German army." Hössler smiled on hearing his name mentioned.

"Well, he seems to like you," observed the officer.

"Harry, I see you're a British major now. Good for you!" continued Hössler. "But I thought you had settled in Hannover. Didn't you marry Karl's sister?"

Harry couldn't understand how Hössler was able to carry on the conversation as if they were at a dinner party rather than in the middle of killing on a scale never before seen. He felt nauseous. How could someone he knew organise mass murder? "Hössler ... why?" asked Harry, with great effort.

"Isn't it obvious?" Hössler replied with a smirk, as if he was party to some kind of universal joke.

"No, Hössler, it's the exact fucking opposite of obvious!" spat Harry.

"Regrettably, this is necessary to build a better future. We don't want Slavic blood or Jewish blood or the taint of homosexuality mixing with pure Aryan blood. I'm not blind. I know this is not a pretty sight, but if the Allies had only given us a chance to finish the job, you would have been most impressed with what we were trying to achieve."

"But, Hössler, these are *people!*" Harry said through gritted teeth.

"Hardly. They're *Un-ter-men-schen.*" He said the last word slowly as if explaining something obvious to a simpleton.

"No, Hössler. They're humans, like all of us, although I may make an exception for the SS."

"Thank you," said Hössler , not getting the point. "But this isn't the largest facility. *Hauptsturmführer* Kramer and I worked together at Auschwitz. There we were able to cleanse the Jewish population far quicker and more humanely.

"HUMANELY?" roared Harry.

"I'm not a monster! I find no joy in taking life. As I said to Goldmann ..."

"Goldmann? You met Goldmann?" interrupted Harry.

"Yes, and his family."

Harry could hold back the wave of nausea no longer and leaned over to throw up. The Allied officers were closely watching the exchange between Hössler and Harry. They were all in a deep state of shock and could not begin to imagine what kind of dialogue was taking place.

Harry wiped the vomit from his mouth. His head was spinning. How much of this was his fault? He had fought for a side that thought nothing of murdering ... what was it, hundreds of thousands? Millions? Could it really be millions of people? How much blood did Harry have on his own hands? Richard Barley had pointed out that Harry had been part of the Nazi war machine; he was, therefore, complicit in their crimes.

Harry took a deep breath and asked the dreaded question. "Wilhelm Goldmann, the man who saved your life on many occasions during the Great War, that Goldmann: what happened to him and his family?"

Hössler's little smirk disappeared as he shrugged, "Orders are orders. He was a Jew, so he and his family were liquidated last ..."

Hössler never finished the sentence. Harry pulled out his pistol and shot him in the temple. After the sharp percussion of the single gunshot, Hössler's body crumpled to the floor. Utter silence descended on the room.

Harry turned and walked away.

***

Four of them sat underneath a great oak tree beside a country road. The sun dappled their shadows as it passed through the budding canopy; the green shoots of spring were pushing through the dirt in the fields nearby. The sun was not strong, but they welcomed its warmth on their skin. A breath of wind brought the scent of damp earth and new grass; birdsong seemed intent on waking the surrounding countryside from its winter slumber. It was a scene of bucolic tranquillity.

All of this beauty should have filled their hearts with joy, but it didn't. They were too exhausted and too hungry to care. All they could think about was food, food of any kind, but they had no idea what they could scavenge. Two nights ago they had tried to make a kind of soup. They had collected water from a stream and added whatever they could find, mainly old nuts and seeds, still on the ground from the autumn. In their desperation they had even added new grass, trying to bulk out their thin gruel. It had been inedible. The grass set their teeth on edge, and something had turned out to be mildly toxic. One of them had thrown up. Their ammunition was precious, and they dared not waste it hunting rabbits, fast moving and skittish as they were.

Erik Zentz wore a grubby camouflage poncho, which they had tried to use as a cover during the long, cold nights. But large as it was, it was not designed for four, and it had taken half an hour after fitful sleep to stop shivering and prime their bodies back into something approaching usefulness. They could stretch and bend all they wanted, but it didn't stop their hunger pangs or their constantly rumbling stomachs.

Erik was the unit's leader. Having joined up in '39 at the age of eighteen, he had been promoted through the ranks of the SS to become a lieutenant. He excused himself from the others and walked over to a nearby thicket where he gulped down low sobs. How had he ended up here? How could he get out of this mess? And when would he have a proper meal again? He blinked away the tears in his eyes and looked down at his broken finger nails, black with dirt and grime. He ran his hand along his itchy chin, a reminder that he had nearly a week's worth of stubble on his face. He felt wet tears on his cheeks and angrily rubbed them off, unintentionally wiping away some of the mud flecks that spattered his face. Tears were for shame;

tears were for the weak, and he was neither weak nor ashamed … but he was fearfully worried. He didn't recognise the world anymore, neither did his men. 'Men' – ha! His three subordinates were barely more than children. Their filthy, ill-fitting uniforms hung from their scrawny frames, but they were all armed and ready to fight. If only they could find someone to fight.

They had been sent to this roadside near Belsen four days ago, with minimal ammunition, even less food and no support. Their objective was to defend the country road where they now sat … except there were no enemy units, and there hadn't been since they'd arrived. Day four was starting like all the others.

Were they to stay until relieved? Were the orders still valid? He didn't know and was getting to the point of not caring. But the others looked up to him; the others expected him to be decisive and have a plan of action. He sat there and sniffed. His weakened state meant he now seemed to be developing a cold, which meant a mild headache and sore throat were new additions to his repertoire of misery, more woe heaped upon his uncertainty. He hefted the shoulder strap of his submachine gun, which had begun to bite into his shoulder. He touched the cool metal casing for reassurance.

He sat there for several minutes, absorbed in his own introspection, trying to ignore the gnawing emptiness of his stomach, when his ears picked up a sound with a regular rhythm. It was man-made, the low whine of an engine - and it was getting closer. He carefully pushed aside some branches and peered out. In the distance were two enemy vehicles, both soft tops, no armour. Good, he thought. At last, a piece of luck. We'll take them out and head back to base, mission accomplished. Then we can finally eat again!

He bolted out of the undergrowth, hunched down so as to keep a low profile, and raced back to his men, who were still lounging around under the oak tree. "Grab your gear! They're coming. We get this right, we can get out of here and finally get some food!"

And with that, the group quickly got into their ambush positions.

***

Harry and Hannigan drove along the road behind the other jeep heading back to HQ. As they left Bergen-Belsen, one of the officers said, "The Americans have found a smaller one of these camps in Ahlem, just a few miles west of Hannover. They think there are lots of them scattered around."

It was just the two of them now, but neither felt like talking; they were deep in thought after the horrors they had just witnessed. Suddenly there was a flash of light from the row of bushes to their right, and the jeep in front exploded. A second *Panzerfaust* hissed past Harry and exploded harmlessly on the grassy bank behind them.

Hannigan jammed on the breaks and swerved to avoid the burning jeep ahead, just as gunfire began to crack angrily at them. Hannigan and Harry scrambled out and ducked behind the jeep. At least one of the men in the other vehicle was still alive, and they needed to get to him. As the shots whizzed past them, Harry and Hannigan grabbed their weapons. Hannigan had swapped his Lee Enfield for Sophie's Thompson machine gun, and Harry and Hannigan fired short bursts of automatic fire in the direction of the enemy. The ambush had been well prepared, but the firing was wild.

Harry threw himself through the hedgerow to the left of the jeep and saw two of the attackers firing their rifles. Harry opened up his MP 40, and they both fell backwards in sprays of red mist. The other German soldiers had Hannigan pinned down, and the British officer from the first jeep lay groaning and vulnerable in the middle of the road.

"Hannigan, I'll cover you, and you make a dash to the right of their position. Got it?"

"Got it!"

As Hannigan raced to the opposite side of the road, Harry popped up from behind the bush and sprayed the area where the shots were coming from. Hannigan disappeared from view as he dived behind the lush green leaves. Thirty seconds of continual exchanges of gunfire followed. Harry quickly reloaded, sprinted across the road and came in from the left flank, hoping to catch the Germans in a crossfire of his own making. As he burst through the bushes, he saw Hannigan lying on his back, red smears on his chest. He was dead, but he had taken two of the enemy with him. The remaining German was an SS soldier in a camouflage poncho. He turned his gun on Harry just as Harry aimed at him.

The two men fired simultaneously. The SS soldier fell backwards, and Harry felt a searing pain in his gut. He stumbled, clutching his abdomen, and felt warm, wet blood trickle through his fingers. He took a step forward and winced as he staggered past the two soldiers that Hannigan had killed and realised they were little more than children. It had come to this: the Nazis were sending their babes to fight the war they could not win. Harry took a few more painful steps and looked down at the SS man. The face looked familiar, but he couldn't place him. He had seen so many soldiers, so many faces; they had become a blur. Was this someone he liked or loathed? Harry didn't care anymore.

He took a lungful of air of as a wave of nauseating pain washed over him, but he willed himself towards the body of Hannigan, lying underneath an oak tree. Harry gazed down at the unblinking eyes of a man he had once thought of as an enemy but who had become a friend. Hannigan looked peaceful; the end had been quick for him. After what they had just seen, Harry knew there were far worse fates that could befall a man.

Harry sat down beneath the great canopy of the tree. He felt shattered, exhausted to the core of his being. It was a weariness born not just of fatigue but of all the horrors he had experienced over years of fighting. He stopped looking at the death around him and, instead, looked out over a countryside that was bursting with life. The bushes rustled in the breeze; the leaves of the oak tree danced in the sunlight. This was a good place to rest.

Doing his best to ignore the agony of his wound, he reached inside his jacket, where he felt the reassuring edges of E.E. Fowler's *Anthology of Melancholy Poetry*. He wiped his bloody hands on his trousers, trying not to spoil the book he had cherished for so long. He pulled it out of his pocket and opened it for the first time since Sophie had given it to him all those Christmases ago. He flicked to a random page and began to read.

The Eternal Moment by A. W. Williams

We may mourn our fallen sons and brothers,

But avoid contemplating their end,

For no death in battle is serene.

Their suffering is now ended;

The cold damp earth their bed.

Unlike the living, they have seen an end to war;

Forever young, they rest always in our hearts.

Close your eyes in silent prayer,

Join them in an eternal moment.

What's Fiction and What's Fact

Harry Woods and his family members are fictional charters, but their lives take place against the backdrop of historic events. A few of the characters in the book are based on real men:

Wilhelm Josef Ritter von Thoma is the character most closely resembling the real man. He fought in every campaign described. His conversations with Harry and his time as the head of security at the Berlin Olympics are fictional, but he fought on multiple fronts in the war and was captured at El Alamein.

Von Thoma was very much the gentleman German officer and not a member of the Nazi party. He said on acts of violence carried out in Russia, "I am actually ashamed to be an officer". He died of a heart attack at home in Germany in 1948.

Franz Hössler is also real but is a far more fictional version of the historical figure. He was too young to have served in World War I although he did end up becoming a senior officer in the Nazi network of concentration and death camps. A fervent Nazi serving in the SS from 1933, he surrendered at Bergen-Belsen (there's a picture of him standing in front of a truck laden with dead bodies) and was tried for crimes against humanity. He was hanged in 1945.

Those mentioned in connection with the Berlin Olympics and the British officers cited in the capture of von Thoma, at the D-Day invasion and at the liberation of the Bergen-Belsen concentration camp are real men who were present at the time.

The research carried out for this book was extensive; the real events that have made their way into this work of fiction are too many to list, but it is worth mentioning that the scene with American soldiers under friendly fire in the Argonne Forest at the end of WWI actually happened, and the message that Harry intercepted was a genuine one the Germans sent back to Allied lines.

Hitler's acceptance speech as chancellor, while abridged, is authentic as are the two oaths of allegiance. The Nazi book-burning campaign is well-known, and examples of Nazi propaganda, including the questions taken from school textbooks are genuine. Finally, the *Volkssturm* was a Nazi militia that existed as described at the end of the war.

Printed in Great Britain
by Amazon